Collins *practical gardener*

FLOWERING SHRUBS

KEITH RUSHFORTH

First published in 2003 by HarperCollins*Publishers*

77–85 Fulham Palace Road, London, W6 8JB

The Collins website address is:

www.collins.co.uk

Text © Keith Rushforth

Artworks and design © HarperCollins*Publishers*

Photography by Tim Sandall & Keith Rushforth

Cover photography by Tim Sandall

Photographic props: Coolings Nurseries, Rushmore Hill, Knockholt, Kent, TN14 7NN, www.coolings.co.uk

Design and editorial: Focus Publishing, Sevenoaks, Kent

Project editor: Guy Croton

Editor: Vanessa Townsend

Project co-ordinator: Caroline Watson

Design & illustration: David Etherington

For HarperCollins

Managing Editor: Angela Newton

Art Direction: Luke Griffin

Editor: Alastair Laing

Illustration: David Graham

Production: Chris Gurney

A CIP catalogue record for this book is available from the British Library

ISBN 0007146531

Colour reproduction by Colourscan

Printed and bound in Great Britain by The Bath Press Ltd

Collins *practical gardener*

FLOWERING SHRUBS

Contents

Introduction

Shrubs are excellent garden plants. They provide colour throughout the year from leaves – including autumn tints – and often feature flowers, fruit and bark. Some of them possess exquisite scents that can fill an entire garden with a pleasing aroma. They give shape and form to a garden, whether it is the low expanse of a bed of heathers, or the welcome spiky splash of colourful Cornus stems during the winter months. What's more, shrubs offer all these qualities for relatively little cost and, once established, they require very little effort compared with lawns, herbaceous plants and summer bedding, yet can be just as colourful.

There is no formal definition of what constitutes a shrub, apart from it needing to be woody in some way. Yet woody plants show a continuous range, from sub-shrubs that are only woody at the base, through to enormous trees, with shrubs somewhere in the middle. The complete range of woody plants is covered by this book and its companion volume in the series, *Trees and Shrubs*, with woody climbers examined in a further companion title, *Clematis and Climbers*.

Included in this book are those woody plants grown primarily for their strong decorative effect – a blaze of colour in the garden – which are also relatively small growing, to approximately no more than 2m (6ft) in

Camellia williamsii 'J.C. Williams'

Cornus alba 'Spaethii'

height. Nevertheless, the book also contains some slow growing shrubs that produce impressive floral displays from a small size but may grow to 4m (13ft) with time. A good example of this type of shrub would be Camellia, but since on average we move house and garden every nine or so years, most of us do not plant Camellia to make 4m tall bushes – we are just too impatient!

Most of the plants in *Flowering Shrubs* are grown for their beautiful displays of flowers, with fruit, foliage and other characters as secondary points of interest. Two additional groups featured are grown for their visual interest but not necessarily for their flowers. Heathers and related genera include many showy plants, but some are only showy because of their leaf colour. Dwarf conifers are a group grown primarily for the colour and texture of their foliage, and they associate well with heathers as ground cover. Finally, there is a special page featuring architectural plants, selected for their outstanding visual interest, as a 'taster' to this exciting area of gardening. For further planting options and information on cultivation, see the companion volume in this series of books, *Architectural Plants*.

How to Use This Book

This book is divided into three main parts. The opening chapters guide you through all areas of garden practice, from assessing your site, through general care and pruning to propagation techniques. A comprehensive plant directory follows, with individual entries on over 125 of the most commonly available flowering shrubs, listed in alphabetical order. All the most colourful and popular flowering shrubs are included, covering many different styles of gardening and uses. This section is followed by pages devoted to heaths, heathers and ling, dwarf conifers and architectural plants. The final section of the book covers plant problems. Troubleshooting pages allow you to diagnose the likely cause of any problems, and a directory of pests and diseases offers advice on how to solve them.

alphabetical tabs on the side of the page, colour-coded to help you quickly find the plant you want

detailed descriptions give specific advice on care for each plant, including planting and pests and diseases

latin name of the plant genus, followed by its **common name**

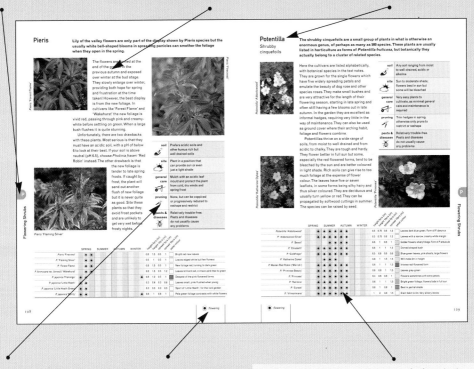

care charts provide an at-a-glance summary of the plant's specific needs. (N.B. Where more than one genus appear on the page, the chart may cater for both plants)

a key at the bottom of the page explains what each symbol means. (N.B. The harvest symbol may relate to berries, nuts, fruit or cones, as appropriate)

variety charts list recommended varieties for most genera of flowering shrubs or the best individual species. These display key information to help you choose your ideal plant, showing:

• when the plant is in flower during the year
• when interesting nuts, berries or other fruit appear
• the optimum height and spread generally achieved over 5 and 10 years (N.B. Running text covers possible heights and spreads beyond this timeframe)
• the colour of the flowers
• additional comments from the author
(N.B. Where more than one genus appears on the page, the chart may list varieties for both genera)

Assessing Your Garden

Existing features

Your garden will be unique in the opportunities it has to offer and the constraints it might impose. So the first task is to assess what features are already there and how they might affect your plans.

Unless you have a newly-built house, you are likely to find some existing plants in the garden. Using a tape measure and some graph paper, draw a plan of the garden showing all established plants, paths and other features. The other features will include 'good' ones such as pleasant views, and 'bad' ones like the oil tank that needs concealing. You should also note down any physical features, such as sloping ground, manhole covers, drain runs, a patio and a driveway.

Next, consider whether you want to keep any of the existing plants. Especially important is to consider whether the existing plants block out any eyesores. Similarly, do you want to keep any of the other structural features of the existing garden design, such as paths and ponds?

Other factors to consider are the physical constraints of aspect, exposure and the characteristics of your garden's soil.

Aspect

The major issue to do with aspect is whether your garden faces north, south, east or west, and where the sun shines at different times of the day (see opposite page). Each orientation will have a different impact upon the climate of the garden, thus determining which plants will thrive and which will struggle.

However, aspect is also determined by geographical and structural features. These may affect the amount of sun a garden receives as much, if not more than, its orientation. These features include the proximity of neighbouring buildings and large trees, and whether your house is situated on a hill.

Exposure

The degree of exposure to the elements that your garden experiences is another determining factor in what plants will grow. We normally think of this in terms of whether the garden is exposed and therefore colder and suiting hardy plants, as opposed to a sheltered garden where more tender plants can be grown. Life is not quite as simple as this, however, as the factor of increased wind in an exposed site complicates matters. For example,

Hydrangea quercifolia 'Snow Flake' suffers in wind

some plants which are perfectly hardy, such as *Hydrangea quercifolia* 'Snow Flake' are ill suited to windy conditions because the large flowers are simply blown over. However, a windy site can give some protection to a plant susceptible to late spring frosts, as these usually only occur in still air conditions.

Soil

The next stage is to work out what kind of soil you have, since each type of soil can vary greatly in drainage capacity, fertility and chemical composition.

The acidity or pH of the soil can have a marked effect upon what it is possible to grow or how the plants will grow. Soils derived from chalk and limestone rocks will be alkaline. These soils are often well drained, with good nutrient-holding capacity, and are excellent for shrubs such as Daphne or Syringa, but Rhododendrons will not grow on them, as they only like acid soils.

Soils derived from sandstone or from sands and gravels are usually acidic in nature. They will grow a wider range of plants, because most plants that tolerate alkaline conditions will still thrive on them. However, they are often too freely drained and thus dry out easily – and they do not tend to hold nutrients well.

Soils derived from clays can be either acidic, alkaline or neutral. However, they are usually poorly drained, and thus wet and heavy over winter, and slow to warm up in the spring, although they have a high nutrient holding capacity. Each of these soils can be improved by the addition of organic matter.

Specific Conditions

Each garden is different, with its own specific, prevailing conditions to take into account. The illustration below is a representation of a 'typical' garden, comprising a number of different elements which often feature in most gardens.

Of course, your own garden may look very different from the one illustrated here, but you will almost certainly need to take the same factors into account when assessing the suitability of your garden for the cultivation of flowering shrubs. Remember that it is always easier to work with conditions as you find them. Don't try too hard to fight Nature, because Nature usually wins in the end. That said, with a few slight changes to your garden, you can improve considerably your plants' chances of growing, without too much effort and expense.

KEY

This symbol denotes the shadiest parts of a garden, typically to be found wherever a tree or building casts a shadow.

The yellow line denotes sunshine in the garden. On one side the sun will shine in the morning, on the other, in the afternoon.

This blue arrow denotes the direction of wind. In this case, the wind swirls over the top of the fence and down the garden.

This green arrow denotes a gradient in the garden floor. In this case, the garden slopes from one side to another.

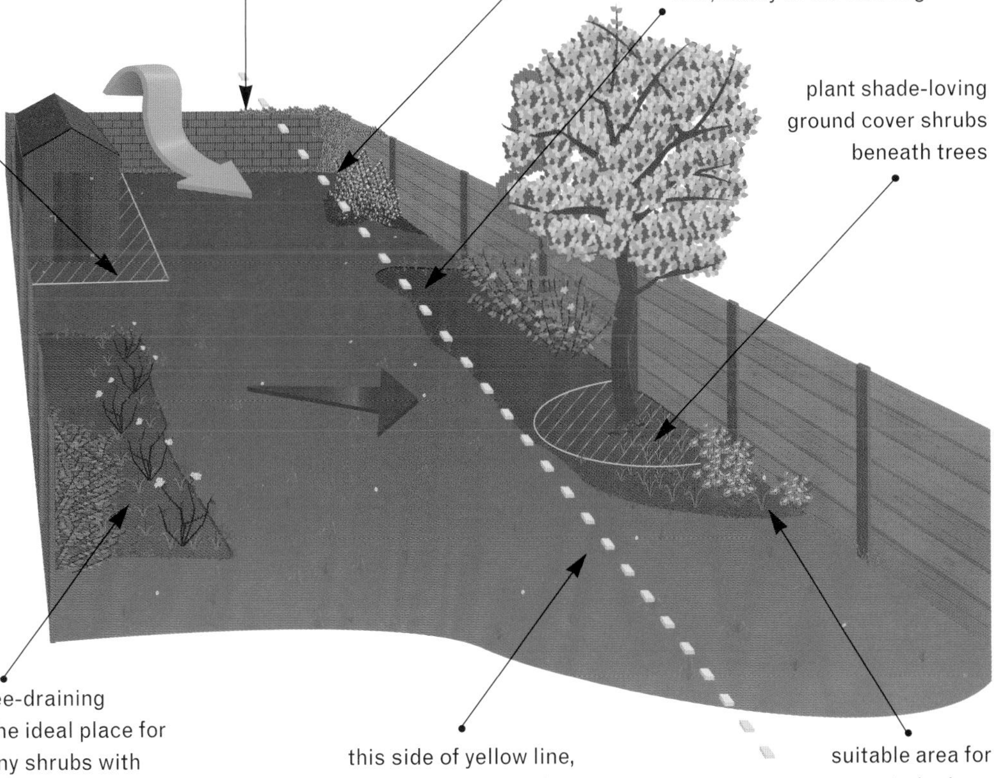

wind turbulence here – do not plant susceptible shrubs in this area

protected corner, good for delicate shrubs

this side of yellow dotted line, shady in the morning

plant shade-loving ground cover shrubs beneath trees

sheds and other buildings will cast shadows for much of the day; avoid planting sun-loving shrubs here

a sunny free-draining border is the ideal place for mixing many shrubs with other sun-loving plants

this side of yellow line, sunny most of the day

suitable area for semi-shade-tolerant shrubs

Choosing & Buying Plants

Selecting your plants

The type of flowers that a shrub produces will probably be the first thing you consider when choosing which plants to buy. However, few shrubs are in flower for more than a few weeks at a time. To maintain colour and variety in the garden throughout the year, you will also need to consider the range of flowering times – you don't want everything flowering at once – and the other features a shrub displays for the rest of the year, such as leaves, fruit, bark and overall shape.

Flowers and fragrance

Most flowering shrubs produce flowers which are displayed alongside foliage, such as Abelia, Buddleja, Corylopsis, Hypericum, Mahonia, Osmanthus, Rosa, Rubus and Weigela. Here, the flowers provide a splash of colour against a background of either leaves or shoots.

Other shrubs produce blooms which totally hide the foliage, such as Brachyglottis, Ceanothus, Chaenomeles, Cistus, Convolvulus, Daphne, Exochorda, Forsythia, Kalmia, Olearia, Prunus, Rhododendron, Ribes and Viburnum. These tend to flower over a relatively short period – often no more than two or three weeks – whereas many of the shrubs that flower in contrast to foliage and shoots do so for longer periods.

The third element of floral effect is fragrance. Many shrubs produce flowers with wonderful aromas that only add to the pleasure of a garden: these include Buddleja; Calycanthus; Choisya; Corylopsis; Daphne; Deutzia; Lavandula; Lonicera; Philadelphus; Sarcococca and

Magnolia soulangeana 'Lennei'

Viburnum. Only a few have pungent flowers that are unpleasant to some noses – Cotoneaster for example – but this is a factor worth considering.

Fruits and foliage

Fruits are features for autumn and winter, on the whole, and only showy when they are fleshy berries. Examples of shrubs with fine berry displays include Berberis, Callicarpa, Chaenomeles, Clerodendron, Cotoneaster, Euonymus, Ilex, Leycesteria, Mahonia, Punica, Rosa, Sarcococca, Skimmia and Viburnum. Shrubs that produce capsules tend not to look so impressive, but some can be attractive, such as the fruiting heads of Hydrangea.

For the majority of the time, foliage dictates the appearance of a shrub. It is said that the human eye can perceive more shades of green than any other colour, and carefully selecting shrubs that exhibit a variety of hues and finishes – light green, dark green, matt or glossy – will create subtle visual contrasts.

Evergreen foliage provides a year-round effect, whereas autumn colour sends the gardening year off in style. Shrubs with coloured foliage have an important role to play, but take care not to over use them. The colour of new foliage can be very strong, whether in the spring with, for example, *Philadelphus coronarius* 'Aureus' and *Physocarpus opulifolius* 'Dart's Gold', or in bursts or flushes through the summer with *Corylopsis sinensis* 'Spring Purple', *Nandina domestica* 'Fire Power' or *Pieris* 'Forest Flame', to name a few.

Purple foliage can be attractive, but is probably over used. Look for varieties which keep a good colour throughout the summer, such as *Acer palmatum* var. dissectum 'Crimson Queen' or *Berberis thunbergii* 'Dart's Red Lady', and avoid those which become a dull, dank green after the first flush of youthful exuberance. Golden foliage can also be very attractive, *Lonicera nitida* 'Baggesen's Gold' is a fine example, but many deciduous shrubs with golden foliage get bleached if positioned in strong sunlight – *Physocarpus opulifolius* 'Luteus', in particular, suffers from this problem. Shrubs with variegated foliage, such as *Cornus alba* 'Elegantissima', can offer variety without exhausting the eye.

Designing with shrubs

The next stage is to draw up some design ideas – no matter how rough – for planting schemes that utilize shrubs. The traditional shrub bed combines many different shrubs of contrasting and complementary forms. Shrubs can also be sited alongside perennials and summer bedding to provide an element of continuity in the planting. Specimen shrubs (generally, the finest ones available), with particularly impressive features can be used as focal points, on their own or in small groups. Or if you are looking simply to fill a large area of the garden, then shrubs make ideal plants for ground cover.

If you are planning a shrub or mixed bed, you will need to select plants with different forms or habits of growth. Upright spiky subjects, such as *Forsythia*

Berberis offers varied form and colour and mixes well

Buxus harlandii makes a good focal point in the middle of a mixed herbaceous border

'Lynwood', *Rosmarinus officinalis* 'Miss Jessop's Upright' or *Ribes sanguineum* 'Pulborough Scarlet', contrast with the rounded mounds of *Acer palmatum* var. *dissectum*, *Daphne tangutica* or *Kolkwitzia amabilis* 'Pink Beauty', or the tiered layers of foliage offered by *Viburnum plicatum* 'Mariesii'. Choose carefully and play around with different planting arrangements. A bed full of spiky subjects is likely to be discordant and unsettling, whereas nothing but rounded bushes can quickly send you to sleep.

Size and vigour of growth should also be considered. Taller growing shrubs should generally be sited towards the back of a border, with lower growing shrubs at the front. But it is good to vary planting schemes with the occasional taller spiky bush planted near the front between lower growing specimens.

Prostrate growing shrubs can also look very effective and are especially useful as ground cover. Most heathers fall into this category, as do some dwarf conifers, for example *Juniperus horizontalis* forms. The more vigorous prostrate shrubs, such as *Rubus tricolor* and Vinca, work well as cost effective temporary planting to fill the gaps between larger shrubs in early stages of growth.

> ### BARK
>
> Bark effect is most often a winter phenomenon, as it is usually not developed until the wood has fully ripened, and in most cases is hidden by the leaves before then. The effect can either be due to a striking bark colour, such as *Cornus alba* 'Sibirica' or *Cornus stolonifera* 'Flaviramea', or to a waxy bloom, such as *Rubus cockburnianus* and *Rubus thibetanus*. However, the corky wings of *Euonymus alatus* or the bristly stems of *Rubus tricolor* are also worth considering.

Buying Shrubs

Shrubs can be bought from a variety of sources – garden centres, general and local nurseries and specialist nurseries. In practice, you will probably visit them all, sooner or later!

Garden centres vs. nurseries

A garden centre will often be the first port of call, as there are usually one or two close by. They are retail outlets, selling on plants that are grown elsewhere, and as such are likely to have a limited range, but what they do have will be of a uniform quality. Apart from anything, they will almost certainly stock the full range of accessories and all the latest gadgets.

General nurseries are likely to have grown the plants sold in the garden centres, so you may find better stock and a wider range, but you will probably need to travel further to find one. Small local nurseries can be good for a number of items, and may be cheaper, but usually have a more restricted range.

Specialist nurseries are well worth considering if you have a particular favourite type of plant or want something less common. Horticultural societies will help you hunt out specialist nurseries and can often provide comprehensive lists.

Container grown plants

Suppliers sell shrubs either container grown, bare-rooted or rootballed. The great advantage of buying plants grown in containers is that you will be transporting them with their complete root system intact, and as such they are much more likely to thrive when planted out. Container plants can be planted throughout the year, not just in the dormant planting season of autumn to spring, although they will need very regular

Check container grown shrubs over thoroughly before buying them

watering if planted during the summer months until they have established roots into the soil. In particular, container grown stock is excellent for evergreens, which can dry out and die if planted bare-rooted.

The main drawback is that container grown shrubs can become 'pot-bound' if left for too long –– shrubs should not spend more than two years, and preferably only 18 months, in a container before being repotted or planted out. With such plants you tend to find that the roots have filled the pot and started to circle around, which means that they are unlikely to establish a new root system in the soil when planted in the garden. Or sometimes the roots escape through the bottom of the pot and grow into the sand or soil beneath. Pot-bound shrubs often show poor growth because they have exhausted the nutrients in the compost.

When buying container grown plants:
- check the roots are not spiralling around inside the pot
- look out for too many roots escaping through the drainage holes
- ensure the top growth is healthy and the soil around the plant is not overgrown with weeds
- check to see whether the level of compost has

TIP

Garden centres sometimes containerize shrubs, such as roses, which have been supplied to them bare-rooted. There are two ways to tell if a plant has been containerized. First, check the surface of the compost; if it is rough then the shrub has probably been newly potted, as a month or two of rain makes it much smoother. Next, try and lift the shrub up by the stem; if the soil is loose and the plant comes away in your hand, this is another sure sign. Return later to buy them, or simply go elsewhere, as if planted out too soon the compost will fall away, damaging the soft new roots.

dropped below the rim of the pot (1cm/⅜in below the top) – all container composts break down over time, so if the level has dropped this is a sure sign the shrub has been there too long.

Bare-rooted plants

Bare-rooted shrubs weigh much less than container grown equivalents and will be easier to transport. However, much of the root system is left in the nursery soil and therefore they can be slow to establish in their new home. On the other hand, they can have a more extensive root system than container grown plants, as in the nursery they will have spread into a much larger volume of soil than if they were grown in a pot.

When buying bare-rooted shrubs:
- look for healthy root systems; avoid plants with damaged, broken or dry roots
- always keep the roots out of strong sunlight, as they can become dried out or overheated, both of which will kill them

Bare-rooted shrubs can be sent by mail provided the roots are wrapped in either polythene or straw to keep them moist. Roses travel particularly well in this manner.

Rootballed plants

Rootballed shrubs are nursery grown plants that have been lifted with the soil attached to the roots. The ball of soil is wrapped in hessian or a coarse cloth to prevent it falling off and causing the roots to dry out.

A rootballed shrub will weigh more than a similar sized container grown plant, because soil is heavier than compost. For some items, rootballing represents a good compromise

between the cheapness of bare-rooted stock with its increased risk of failure, and the expense of container grown stock.

With some evergreens, such as field-grown conifers, the rootball should be handled with extra care, as the more soil knocked off, the greater the risk of the plant failing to grow well once it has been re-planted. However, plants which make dense fibrous root systems, such as Rhododendrons, are very resilient and the technique is excellent for these.

> **SIZE MATTERS**
>
> Avoid buying shrubs which have nearly attained their full size as they are less likely to thrive than ones bought at a third to a half their full size. Equally, if the plant is too small, it will be vulnerable to damage and slow to make a reasonable size. Aim to buy plants which are between a quarter and a half of the intended full size, if that is up to 2m (6ft), and aim for a minimum 0.5m (1½ft) for taller growing plants. But do not be inflexible about this – items that grow vigorously from buds low down on the plant, such as roses, can safely be bought smaller.

Ensure that bare-rooted plants have healthy root systems (*left*) and handle rootballs carefully (*right*)

Planting

In order to get the best from your newly acquired shrubs, it is important to learn how to prepare soil, deal with weeds and plant correctly. Again, different rules apply for container grown, bare-rooted and rootballed shrubs.

Preparing the Site

Preparation is half the battle when it comes to planting. The site needs to be in as good a condition as possible and you need to have planned exactly where you are going to place each shrub.

At this stage, there are three other aspects of soil preparation to consider: compaction, waterlogging and weeds. Some plants simply will not thrive in certain soils, however, no matter how much preparation is carried out. (Alkaline soils generally present the most problems in this respect.) Check in the plant directory before buying and see page 8 for more on this subject.

Compacted soil

Shrubs will not grow in compacted soils for several reasons. Without an adequately porous structure, air cannot circulate and water cannot drain away. Perhaps most importantly, newly planted shrubs will not take hold since the roots need to be able to penetrate the earth and the sheer density of the compacted soil will prevent this.

Compaction is unlikely to be a serious problem if you have an old garden, but with almost all new houses you will find the soil has been compacted by the builders' heavy machinery. A lot of hard work is the only solution. First, start to break up the surface with a fork, then dig out about two fork-depths of the topsoil. Take a pickaxe and break up the subsoil underneath, then replace the topsoil.

Waterlogging

Waterlogged soil prevents a shrub from growing by drowning the roots. Very few plants can actually grow with their roots under water. Many shrubs, however, will tolerate short periods of waterlogging during the dormant season. This is because the fine roots that absorb water, air and nutrients from the soil, and are very susceptible to being drowned, are not actually produced during the dormant season.

Waterlogging is usually either caused by compaction or poorly draining soil. Follow the method just described to break up compacted soil. With naturally heavy soil, digging in organic matter and applying a layer of organic mulch will help to make it more free draining, and has the additional benefit of improving soil fertility.

If the soil in your garden is persistently waterlogged, short of introducing complicated drainage systems, another technique to try is to make a series of mounds and then plant the shrubs into the mounds. However, you will still need to choose more tolerant shrubs for this to be effective.

Weeds

Weed control is well worth achieving before you plant, to ensure that new plants are not competing with weeds for nutrients, and because weeding is more difficult with planting in place. Larger weeds can be removed by hand, hoeing, or by forking over the soil. Perennial weeds, such as couch grass, are the biggest problem, as even if their upper foliage is killed, they survive through their underground food stores and return each year. To remove perennial weeds properly you need to kill them off at the roots. For this it is best to use translocated chemical

Remove weeds from around shrubs to reduce competition for the nutrients in the soil

weedkillers, such as those containing glyphosate, which are applied to the foliage and then travel down through the plant to attack the roots. However, translocated weedkillers tend not to be selective and will attack weeds and garden plants alike – another reason why it is better to achieve a weed-free soil prior to planting. Most weedkillers require at least several days to take effect, and often as long as several weeks or more, before any planting can occur, so always read the label.

If you dislike using chemicals, try laying sheet mulches (woven polypropylene and black polythene) for several weeks or months before planting to kill the weeds. An organic mulch is another option, provided you apply a layer at least 5cm (2in) thick, and this has the added benefit of enriching the soil.

Planting the Shrub

No shrub likes to be planted deeper than it has been growing. Always plant at the soil mark on the stem made by the nursery soil, or the level of the container. If in doubt, plant on the shallow side.

If you have already had to deal with any compaction by digging over the soil, then simply excavate a hole sufficient to accommodate the root system as normal. Otherwise, employ the 'two holes' method to give your plant the best possible start. First, dig a hole as large as possible, but at least 15cm (6in) larger than needed. Fill the hole back in completely, resisting the temptation to plant as you do so. Then dig another hole of the correct proportions out of the hole you have just filled in. This may seem like needless extra work, but by digging two holes you are breaking up the soil around the plant so that the roots can freely extend out.

Container plants

Before planting, check if the compost has dried out, since it is unlikely to rewet when planted in the ground. Soak the compost in a bucket of water for an hour or two, but do not leave it soaking too long or you will kill all the fine roots. Also, trim back any damaged top portions to good shoots.

Container grown shrubs can be planted at any time of the year, but if planted during the summer months they will require regular watering.

To plant a container grown shrub: dig out a hole of the correct depth but at least 5cm (2in) wider than the container [A]. Remove the shrub from its pot. Tease out the roots if they have formed a circular mass in the

bottom of the pot, so that they are spread out in the hole as widely as possible, and place the rootball in the hole [B]. If there are woody circling roots which cannot be teased out, cut them with secateurs at three points equally spaced around the circle, so that new roots can form. The objective is to prevent the roots growing in a circling manner, as shrubs with circling roots usually blow over sooner or later. Replace the soil in layers no more than 10–15cm (4–6in) thick, firming each layer with your feet as you go along [C]. Use the sole of your foot to firm, taking care not to compact the soil unduly as you do so. Water the plant in thoroughly [D].

When planting into a grassy site, you will need to remove the turf. The best place to put the turf is at the bottom of the planting hole – breaking it up first – where it can act as a compost for the roots. Never, ever place it around the shrub, as the grass will grow vigorously to the detriment of the shrub, even if you turn it upside down!

A

B

C

Bare-rooted plants

Bare-rooted shrubs should only be planted when the plant is dormant, between late autumn and early spring. If in leaf, the plant will not be able to absorb sufficient water to compensate for the loss of roots.

Check the condition of the roots. If dry, soak them in a bucket of water for up to 12 hours. If some are broken or damaged, cut them back to undamaged root using a knife or secateurs.

To plant a bare-rooted shrub: dig the hole to the correct depth and width to hold the roots. If any roots are bent so that they are growing into the centre of the shrub, bend them back outwards [A]. If this is impossible, prune them off, otherwise you risk the root girdling the other roots and causing the shrub to blow over in the future. Backfill round the plant, firming the soil as you go [B]. Water the plant in thoroughly [C].

Rootballed plants

Rootballed shrubs can be planted over a longer period than bare-rooted shrubs, but avoid the late spring to early autumn period. Fibrous-rooted plants, such as Rhododendron, can safely be soaked if the rootball has dried out, but most rootballed shrubs have coarser root systems which will fall apart if thoroughly wetted. Wait till after planting to give these a thorough watering in. To plant a rootballed shrub: dig a hole to the same depth as the rootball but at least 5cm (2in) wider to allow for the roots. Place the shrub in the centre of the hole and

untie or cut the hessian or other material used to make the ball. Spread out the hessian but don't try to remove it or you will damage the rootball – it can safely be left in the ground to rot down. Tease out any roots that are free from the soil of the rootball and spread these out, checking that there are no girdling or circling roots. Backfill with soil in stages of 10–15cm (4–6in) in thickness, firming as you go.

Planting a wall shrub

When planting a shrub beside a wall, dig the planting hole 30–50cm (12–20in) out from the wall if possible. This is because the soil directly beside a wall is often drier than elsewhere – especially on house walls due to the overhang of the roof – and frequently full of rubble. If the shrub is to be tied into support wires or trellis on the wall, plant it at an angle towards the wall, using a cane as a temporary stake to bridge the gap.

Supports are needed for two functions, to keep the shrub in place and as a route along which growth may be trained. On both counts, using a system of wires and/or trellis is the best option for growing wall shrubs.

Place the plant carefully in the hole [A]. Attach wires to a wall using 'eyes' which are screwed into the mortar using a plastic plug. Alternatively, use a network of wooden battens or trellis to support the wires, as shown [B]. The wires should start from 30cm (12in) above ground level.

A

B

C

When attaching plants to the wires or trellis, make sure that the ties you use do not cause damage by completely girdling the stems [C].

As the shrub grows, train it by removing branches which extend in the 'wrong' direction, keeping only those which fit neatly against the wall.

Staking

Newly-planted shrubs often need staking to help them get established. The purpose of a stake is to hold the roots firm so that the very brittle feeder roots are not damaged by the plant rocking in the wind – it is not to keep the stem rigid. Once the fine roots have become woody (lignified) the shrub should not need further staking.

Stems of flowering shrubs are designed to flex in the wind to dissipate the wind's energy. Holding the stem rigid confuses the plant, as it uses the flexing of the stem to determine how much wood it needs to make. Thus, rigidly-staked shrubs can be stronger above the top of the stake, and often when the stake wears out and snaps, the stem is unable to support the top of the plant.

The solution to this problem is, wherever possible, to stake using no more than a thin batten or bamboo cane, which provides adequate protection against wind rock but which still allows the stem of the plant to flex. Tie the stem to the cane with tape, rather than wire or twine, which will be unyielding when the stem thickens and will also cut into the plant, causing it damage.

Normally a shrub should not need staking for longer than a year, and often for only a few months. If after a year it still needs staking, it is probably because it has been planted too deep. It is better to trim it back rather than to continue staking.

Transplanting

Moving established plants can be an alternative to getting rid of unwanted plants or to those which do not fit in their existing position in the new design.

Small plants – that is plants that have reached less than half their mature size – can be dug out quite easily with a spade and moved bare root. Very small plants can be lifted with all or nearly all their roots.

Transplanting a mature plant that has almost reached full height involves a careful operation to dig out the rootball. Transplant between early autumn and late spring, though evergreens such as Ilex are best moved in early autumn when the soil is still warm. They should also be thoroughly watered in once they have been transplanted.

First, make a circle guideline around the shrub, digging a vertical slit a minimum of 30cm (12in) from the stem, or 50–60cm (20–24in) for shrubs 3–4m (10–13ft) high. Remove a spadeful of soil from outside the guideline, then work backwards to dig a circular trench around the shrub approximately 30cm (12in) deep. Next, use the spade to cut horizontally across from the base of the trench, freeing the shrub from the soil. Slip a folded sheet of polythene, or some other material, all the way underneath by gently rocking the shrub. Then either lift the shrub or dig a ramp on one side and drag it to its new position. Plant as described for a new rootballed plant. You should not need to stake the replanted shrub if the rootball has remained intact.

Dig well under the rootball when transplanting a hydrangea or any other shrub

Care & Maintenance

All plants need a little care and attention if they are to thrive. Simple maintenance, as outlined here, will mean that you get the best from your shrubs and will help to ensure a fantastic garden all-year round.

Mulching

Mulches are effective labour-saving applications and greatly benefit shrubs. The primary purpose of a mulch is to protect the soil surface; it helps to prevent weeds from germinating, it provides moisture retention by restricting evaporation from the soil surface, and it also helps to regulate soil temperature so that it is cooler in the summer and warmer in the winter.

Applying organic mulches that are eventually broken down and incorporated into the soil also benefits the soil texture by improving the water retention of lighter soils and lightening heavy soils so that they drain more easily. Organic mulches with high nutrient contents will also help to feed the soil and boost fertility.

Organic mulches

Bark is an excellent organic mulch, as it is long-lasting, looks good and is a by-product of timber production. Cocoa shells make an effective alternative to bark. You could also use wood chippings, but these are better suited to making paths through shrub areas rather than as mulches for beds. None of these wood- or husk-based mulches provide significant nutrients. A peat mulch will provide lots of nutrients but is only suitable for plants that flourish in acid soil, such as rhododendrons and heathers. To stay environmentally friendly, however, choose a peat-substitute instead, as the manufacture of peat composts has resulted in the large-scale destruction of some wetland areas. Leafmould is formed from composted leaves and will greatly improve the soil, as will manure, but here mulching turns into feeding, and with manure in particular you can be encouraging weeds to grow.

Spread a layer of organic mulch between 5–10cm (2–4in) thick. Any thinner, and the mulch will not work and birds and animals are likely to create bare areas. Any deeper, and you may swamp the plants and cause the mulch to overheat as it breaks down, thus scorching the stems of your shrubs.

Inert mulches

The two main types of inert mulches are pea gravel and synthetic sheeting (woven polypropylene or polythene). Although highly effective at controlling weeds, they do not provide any nutritional benefits. The open nature of pea gravel prevents weed growth whilst providing a surface which can be walked on without showing, and it sets off beautifully small shrubs, such as dwarf conifers. As with organic mulches, lay pea gravel in layers 5–10cm (2–4in) thick. However, if you need to raise the soil surface for any reason, a layer of pea gravel 30cm (1ft) thick will not harm plants, provided they are greater than 30cm (1ft) in height.

Sheet mulches work by allowing rain and water to percolate through the sheet whilst greatly reducing evaporation from the surface. Established weeds and those which germinate beneath the mulch are starved of light and eventually die, whilst the seeds which germinate on the top of the mulch are unable to root through the sheet. Woven polypropylene is the best material, but black polythene sheeting of a minimum 500 gauge or old polythene bags, such as compost bags, can also be used. These do not allow water to percolate, but provided they are no larger than 1m (3ft) square the water will run in from the sides.

Laying sheet mulches

A full sheet is best for covering an entire shrub bed. Lay it over the ground before planting but after initial preparation of the soil. Mark out the positions of the

Cocoa shells will provide an effective mulch but offer few nutrients

shrubs on the sheet and cut a cross for each one [A]. The size of the cuts will obviously depend upon the size of the shrub and its root system. Fold back the four flaps and plant the shrub through the centre, laying the flaps back around the stem after planting [B]. Mulch around the plant [C].

For shrubs that are scattered around the garden or for specimen shrubs, individual squares of sheeting are more appropriate. Cut a cross-shaped notch if the shrub is small and will go through the hole. For larger shrubs, cut a slit from one side into the middle of the square, then place it around the shrub and overlap the sheeting to close the slit. Squares should be a minimum of 0.5m (1ft 6in) square, but 0.7m (2ft 3in) is better and 1m (3ft 3in) square even better still. Squares are held down in one of two ways. Either use a spade to make slits in the turf just in from each edge and then force the sides into the slit, or hold down the corners with turf or stones.

> **TIP**
> Synthetic sheeting is not particularly attractive to have around the garden. Cover it up with an organic mulch, which will disguise the material and also hold it down firmly. The depth of the organic mulch can be thinner when you are laying it over sheeting, but aim for a minimum of 5cm (2in), and avoid mulches with a feeding action.

Feeding

Shrubs require adequate amounts of nutrients but generally do not require much additional feeding unless the soil is poor. You can test the amount of nutrients in your garden soil with kits available at garden centres. These work in a similar manner to the widely available pH soil testing kits. On poor soils, the best solution is to apply a mulch of well-rotted manure or leafmould at the rate of a barrow load for every 3m (3yd) square. Dried manures, such as poultry dung, should be applied at the lower end of the recommended range.

Inorganic chemical fertilizers can also be applied, but be wary of the recommended dosage values, which tend to be on the generous side. Too many added nutrients will only result in lush growth at the expense of flowers. This is especially the case if there is an excess of nitrogen in the fertilizer. Unless your plants are showing signs of deficiency in a particular mineral (see pages 154–157), apply a balanced general fertilizer at a rate of 60g (2oz) per 1m (1 yard) square, feeding once a year, preferably in spring. Soluble fertilizers can be applied using a watering can or by hose attachment, and are particularly effective on light sandy soils.

Digging well-rotted manure or compost into your garden soil will help enrich it and will greatly benefit your shrubs

Weeding

Weeds take water and nutrients intended for the shrubs, they can smother small shrubs and they look untidy. These are all good reasons for controlling weeds and there are several ways of doing so. Sheet mulches are particularly effective when applied to new plantings but are inconvenient for established beds, and organic mulches will control germinating weeds but are less effective where there are established weeds.

Chemical weedkillers, or herbicides, require the least effort, but you do run the risk of harming the shrubs, especially if you over use them. Herbicides containing glyphosate will kill most weeds. The herbicide is sprayed over the foliage of the weeds and kills by disrupting respiration. It should not be sprayed onto the foliage of shrubs and it may damage plants in the rose family by soil uptake, but it is generally a very safe material. Paraquat and diquat are also applied as foliage sprays but only kill the foliage onto which they are sprayed, not the root systems of established weeds. Some persistent herbicides are available from garden centres, such as products containing dichlobenil. As with all chemicals, these should be used strictly in accordance with the manufacturers' recommendations.

The third method of weed control is pulling or digging weeds out by hand. Take care when hoeing, as even shallow hoeing can damage the root systems of shrubs. Hoeing is most effective when the weeds are young and the weather is hot and dry, so that the uprooted weeds quickly wither. If the weather is wet, many will simply root into the soil again. Pull up large weeds by hand.

Watering

Water is essential for the growth of shrubs but they can easily be drowned. Therefore make sure the shrub has adequate water, but is not swimming! Also, if kept too moist some shrubs will grow well but fail to flower.

Working out quantities

First work out how much you will need to apply to each shrub. There are differences between the first year after planting, where watering is needed to give quick establishment, and later years when water may be needed to promote healthy and balanced growth.

Little water is needed during the winter months, apart from newly-planted evergreens if there are prolonged dry periods just after planting, especially in early spring or late autumn. The amount needed during the summer half of the year increases with the strength of the sun. In average temperate climates, the strength of the sun in mid-spring and early autumn is sufficient to evaporate roughly 1.5cm (½in) of water per week, in late spring and late summer this increases to 2cm (¾in) per week, and in high summer reaches 2.5cm (1in) per week. To work out exactly how much you need to water, measure with a rain gauge how much rainfall has fallen during the past week [A], noting the results [B], then only apply the above amounts less the rainfall.

A  B

You will also need to take into consideration the water-holding capacity of the soil. Well drained fertile soils, such as loams, will hold almost three times as much water as sandy soils. If you live in a high rainfall zone and have a good loam soil and never have droughts longer than four to six weeks, you need only water new plantings to establish them in the soil. However, if you live in a dry zone and garden on a light sandy soil, almost any drought will put your plants under pressure and weekly watering will be very beneficial.

Watering equipment

Watering cans, hand-held hoses and sprinkler systems are cheap and easy to use, but a significant amount of water is lost to evaporation and it is easy to apply too much. A more efficient, but expensive, alternative is to install a network of pipes or buried hoses, which can be supplied as fully automatic systems complete with pop-up sprinklers. Seep hoses and trickle irrigation devices provide a cheaper option. A seep hose is full of small perforations through which the water slowly oozes out into the soil. In trickle irrigation systems the water drips out of nozzles either onto the soil surface or just below.

With these systems virtually no water is lost through evaporation, but it is not so easy to measure how much is being applied and seep hoses in particular are liable to become blocked after a year or two.

Protecting Plants

Some flowering shrubs will require protection from the vagaries of the weather at various times, particularly if you live in a cool climate.

Winter protection

Winter protection is appropriate for some plants but is not really feasible for larger shrubs. Straw is ideal for wrapping plants or covering vulnerable parts. To prevent semi-hardy shrubs being killed by winter cold, cover over the crown of the plant (around the base) with a layer of straw or mulch. Frost damage may still cause the plant to be cut back, but new shoots will grow from the protected base in spring. To protect shrubs which are not frost hardy, wrap them up in straw, then hold the

TIP

To protect against late spring frosts, either insulate by covering plants with a lighter material, such as fleece or net curtains, or spray susceptible foliage with water, which protects because heat is given off when water changes from liquid into ice. Always keep an eye on the weather if air frosts are forecast, as these can be disastrous.

straw in place with a sheet of polythene or hessian. The perennial problem with winter protection is exactly when to remove it – too early and a cold snap or hard frost may kill the plant, too late and the plant may be making soft growth beneath the protection, which will be susceptible to fungal attack.

Protection from animals

You may need to protect your plants from animals that like to strip bark or feed on the foliage. The most effective method of protection is to fence off vulnerable plants. Use hexagonal wire netting with a mesh size of no more than 3cm (1¼in) and at a height of 1m (3ft 3in) for smaller animals or 1.5m (5ft) for larger animals. Make sure the bottom 15cm (6in) of netting is bent outwards and covered by a thin layer of soil, otherwise burrowing animals will break through.

Pruning

Shrubs vary greatly in their requirements for pruning. The main reasons for pruning are to control the size of the shrub and the direction of growth, or to promote vigorous new growth.

Equipment and technique

A pair of secateurs is the best tool for most pruning and will cut through shoots up to 1cm (½in) thick. Secateurs come in two styles. By-pass secateurs have a sharp blade and a blunt blade which cut by a scissor action. In anvil secateurs the sharp blade cuts against the middle of a blunt anvil, rather like a knife on a chopping board. By-pass secateurs cause less bruising to the shoot and are thus better for finer pruning.

Shrub pruners are larger versions of secateurs and can handle branches up to 3cm (1¼in) in thickness. Use a pruning saw for larger branches or stems. Shears are useful for trimming hedges and similar bushes.

Pruning current or one year wood requires fine cuts. These should be made at a point on the branch where there are identifiable buds from which new shoots will grow. Make the cut about 0.5cm (¼in) above a bud or pair of buds. Where there are opposing buds cut straight across the stem, and where there are alternate buds cut at an angle. Choose buds which will grow outwards, so that the shrub develops an open framework of branches. For cuts into larger stems, where regrowth will not be from identifiable buds but from dormant buds, the cuts should be made at an angle so that water drains off the cut surface.

Secateurs, pruners and saws handle progressive degrees of pruning

Training pruning

Training is the simplest type of pruning and involves general maintenance to remove dead branches and defective or crossing limbs, or where limbs which spread in the 'wrong' direction occur, such as with a shrub growing against a wall. Most newly planted shrubs will also need some initial training to encourage healthy growth and a balanced, open shape. Immediately after planting, prune back any dead or damaged stems and any stems that are crossing, and if necessary thin out to encourage an open branch structure. Remove errant branches at a suitable point, either where they originate on the main stem or at a side branch (or a suitable bud).

use secateurs to cut out any dead or damaged wood and weak, crossing stems

cut back hard all the plant's stems to about 7cm (2¾in) from the ground

COPPICING A SHRUB

Coppicing can be used on shrubs which have strong stem colour. To promote vigorous, colourful new growth, cut the plant back hard before new growth begins in spring.

Coppicing

With shrubs which have grown too large for their setting, the choice is either to cut them back hard ('coppice') or to reduce their size more tactfully. Coppicing offers a quick way both to reduce and rejuvenate the plant. Not all shrubs can be coppiced, however, as it requires a shrub that can regrow from dormant buds in the bark.

Many broadleaved shrubs will respond, but there are some which are very sensitive and likely to die. Coppicing is not advisable for Cistus, Cytisus, Daphne

TRAINING PRUNING

When planting a young shrub, prune it carefully all round to create a balanced form and encourage vigorous growth. Cut back any weak, damaged or dead wood. Crossing or congested shoots should also be removed.

TIP

Shrubs with beautiful coloured bark can be coppiced to encourage a vigorous display of stems. Such shrubs include Cornus and some Rubus. Cut back the shrubs to near ground level in early spring, removing all the stems, for a colourful display in winter. It is worth the few months' wait for the effects coppicing can bring about.

and Hebe, and almost all conifers, with the exception of Taxus, will die if cut back hard as they must have green foliage from which to make new growth. Also, be wary of coppicing a shrub which has been propagated by grafting, as you will probably encourage the rootstock to grow, rather than the scion variety.

To coppice a shrub, cut all growth back down to 7cm (2⅜in) above ground level, or alternatively leave the shrub on a short stem or 'leg'. You may need to thin out the new growth after the first season to form a natural shape. This will involve removing surplus stems, and possibly shortening the new growths. Coppicing is best carried out in spring, but it can be done at any time of the year; however, avoid early autumn, as any new growth is likely to be killed by winter cold.

Pruning to flower

Pruning is also used to increase flowering. To practise this successfully requires an understanding of what makes each particular shrub tick, as there are two main categories for this type of pruning and knowing which one you are dealing with can make all the difference between colourful flowers and undistinguished foliage.

The difference between the two groups is whether they flower from buds laid down last year (Group 1) or whether they flower on the new growth (Group 2). Generally, Group 1 shrubs flower over winter, in spring or early summer, whilst Group 2 shrubs flower in summer and autumn. Ceanothus provides an example of a genus which includes varieties in both Group 1 and Group 2. *Ceanothus thrysiflorus* flowers in spring and is a Group 1 shrub, whereas *Ceanothus* 'Burkwoodii' flowers in late summer and autumn and is in Group 2. If *Ceanothus thrysiflorus* is hard pruned in late winter or early spring, it will not flower until the following season, as you will have removed the previous year's growth. Whereas if you were to hard prune *Ceanothus* 'Burkwoodii' in late winter or early spring, it would produce more new growth and therefore lots more flowers.

Group 1 shrubs

Group 1 shrubs include Abelia, Berberis, Camellia, Chaenomeles, Clethra, Cornus, Deutzia, Exochorda, Forsythia, many Hydrangea and Spiraea and most other shrubs.

Group 1 shrubs should be pruned immediately after they finish flowering. The level of pruning will range from limited removal of crowded shoots, for example with Abelia, Camellia and Chaenomeles, to genera where the pruning will consist of removing two or three year old shoots with the intention of concentrating the new growth into a limited number of shoots, for example with Forsythia. The main thing to remember with Group 1 shrubs is that, in general, you should restrict your pruning to the older shoots, leaving the newer shoots intact, as these shrubs tend to flower better on the spur shoots which are formed in the second year of a stem's life. That said, some do react well to being hard pruned annually. *Berberis stenophylla*, for instance, can make a floriferous hedge if hard trimmed annually after flowering in mid-spring, but this means that you will not get the attractive waxy blue fruits that distinguish this plant. One solution is to plant two shrubs and hard prune them after flowering in alternate years.

hard prune older stems immediately after flowering to encourage new growth

PRUNING GROUP 1 SHRUBS
Group 1 shrubs vary in terms of the amount of regular pruning they require, but as a rule you should avoid pruning new and one year old stems. Concentrate on removing older shoots, directly after flowering.

Group 2 shrubs

Group 2 shrubs include *Buddleja davidii*, Caryopteris, some Ceanothus, Ceratostigma, *Hydrangea paniculata*, Hypericum, Lavatera, *Lupinis arboreus*, Perovskia and *Spiraea japonica*. As they flower on this year's shoots, they can be hard pruned just as growth is starting in the spring. This will encourage them to make vigorous new growths and these will either bear large trusses of flowers, as with *Buddleja davidii*, or simply a greater number of flowers, as with Hypericum and Lavatera.

Group 2 shrubs can either be cut down to 7cm (2¾in) above ground level, or to the bases of branches – either way they will make new growth from dormant buds. Shrubs pruned in this manner will tend to flower later in the summer than if unpruned. For example, unpruned specimens of *Buddleja davidii* flower in mid-summer with many small trusses, whilst hard pruned specimens flower in late summer with fewer but much larger trusses. As this plant is grown both for its floral beauty and because the honey scented nectar is a favourite food for butterflies, it is possible to extend both flowering and butterfly attraction seasons by planting two specimens, hard pruning one as per Group 2 and lightly pruning the other as per Group 1.

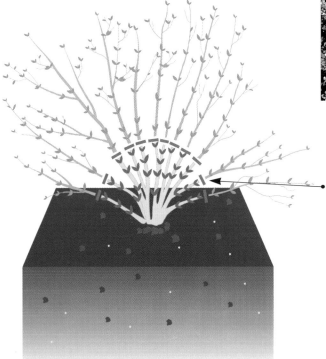

cut the shrub back hard to an even shape, 7cm (2¾in) above the ground or to the bases of branches

PRUNING GROUP 2 SHRUBS

Since Group 2 shrubs flower on new stems and shoots produced in the same year, for the best show they need to be hard pruned just as new growth is beginning in the spring. This will encourage an immediate response in the overall growth of the plant, followed by a more floriferous show of flowers that are larger in size.

Evergreen shrubs

Evergreen shrubs may fit either Group 1 or Group 2, but most of them require little pruning apart from 'tidying up'. Where they do need specific pruning is if any parts suffer from winter cold damage. This can happen when the severity of the cold kills parts of the shrub or when there are cold dry winds that freeze roots so that they are unable to provide water to the branches, causing the foliage to dry out and die. Because most evergreens tend to produce new leaves later than their deciduous counterparts, damage may not show until 'normal' growth has been made. Evergreens damaged in this manner require minor trimming to remove any damaged areas, mainly by cutting back to suitable side branches. Otherwise, prune as per the above groups, if more active pruning is appropriate.

Large-leafed shrubs should be pruned with secateurs

Snap dead flowers off between forefingers and thumb; be careful not to tear the stems

Dead-heading

Dead-heading refers to removing the old faded blooms. It is most often practised in flowering shrubs like Rhododendrons, where the flowers are picked off to prevent the bush exhausting itself by making seeds. By removing the flowers, energy is diverted into new growth, so that the side buds will mature in time to set flower buds for next year. To remove, hold the flower between the thumb and first two fingers just above the dormant buds in the leaf axils and snap it off. Don't worry if the leaf and bud come away with the flower, as there will be several others remaining.

Dead-heading is very valuable where the faded flower contrasts with remaining flowers. *Buddleja davidii* 'White Profusion' and *Buddleja fallowiana* 'Alba' can be very attractive when the large trusses of white flowers first open. However, after the flowers have finished, the petals turn brown and this contrasts poorly with the bright white flowers of later flushes. Snip off the faded trusses at the base of the flowers above the last leaves and you may get a further smaller pair of trusses. Other flowers which contrast poorly when they fade include the *Camellia japonica* forms, where frost damage to the petals can hasten their demise.

> **TIP**
>
> Roses, like rhododendrons, are commonly dead-headed, but this will not benefit the shrub species of Rosa, most varieties of which are equally attractive in fruit as in flower and only have a single flowering season. Hypericum can also be dead-headed, as this will encourage the side buds of these shrubs to flush and flower

Propagation

Plants may be propagated by either sexual or asexual means of reproduction. Sexual reproduction occurs when plants are propagated by seeds, as there has been an exchange of genes between the two parent plants to produce the seeds, with the result that each plant is uniquely different. Shrubs are propagated through asexual reproduction mainly by taking cuttings from the parent plant to produce a mirror image of the original. The main benefit of growing from cuttings is that, for many shrubs, this will provide usable plants more quickly than from seed, and you need not wait for the parent plant to produce viable seed in the first place. Asexual propagation is essential, however, if you wish to propagate a particular form or cultivar, as these tend not to come 'true' from seed.

Either technique can be employed to grow extra quantities of plants from existing stock. This might be in order to bulk up the numbers of shrubs you have so that you can make larger plantings for minimal expense, or to share plants with other gardeners. Or you could even set up your own little industry by selling them on!

By Seed

Raising plants from seeds is a quick method for many shrubs and for some it is the only practical way. Another advantage is that seed-raised plants have a natural root system, whereas cutting-raised ones can develop unbalanced roots which makes them prone to being blown over. Raising plants from seed also normally gives you diversity in the offspring, so that you are growing something 'new' and may even create a spectacular original cultivar. (However, a few shrubs, such as many Cotoneaster varieties, form seeds without going through the full sexual process and for these the offspring are exact copies of the mother plant.)

To raise plants from seed you must first obtain viable seeds, which then need to be treated so that they will germinate. The resultant seedlings must be nurtured to produce a healthy plant that can then be hardened off and planted out.

Collecting and storing seeds

Seeds can be collected from your own garden or that of a friend, or you can buy them from garden centres or nurseries; otherwise, obtain them in packet form by mail

order – horticultural societies may also run seed distribution schemes.

Collect your own seed as soon as the fruit is ripe – any later and you risk losing them to hungry birds. Most fruits ripen in the autumn, and some late into the winter. For shrubs that produce fine seeds in capsules, such as Buddleja and Hydrangea, there will be some seed in old capsules through to spring.

The next stage is to extract the seed. Fruits which are in capsules will need drying to release the seeds. Lay these out in small trays to dry and avoid using heat except for a few items such as pine cones. With fleshy fruits, especially juicy ones like Gaultheria, it is usually best to remove the flesh to prevent it rotting, which may kill the seeds, although Cotoneaster fruits can be sown with the flesh intact. Larger individual fruits that contain a single seed, such as Acer, only need surface drying before being put into storage.

Store seeds in polythene bags or in small paper envelopes. Make sure the surface of the seeds are dry, otherwise the paper will disintegrate or in polythene they may rot. Store seeds in the fridge to keep them viable for longer.

Collect seeds as soon as they are ready – or you will lose them

Germination

Having got your seed, the next phase is to germinate it. Most really fine seeds will germinate immediately, but many shrub seeds have dormant periods before they will germinate. Only larger seeds tend to go through dormancy, as there are fewer produced which means they need to be sure conditions are right, and with their own food reserves they can afford to wait. For example, a seed may remain dormant until several weeks of cold soil temperatures have passed. That way it can be sure the worst of the winter chill period is over and it is now safe to start putting down roots. Such seeds can simply be sown in autumn in trays placed in a cold frame and left over the winter, where the chill requirement should be supplied by the cool of the cold frame.

Another fairly common form of dormancy is when there is a hard or thick seed coat which needs to be broken down before the seed can germinate. Shrubs with the hardest coats include Cotoneaster and Juniperus, where the seeds may take up to five years to germinate. The seed coats are so hard because these plants produce fruits that are designed to be eaten by birds, with the seeds passing through the gut and released with a pellet of nutrients. Feeding these fruits to a tame parrot or canary will speed up the process naturally, or on a commercial scale strong acids are used to erode the seed coats. Most species with this type of seed coat will also then require a cool period of further dormancy before germinating. The thinner waxy coat of shrubs in the Legume family, such as Lupinus, can be mechanically scoured or scarified. This involves using a file to break through the waxy layer in a section of the seed, thereby enabling it to absorb water and so germinate.

Some shrub seeds experience a two-stage dormancy, whereby roots are put out after one condition is satisfied, but the shoot only grows later after a further dormancy requirement is met. An example in this category is Paeonia. In practice, sow in the autumn and be prepared to wait.

Sowing

Seeds are usually sown in autumn in seed trays and then kept over winter in a cold frame outside if they can withstand the low temperatures, or under cover in a greenhouse or propagator if they are less hardy. Some temperate plants should only be raised in a greenhouse in spring.

Sow seeds in trays and cover for the winter

To stimulate germination, soak larger seeds overnight before sowing. To decide if the seeds are large enough to soak, consider whether you will still be able to handle them when wetted. If the seed is fine dust then the answer is no, but if each seed is 2–3mm (⅒in) or larger the answer is yes.

Seeds require a fine compost for sowing, which does not need to be rich in nutrients but should be moist and freely draining. Sow seeds with enough space in between to allow them to grow without being crowded, then cover them over according to their size. The small dust-like seeds of Buddleja and Deutzia will require no more than a fine dusting of sand to hold them in place, whilst larger seeds should be covered by a depth of compost equivalent to the size of the seed.

Thoroughly soak the compost prior to sowing and do not allow it to dry out. With fine seeds, if the compost is suitably moist from the start then you may not need to carry out any further watering before germination occurs. If watering is required, however, do so from below by standing the pot in a bowl of water. Larger seeds protected by a layer of compost can be watered gently from above.

When the seeds have germinated, they can either be potted up individually as soon as convenient to handle, or left to grow until the second spring. Avoid potting up until there are two adult leaves and never hold a small seedling by its stem, always use a leaf or cotyledon (seed leaf). Pot on using a compost with sufficient nutrients to support growth, or failing that provide weekly feeds.

Protect seeds from hungry mice and birds by covering them over with wire netting. Germinating seedlings make tasty meals for slugs, whilst scarid flies in the compost will eat the roots. Fungal diseases can also be a problem, more so if the seedlings are densely packed, but this can be avoided by spraying regularly with a fungicide.

By Cuttings

Cuttings can be taken as softwood, semi-ripe and hardwood cuttings. When raising plants from cuttings, the main requirement is to keep the cutting alive whilst it forms roots. The shorter this time is, the quicker and better will be the resultant plant. Some plants will form roots at most times of the year, others will only do so at particular times. The speed and timing of rooting is largely determined by the presence of plant hormones, or 'auxins', but these can be introduced artificially by dipping the cuttings into proprietary hormonal rooting powders. These consist of a small quantity of one or more hormones in a talc powder, and some also contain a fungicide which helps to prevent the cutting from rotting. Rooting powders are worth using for all cuttings unless you are certain you have hit the optimum time for an easily rooted shrub (such as Hypericum).

Suitable composts for propagating cuttings should hold moisture to allow water to be absorbed, but should also be free draining so that the cutting can absorb oxygen from the air in the compost, and must be sterile to prevent the cutting from rotting. Suitable composts include peat (or peat substitute), sand, vermiculite and perlite. Mix peat and sand in proportions of three parts peat to one of sand, or half and half for maximum drainage. Vermiculite and perlite can also be used in combination with peat but are often used on their own. Proprietary compost mixes specifically tailored to propagating by cuttings are also widely available.

Softwood cuttings

Softwood cuttings are taken from shoots in late spring or early summer when the current season's growth is soft and has not become woody at the base. Using a pair of secateurs, cut off a young shoot approximately 10–15cm (4–6in) in length, or shorter for slower growing shrubs [A]. Make sure the bottom of the cutting is cut off neatly [B]. Then remove the lower leaves, leaving two to four pairs of leaves at the tip.

Dip the base of the cutting into hormone powder, shaking off any surplus [C], then insert the cutting into a tray or pot filled with suitable compost [D] and gently water it in. Do not push the cutting directly into the soil or you will rub off the rooting powder. Use a dibber to make the planting hole instead. Keep the planted cuttings in a humid atmosphere by placing them in a propagator or by covering them with polythene sheeting

– pots can be covered with a polythene bag. Cuttings need light to continue growing whilst waiting to root, but they should be protected from strong sunlight, which can kill by drying them out or cooking them.

Rooting may occur within a fortnight but can take several months, particularly for slow growing shrubs. After rooting has occurred, pot on the cuttings into separate pots and, once they are established in their new pots after a few days, gradually harden them off by letting in more air. If at any time they become wilted, return them to the frame or cover them with polythene once again.

Semi-ripe cuttings

Propagating with these types of cuttings works especially well with evergreen shrubs, such as Berberis. Semi-ripe cuttings are taken from new shoots later in the growing season, in late summer or early autumn, which are woody at the base but still soft at the tip. They can either be cut with a 'heel' of the old wood at the base or just below the node of a leaf, shoot or bud on the stem.

A B

C D

surface of the wound is covered [C], then plant into a ready-made hole in some compost [D] and lightly water in.

If propagating with pots in a cold frame, keep them covered over winter and insulate if necessary, then harden them off over the next growing season and either plant out in the autumn or pot on and wait until the following spring. Cuttings grown in a propagator over winter can usually be potted on or planted out the following spring.

Hardwood cuttings

Deciduous shrubs do not give successful cuttings in late autumn, but they can be propagated from hardwood cuttings in late winter when the shrubs are leafless or almost leafless, particularly Forsythia, Ligustrum and Salix. Cuttings are taken from shoots of this season's growth when the whole shoot has turned woody.

First, select a free bed in a shaded part of the garden and dig a trench about 17cm (7in) to hold the cuttings. Place sand in the bottom of the trench to assist with drainage. Select healthy, vigorous, fully matured sideshoots and cut them off just above the junction with the older wood of the main stem. Remove any remaining leaves and trim each cutting to a length of 25cm (10in). Treat the base of the cutting with hormone powder, cutting a wound if necessary. The cuttings are then buried in the trench to two thirds of their length at a spacing of 20cm (8in) apart. Lift the cuttings in the following autumn and either plant them out, for example as a hedge, or grow them on in a nursery bed for a year.

Root cuttings

Another option for propagating with cuttings is to take root cuttings. These are taken in late winter when the plants are still dormant and are particularly useful for suckering shrubs, such as some Rubus.

Expose some of the root system of a plant or lift it entirely from the ground. Select undamaged, young roots of a pencil thickness, and cut them off near the stem. Trim the roots into 5–7cm (2–2¾in) lengths, making a straight cut at the portion nearest the stem and a slanting cut at the opposite end – this is so that the cutting is potted up the right way round. Insert each cutting into a container filled with rooting compost, at intervals of about 5cm (2in) with the slanting end buried in the compost.

The cuttings will require an initial thorough watering in, but will need little if any watering until the shoots appear. After about a couple of months, the cuttings will have rooted and can then be potted on if growth is vigorous, or left to grow for another year and then planted out.

Making a cut below a node or with a heel will assist with rooting as growth hormones concentrate in these areas.

The method of propagation follows the basic pattern of softwood cuttings but with a few differences. After making the cutting [A], as well as removing the lower sets of leaves you will need to cut off the soft tip and if there are any sideshoots these should also be removed [B]. In addition, the base of the cutting can be wounded to improve rooting. To cut a wound, remove a thin sliver of bark at the base of the stem on one or both sides, about 3cm (1¼in) long. The wound increases the cut surface, so that water and hormone powder are more readily absorbed, and the damage also increases the production of hormones. Dip the cutting into hormone powder, making sure the entire

Grow young cuttings on in a propagator over winter

Planting Combinations

Some plants go well together, and it is very obvious, at least after the event, that some combinations do not. The success of any combination is partly a matter of taste – whether you accept such a concept as good taste – but also a question of whether it actually 'works'. A multiplex of different colours, forms and foliages mixed together can be very discordant, although occasionally it works. So how can we increase the chances of a scheme looking as good in practice as when we first conceived it?

Personally, I think there are several elements, but your own individual taste may suggest others.

Use of natural or contrived features

Most of us are familiar with the fall of land from a mountain top into a valley whether seen from above or from beneath, or the view over water and the marginal vegetation. This style of landscape can be

Ribes growing in conjunction with *Magnolia soulangeana* 'Lennei'

utilized on a small scale in the garden. For instance, if the garden slopes, you can use a series of tumbling beds of heathers, low growing Cotoneaster or dwarf conifers to create the impression of a natural fall of land; other plants which can give this effect are some of the brooms, such as *Cytisus praecox* 'Warminster', or *Ceanothus thyrsiflorus* var. *repens*, which can be very effective if planted at the top of a small wall or bank. A variant is to site *Acer palmatum* 'Dissectum' – or one of the other dwarf maples, evergreen azaleas or *Spiraea* 'Arguta', with its arching branches massed with trusses of small white flowers – around the far side of the pond, so that they both tumble over the water's edge and are reflected in it. Alternatively, use a conical evergreen such as *Abies lasiocarpa* 'Arizonica Compacta' to rise out of the planting. One of the most effective plants around my pond is a cobra lily (Arisaema) I collected in Vietnam; this is much more attractive in its reflection than when viewed directly. A level lawn stopped by a bed of shrubs is similar to the hedge around a meadow and thus has a rustic charm.

Plants can be used to create the appearance of high land tumbling down to the valley bottom. In essence, the use of taller plants at the back of a bed and lower ones at the front achieves this effect. Evergreen azaleas and vigorous Berberis, like *B. stenophylla*, can be trimmed immediately after flowering to make a plant plateau, or *Lonicera nitida* clipped as a topiary.

Scale

Scale is very important, as however much we might want to recreate an expansive moorland in the garden, the plants have to relate to the space available. Sometimes we can 'borrow' space from next door – perhaps using their tree or large shrub as a focal point – but generally we have to use the space within the garden. Therefore, the plants used have to fit together well. If you want a punctuation mark, for instance, like a Lombardy poplar, choose a shrub which will not grow too tall for the situation. Lombardy poplar (see *Trees & Shrubs* in this series of books) may be fine if you want a tree 20m (66ft) tall and have the corresponding space, but it will be out of scale in a small back garden. *Juniperus communis* 'Compressa' will achieve the same effect in a setting of flat Cotoneaster, heathers and other low growing shrubs, or you could try *Berberis thunbergii* 'Helmond Pillar' if you want a deciduous shrub with purple foliage instead.

Rhododendron 'Blue Diamond', showing colourful flowers and strongly contrasting foliage

Variety but conformity

Too much variety is uncomfortable, like a choppy sea making one seasick. However, although a placid flat sea may suit those of a nauseous disposition, it soon becomes tiresome for those seeking a modicum of stimulation. For example, the rounded globe shape of *Thuja occidentalis* 'Little Gem' can be very useful, but if there is one every half metre (20in) it may appear depressing. A good planting scheme will achieve a combination of variety, so that each aspect of the scheme has its own character, whilst holding together as a planned setting.

Timing

Plants do their things at different times. This has two benefits; for instance, two plants whose flowers would clash if in bloom at the same time can be grown together because they flower at different times. It is difficult to think that the cerise pink of *Camellia williamsii* would look good when flowering beside the purple pink of *Cistus argenteus* 'Peggy Sammons', or the rich blue of *Ceratostigma willmottianum* against the bright blue of *Ceanothus* 'Cascade', but because they flower at different seasons they can be grown in proximity without

Hebe and Ramnus combine well with a conifer to make a distinctive garden backdrop

Viburnum burkwoodii is a handsome, reliable shrub that will combine well with many others and make a statement

clashing. The other benefit of timing is that you can plant a variety to give colour over an extended season. A garden should be designed to look good throughout the year, not just for one short period.

Quality plants

Choose and use quality plants. Just because a garden centre will sell you a plant does not mean that it is a good one for you or your garden. Many plants are selected for ease of propagation as much as quality of flower, fruit and foliage; an example is the common form of Leyland cypress which is inferior to some of the other clones, but these are harder to raise and therefore not commercially viable.

Select plants which look good after they have been grown in a garden for several years, not because they look good in a garden centre. An example here is *Chamaecyparis pisifera* 'Boulevard'; it requires constant moisture and nutrients to look outstanding. In a nursery it gets this attention, but we generally expect plants once they are established to get on with life; 'Boulevard' will do just that, but in a dry spell unless watered the older, weaker foliage will turn brown, seriously detracting from the bright blue foliage.

Be prepared to be different

Finally, be different. Too much of modern culture is based on having (or wanting) whatever everyone else has. But never forget that your garden is your own, not anyone else's. And be prepared to experiment; if it doesn't work there is always the compost heap....

Photinia fraseri combines superbly with hornbeam for two-tier hedging

Flowering Shrubs

This section comprises most of the flowering plants included in the book. There are separate sections for Heathers and closely related plants (pages 137–141), and Dwarf Conifers (pages 142–150), as well as a single page on Architectural Plants (page 151). The plants covered range from low-growing, ground-hugging forms, such as *Rubus tricolor* and Gaultheria, to upright shrubs which can, with time, make large shrubs. The main unifying feature in this section is the beauty of the blooms, although a few are more showy in foliage or autumn fruit.

The sizes and spreads listed for shrubs after five and ten years' of growth respectively are indicative of what may be expected if the soil is well drained and reasonably fertile. If given lush conditions, many plants can exceed the suggested dimensions; similarly, on weedy or barren sites, they may take twice as long to grow to any size. The sizes assume that the planting stock is of a normal size for the individual shrub. Most of the time, planting stock will be circa 0.4m (16in) in height, but low-growing or slow-growing shrubs will be smaller and the indicated sizes try to make allowance for the likely planting size. Larger planting stock can give an immediate impact, but it is often slow to get established and may not be any larger over a five or ten year period.

Abelia
Abelia

Abelia are shrubs which are grown for both flower and foliage and come from China, Japan, the warmer parts of the Himalayas and Mexico. The flowers are tubular to bell-shaped in a fusion of the petals, and show that the genus is related to the honeysuckle (Lonicera). Their colour can range from white through to red.

Individually, the flowers are rather small, but they are freely carried and over a long period can make a very attractive display with one to four blooms from every leaf axil when really doing well. Colour is also provided by the two to five sepals at the base of the flower which persist when the petals fall and develop as a crown to the fruit (which contains a dry single-seed). The leaves are in clusters of two or three on the shoot and are no more than 6cm (2⅜in). Abelias can be either deciduous or semi-evergreen. They are not reliably hardy in cold areas, where they will benefit from the protection of a wall or a sunny aspect. Pruning need only include the removal of weaker growths. The early flowering forms should be pruned after flowering has finished (Group 1) but the forms which flower after

soil	Plant in any suitable, well-drained soil, including chalky soil
site	Enjoys being situated in full sun and will not flourish with much shade
general care	Likes plenty of organic matter in the soil, so dig in a mulch and fertilize the plant in the spring
pruning	Prune to restrict and remove dead and damaged shoots for a healthier shrub
pests & diseases	There are usually no problems from pests and diseases with this particular shrub

Abelia grandiflora

Abelia schumannii

mid-summer can be hard pruned in spring as Group 2 shrubs – which is just as well if a severe winter cuts them down to ground level (see pages 23–4). Propagation is by semi-hardwood cuttings in mid-summer.

	SPRING	SUMMER	AUTUMN	WINTER	height 5yrs (m)	height 10yrs (m)	spread 5yrs (m)	spread 10yrs (m)	petal colour	
Abelia 'Edward Goucher'		● ●	●		1.2	1.5	1.2	1.5		Glossy, semi-evergreen foliage
A. 'Confetti'			●		0.9	1.2	0.9	1.2		Glossy leaves are edged with white
A. grandiflora		● ●	● ●		1.2	1.8	1.2	18		Glossy semi-evergreen foliage, purple in winter
A. grandiflora 'Francis Mason'		● ●	● ●		1	1.5	1	1.5		Leaves are flushed orange when young
A. grandiflora 'Gold Spot'		● ●	● ●		1	1.5	1	1.5		Leaves variegated yellow
A. schumannii		● ●	● ●		1.2	20	1.2	2		Flowers larger, carried single in leaf axils

● *flowering*

Abeliophyllum
White forsythia

This shrub is grown for its highly fragrant flowers in later winter/early spring. The name means Abelia-leaf, but it is actually a member of the Olive family like Forsythia and comes from Korea.

Abeliophyllum distichum

The flowers are carried in racemes of three to fifteen blooms along the shoots and have four notched petals which are spread out in a star shape. These may be followed by rounded winged fruit. The shoots are warty and square in section. The leaves may turn purple in autumn before falling.

White forsythia is excellent for an open, sunny site in a border or when grown against a wall, where it will make a taller plant. It can be propagated from softwood or semi-ripe cuttings in summer, or the long trailing shoots can be layered.

soil	Well drained. Abeliophyllum: any, including chalky ones. Abutilon: fertile preferably
site	For best results, both these shrubs need a hot sunny site, particularly against a wall
general care	Abeliophyllum: propagate from semi-hardwood cuttings. Abutilon: propagate from soft/semi-hardwood cuttings
pruning	Abeliophyllum: trim flowering shoots when blooms fade. Abutilon: cut back in spring
pests & diseases	Abeliophyllum: generally trouble-free. Abutilon: watch out for white fly and red spider mites

Abutilon
Indian mallow *or* Flowering maple

Abutilon is in the mallow family, like Hibiscus and Lavatera. This is shown by the stamens of this plant, which are united into a tube around the style.

Abutilon suntense

The flowers have five showy petals which are united into a tube at the base. The calyces can also add to the display. Abutilon is a large, mainly tropical genus and not long lived in the average garden. In cold sites, it needs protection against a wall, or in a conservatory, and likes full sun or light shade at most. They should be kept well watered when growing, and will respond by making fast growth and flowering over an extended period. Propagate by softwood or semi-hardwood cuttings in summer.

	SPRING	SUMMER	AUTUMN	WINTER	height 5yrs (m)	height 10yrs (m)	spread 5yrs (m)	spread 10yrs (m)	petal colour	
Abeliophyllum distichum	● ● ●			●	1	2	1.2	2	□	Deciduous early flowering shrub for sunny site
A. distichum Roseum Group	● ● ●			●	1	2	1.2	2	▨	Deciduous early flowering shrub for sunny site
Abutilon megapotamicum		● ● ● ●	● ● ● ●		2	2.5	1	1.5	▨	Glossy, dark evergreen leaves; flowers pendent
A. megapotamicum 'Variegatum'		● ● ● ●	● ● ● ●		2	2.5	1	1.5	▨	Leaves blotched yellow
A. suntense	●	● ●			3	2	4	3	□	Deciduous, fast growing; flowers bowl-shaped
A. vitifolium	●	● ●			2.5	1.5	4	2.5	▨	Grey, green-toothed leaves

● *flowering*

Acer
Maple

Most maples form large trees, or at least large shrubs. They make excellent structural plantings for the garden, whether for shelter, foliage (especially autumn colour) or their barks. However, there are a number of forms of the Japanese maple which are low shrubs and clearly fit within the remit of this book. They are valuable tumbling over a low wall, or in the rockery to give scale, and also add autumn colour to the planting.

A. p. var. d. Dissectum Atropurpureum Group

soil	Acers will perform best when planted in fertile, well drained soil
site	Situate in the semi-shade and protect from hot sun and cold winds
general care	Feed and keep moist during the growing season. Important not to over-water or let the plant dry out
pruning	No great pruning is required, apart from removing twigs which die back over winter
pests & diseases	Vine weevil can be a problem to look out for, especially when growing in containers

Acers are excellent in containers, provided they are suitably pampered (watered) during the summer and have free drainage. They do not like to be in hot dry situations, preferring some shade and that their roots are kept cool. Their foliage is their main feature, ranging in colour from bright green to red, and in shape from a 'regular' maple leaf to deeply dissected ones. They do flower – these are purple and carried with the new foliage in spring – although you will need to keep an eye out if you want to see them as they are scarcely showy by normal criteria. Japanese maples grow best on neutral to acidic soils and are not really suited to chalky ones. They can be difficult to propagate from cuttings, as they must make new growth before losing their leaves in the autumn, so most of the small cultivars are grafted onto seedling rootstocks. This is carried out in mid-summer and the rootstock must be dry (but not wilted) or its sap will flood and kill the scion.

Acer palmatum var. *dissectum* Dissectum Viride Group

	SPRING	SUMMER	AUTUMN	WINTER	height 5yrs (m)	height 10yrs (m)	spread 5yrs (m)	spread 10yrs (m)	petal colour	
Acer palmatum 'Red Pigmy'	●				0.9	1.5	0.9	1.5		Leaves reddish-purple, long slender lobes
A. palmatum var. *dissectum*	●				0.7	1.2	0.8	1.2		Leaves green, turning yellow in autumn
A. p. var. *dissectum* 'Crimson Queen'	●				0.7	1.2	0.8	1.2		Leaves red-purple, turning scarlet in autumn
A. p. var. *dissectum* 'Inaba-shidare'	●				1	2	1	2		Leaves deep purple-red, crimson in autumn
A. p. var. *dissectum* 'Ornatum'	●				0.7	1.2	0.9	1.2		Leaves deeply cut, reddish-purple
Dissectum Atropurpureum Group	●				0.7	1.2	0.9	1.2		Leaves deeply cut, reddish-purple
Dissectum Viride Group	●				0.7	1.2	0.9	1.2		Deeply dissected green leaves, turning yellow

● *flowering*

Albizia
Pink siris

This is a genus of tropical trees which is not reliably hardy in many climatic conditions. However, when this single species does flower it is well worth having in the garden, which is why it is included here.

The reason it is not fully hardy is a combination of summer heat and winter cold/frost. It has a wide distribution, from Iran to China and Korea. It requires more summer heat than is available in many climates to ripen the wood so that it can withstand the vagaries of winter. However, it is grown for the beautiful pink flowers which are carried in late summer, even on young plants. It is also grown as a summer foliage plant, for the doubly pinnate foliage.

Propagation is by imported seed. This will have a hard waxy seed coat. To break this down, pour a quantity of boiling water equal to the volume of the seeds onto them, then soak for twelve hours before sowing. The boiling water breaks through the waxy coat and allows the seeds to imbibe water and germinate.

Albizia julibrissin

soil	Both prefer light, sandy, moderately fertile and well-drained soil
site	For best results, position both in as much full sun as possible
general care	Albizia: Plant out in early spring after the winter frosts. Arctostaphylos: no particular requirements
pruning	Generally, no pruning is required, apart from removing any dead twigs
pests & diseases	On the whole, these plants are fairly trouble-free from any pests and diseases

Arctostaphylos
Bearberry *or* Manzanita

This is a genus of shrubs mainly native to California but the species featured here is a British native. The bell-shaped flowers indicate that they belong to the heather family.

Arctostaphylos uva-ursi 'Vancouver Jade'

The fruit is a berry-like drupe, ripening red. The species of Arctostaphylos are mainly evergreen, with thick small paddle-shaped leaves. They tolerate a wider range of soils than most members of the heather family, being as happy on humus-rich soils as on those derived from limestone, but demand full sun to flourish. They are useful as ground cover, but the taller growing species are suited to shrub borders and some have smooth polished mahogany coloured barks.

	SPRING	SUMMER	AUTUMN	WINTER	height 5yrs (m)	height 10yrs (m)	spread 5yrs (m)	spread 10yrs (m)	petal colour	
Albizia julibrissin 'Rosea'		● ● ●			3	3	2	3		Requires good summer heat for strong growth
Arctostaphylos uva-ursi	●		⬿		0.15	0.2	1	2		Long drooping wands
A. uva-ursi 'Vancouver Jade'	● ●	● ● ●	⬿		0.15	0.2	1	2		Arching habit with glossy leaves

● *flowering*   ⬿ *harvest*

Aronia
Chokeberry

This is a genus of woodland, swamp and scrub margin shrubs from eastern North America. They are related to Sorbus and Photinia and belong to the apple subfamily of the Rosaceae.

Aronia make excellent plants for shrub beds or for wild parts of the garden. They are particularly suited to damp sandy soils, and generally tolerate wet sites but are not suited to shallow chalky soils.

The flowers of this plant are carried in mid-spring, in white clusters at the ends of the shoots. These are followed by the fruits, which ripen in early autumn. The best feature of aronias, however, is the stunning tints which the leaves adopt in early autumn before falling to the ground, turning vivid reds and crimson.

Aronia arbutifolia

Artemisia
Wormwood *or* Sage brush

This is a large genus with members ranging from annual herbs to woody plants. They have deeply divided and often silky hairy leaves which makes them useful as foliage plants.

Artemisia 'Powis Castle'

The leaves of many are aromatic if touched: the herb tarragon belongs to this genus. They are members of the dandelion family or Compositae. They need well drained soils and will not tolerate wet conditions. They are extremely drought tolerant and must have full sun. Propagate by softwood or semi-hardwood cuttings in summer. They are used to discourage mosquitoes and to get rid of leeches in the Far East.

soil	Aronia: damp, rich and wet fertile, but not chalky. Artemisia: well drained
site	Aronia: half sun to dappled shade. Artemisia: Full sun, as much as possible
general care	No particular requirements. Propagate both by cuttings, or seed, which may be slow to germinate
pruning	No pruning required, but older shoots can be removed to keep the shrubs vigorous
pests & diseases	No particular problems from pests and diseases, although with Aronia, birds may quickly eat the fruits

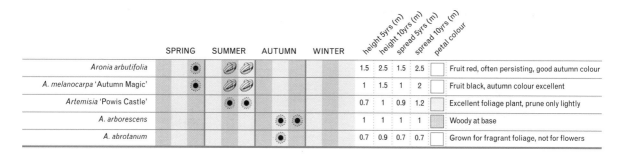

	SPRING	SUMMER	AUTUMN	WINTER	height 5yrs (m)	height 10yrs (m)	spread 5yrs (m)	spread 10yrs (m)	petal colour	
Aronia arbutifolia	●	🌰🌰			1.5	2.5	1.5	2.5	☐	Fruit red, often persisting, good autumn colour
A. melanocarpa 'Autumn Magic'	●	🌰🌰			1	1.5	1	2	☐	Fruit black, autumn colour excellent
Artemisia 'Powis Castle'		● ●			0.7	1	0.9	1.2	☐	Excellent foliage plant, prune only lightly
A. arborescens			● ●		1	1	1	1	▨	Woody at base
A. abrotanum			●		0.7	0.9	0.7	0.7	☐	Grown for fragrant foliage, not for flowers

● flowering	🌰 harvest

Berberis
Barberries

Berberis adds a colour dimension largely missing elsewhere in flowering shrubs – stunning orangey yellows, as displayed by some of the South American species such as *B. darwinii*, *B. linearifolia* 'Orange King' and *B. lologensis* 'Apricot Queen'. However, unusual flower colour is not this plant's only contribution to horticulture. The genus is large, with species occurring in all the continents except Australia and Antarctica. Berberis are tolerant of a wide range of soil types, whether alkaline from chalk or acidic from barren sands, but they do require reasonable drainage. These plants flourish in the average garden soil.

The flowers are carried on last year's shoots in spring and early summer, but just occasionally will some precocious flowers develop in the autumn in the more floriferous varieties like *B. darwinii*. They should be pruned as Group 1 shrubs (see page 23). The flowers are followed by the berries; these are colourful, either red or blackish-blue and are worthy of garden space for fruit effect alone. If you prune as Group 1 you will miss this berried treasure. The berries are also juicy and edible, and can be used for conserves.

One feature of Berberis which can be seen as either a drawback or an added advantage is that the stems have spines. These are borne at the base of the leaves and are usually three spines, up to 2.5cm (1in) at right angles. They can hurt small children (an obvious drawback!), can puncture plastic footballs and similar air-filled toys (this could be either a drawback or an advantage – perhaps they should play elsewhere!) and can be used to create effective hedges which discourage intruders (a definite advantage).

The species divide into evergreen and deciduous species which gives them different roles to play in the garden. The

Berberis thunbergii 'Rose Glow'

Berberis darwinii

soil	This plant likes any well drained soil, and is good for chalk soils
site	Position in full sun, but this plant also performs well in light or partial shade
general care	Propagate by semi-hardwood cuttings in summer or hardwood cuttings in a cold frame taken in autumn
pruning	Prune to remove weak or broken branches; can be trimmed for hedges.
pests & diseases	Some species host the fungus which causes rust on wheat and can cause leaf spotting and early leaf fall

Berberis thunbergii 'Red Chief'

evergreen species all have bloomed blue-black berries whereas the deciduous species all have red berries (apart from a small group of species in southeast Tibet and Bhutan). The evergreen species are listed beneath the deciduous species in the table below.

Deciduous Berberis include the outstanding *B. temolaica*, a quality specimen shrub with glaucous foliage which turns plum purple in autumn and sports white bloomed shoots. *B. wilsoniae* is a low shrub, attractive in habit, leaf (especially autumn colour) and for the red fruits. *B. thunbergii* comes in a wide variety of foliage colour forms, both purple-reds and golden greens, whereas the normal species is notable for its sealing wax red fruits and autumn colour. This species is excellent for hedging, especially the smaller growing forms which need little trimming.

	SPRING	SUMMER	AUTUMN	WINTER	height 5yrs (m)	height 10yrs (m)	spread 5yrs (m)	spread 10yrs (m)	petal colour	
[DECIDUOUS] *B. ottawensis* 'Superba'		●	harvest		1.5	3	1.2	2		Leaves purple-green, fruit red
B. temolaica	●		harvest		1.2	2	1.2	2.5		Good autumn colour, suckering on own roots
B. thunbergii	●		harvest		0.8	1	0.8	1		Fruit sealing wax red, good autumn colour
B. thunbergii 'Aurea'	●		harvest		0.8	1	0.8	1		Leaves golden-yellow
B. thunbergii 'Bagatelle'	●		harvest		0.2	0.3	0.2	0.3		Dwarf form
B. thunbergii 'Dart's Red Lady'	●		harvest		0.8	1	0.8	1		Leaves deep purple, red in autumn
B. thunbergii 'Golden Ring'	●		harvest		0.8	1	0.8	1		Leaves reddish purple with a gold margin
B. thunbergii 'Harlequinn'	●		harvest		0.6	0.8	0.6	0.8		Leaves pink variegated
B. thunbergii 'Helmond Pillar'	●		harvest		0.5	0.8	0.2	0.3		Leaves rich purple; narrow upright habit
B. thunbergii 'Red Chief'	●		harvest		0.4	0.6	0.2	0.3		Leaves reddish purple, scarlet in autumn
B. thunbergii 'Rose Glow'	●		harvest		0.6	0.8	0.6	0.8		New leaves purple, maturing to silver-pink
B. thunbergii f. *atropurpurea*	●		harvest		0.8	1	0.8	1		Leaves purplish red in spring and summer
B. wilsoniae		●	harvest		0.6	1	1.2	2		Deciduous/semi-evergreen, scarlet in autumn
[EVERGREEN] *B. buxifolia* 'Pygmaea'					0.3	0.5	0.3	0.5		Dwarf form, virtually thornless
B. candidula	●		harvest		0.4	0.7	0.3	0.7		Forms dense domed bush, leaves silvery beneath
B. darwinii	●		harvest		1	1.8	1	1.8		Excellent flowering shrub
B. frikartii 'Amstelven'		●	harvest		0.8	1	0.8	1		Branches compact, leaves glaucous beneath
B. julianae		●	harvest		1	2	1	2.5		Can make 4m in time
B. linearifolia 'Orange King'	●		harvest		1	1.5	0.5	1		Upright habit, flowers 2cm across
B. lologensis 'Apricot Queen'		●	harvest		1	1.5	0.5	1		Erect growing floriferous shrub
B. stenophylla	●		harvest		1.5	2.5	1.5	2.5		Excellent hedging shrub if clipped after flowering
B. verruculosa		●	harvest		1	1.2	1	1.2		Twigs warty, leaves grey beneath

● flowering   harvest

Brachyglottis

New Zealand Senecio

These evergreen shrubs are better know as species of **Senecio**, but as this genus includes weeds like groundsel and ragwort, from a horticultural perspective their separation into a distinct genus is to be commended. The **New Zealand Senecio** are particularly good for exposed coastal sites, as they tolerate salt spray, but are worth their place in less challenged gardens.

They produce masses of yellow dandelion flowers in summer, when few other plants are in full bloom. However, their most endearing feature is the foliage. This is silvery or buff coloured due to a dense covering of matted hairs producing a felted texture. The felt remains on the shoots and leaf undersides, but is soon rubbed off the leathery upper surface of the leaf, which becomes mid- to dark green or grey. New Zealand Senecio fit well into mixed and shrub borders provided they are given full exposure to the sun, and preferably a hot part of the garden. They should not be planted in shade, nor on poorly drained soils. They can be hard pruned in spring (Group 2) (see page 24) to maximize the foliage, but this will be at the expense of flowers. Otherwise, lightly trim after flowering to retain a neat shape; this is particularly relevant for 'Sunshine', which tends to be rather sprawling in its

Brachyglottis senecio 'Sunshine'

soil	This plant performs excellently in any well drained soil
site	Position in the full sun, preferably in the hottest spot in the garden
general care	Little care and maintenance is required but this plant can be damaged by hard winters
pruning	Can be pruned hard in spring to maximize foliage, or trim after flowering
pests & diseases	Generally, this plant is fairly robust and trouble-free from most pests and diseases

habit. Propagate by semi-hardwood cuttings in summer, or by seed. The Latin name translates as short (*brachy*) tongue (*glottis*) and refers to the short ray florets.

Brachyglottis senecio 'Sunshine'

	SPRING	SUMMER	AUTUMN	WINTER	height 5yrs (m)	height 10yrs (m)	spread 5yrs (m)	spread 10yrs (m)	petal colour	
Brachyglottis monroi		● ●			0.7	1	1	1.2		Dense habit; leaves with undulating margins
B. senecio 'Sunshine'		● ●			0.8	1	1.2	2		Leaves silvery-grey when young

● *flowering*

Buddleja
Butterfly bush

These are some of the commonest and most popular garden plants, self-seeding as effectively as sycamore but without the opprobrium that it attracts. They are primarily grown in the flowering garden for their large flowers which are honey-scented and which butterflies visit by the score in mid-summer.

The species listed here flower on the new growths, and thus are Group 2 for pruning (see page 24). They do not have to be hard pruned in spring, and the unmanaged Buddleja makes an excellent small tree. Untrimmed bushes flower in early summer a couple of weeks or more before their pruned cousins. However, for the brightest and best flowers, hard pruning to several centimetres (inches) above ground level (or back to main stems) in late winter is recommended. Vigorous regrowth will follow, terminating in large trusses containing myriad small flowers. The blue and purple flowered forms are not unattractive when the petals wither to brown but the white flowered forms tend to look ragged at this stage; it is worth dead-heading these, which will encourage side shoots to develop flowers.

Buddleja require good drainage and full sunlight; for the largest flowers they need a fertile soil, but they will grow on any well drained substrate, self-seeding into piles of gravel and chalk cliffs. They are propagated by semi-hardwood cuttings in summer, by seed.

soil	Performs in any well drained soil, but perhaps best in fertile loams
site	Position in the full sun, avoiding any intensity of shade
general care	For best results, give a good mulching and feed in the spring to produce the largest flowers
pruning	Hard prune to just above ground level in late winter to get the largest blooms
pests & diseases	There are no particular problems, but watch out for capsid bugs, caterpillars and red spider mites

Buddleja davidii 'Nanho Blue'

Buddleja davidii 'White Profusion'

	SPRING	SUMMER	AUTUMN	WINTER	height 5yrs (m)	height 10yrs (m)	spread 5yrs (m)	spread 10yrs (m)	petal colour	
Buddleja crispa		● ●	●		1.5	2	1.5	2		Silvery white foliage, needs a sheltered site
B. davidii 'Black Knight'		● ● ●	●		2	2.5	2	2.5		Excellent form with large trusses
B. davidii 'Dartmoor'		● ● ●	●		2	2.5	2	2.5		Unusual flower colour, can make 4–6m
B. davidii 'Empire Blue'		● ● ●	●		2	2.5	2	2.5		Attractive to butterflies, can make 4–6m
B. davidii 'Harlequin'		● ● ●	●		1.5	2	1.5	2		Leaves with creamy white variegations
B. davidii 'Nanho Blue'		● ● ●	●		2	2.5	2	2.5		Narrow leaves
B. davidii 'Royal Red'		● ● ●	●		2	2.5	2	2.5		Large trusses
B. davidii 'White Profusion'		● ● ●	●		2	2.5	2	2.5		Excellent when first out
B. fallowiana 'Alba'		● ●	●		2	2.5	2	2.5		Leaves white woolly, requires shelter

● *flowering*

Buxus

Box

Box has small evergreen leaves and much smaller insignificant flowers. It is valuable in the garden because it is very tolerant of clipping. This makes it one of the best shrubs to use for topiaries and living sculptures. It is also excellent for hedges of all sizes; outstanding in this respect is the cultivar 'Suffruticosa', which can be trimmed to make a hedge only a few centimetres (inches) in height.

Box is a genus of about 70 species that is found in a variety of habitats throughout Europe, Asia, Africa and Central America. It can be used as neat markers for vegetable gardens and displays of summer bedding, or to emulate mediaeval garden design. Untrimmed, this variety may make 1.2–1.5m (4–5ft). *Buxus sempervirens* as a wild species can make a narrow crowned tree over time.

Box is often found in the wild on soils derived from chalk and limestone, but it is perfectly happy over a wide range of soil pH, from about 5.5 to 7.4. However, what these plants do need is good drainage. Box is easily raised from cuttings, taken either in the spring or autumn.

soil	Does well in any well-drained soil, but has a slight preference for alkaline soils
site	Does not like full sun. Much prefers moderate sun to moderate shade
general care	Full sun can lead to foliage scorch, as can strong winds, so ensure plant is in a sheltered spot with protection
pruning	None needed but tolerant of hard pruning in the late spring for shaping
pests & diseases	Generally trouble-free from pests and diseases but can be affected by red spider mite

Buxus sempervirens

	SPRING	SUMMER	AUTUMN	WINTER	height 5yrs (m)	height 10yrs (m)	spread 5yrs (m)	spread 10yrs (m)	petal colour	
Buxus sempervirens 'Elegantissimum'	●				0.5	1.2	0.5	1.2		Leaves with a creamy white margin
B. sempervirens 'Suffruticosa'	●				0.3	0.5	0.2	0.4		Slow growing variety

● *flowering*

Callicarpa
Beautiful fruit

The scientific name for this plant is from the Greek *kallos* (beauty) and *karpos* (fruit) and admirably describes these deciduous shrubs. The berries are a remarkable violet purple in 'Profusion', a colour not found in any other shrub, whereas in others they are white.

The fruits are carried in dense, rounded clusters and ripen in late autumn. Individually, each fruit is small, only 3–4mm (⅛–⅛in) in diameter but each cluster contains a few dozen fruits, and there are two clusters at each node along the length of the shoots, giving a stunning display like an

soil	Grows well in moist soils and moisture retentive soils in particular
site	Prefers sun to light shade. In dense shade it will not fruit reliably
general care	Fruiting may be more prolific with these plants if two or more clones are grown together
pruning	Only prune to restrict size or to remove old unproductive shoots
pests & diseases	In general, there are no particular problems with these plants from pests and diseases

Callicarpa bodinieri var. giraldii 'Profusion'

Callicarpa bodinieri var. giraldii 'Profusion'

enlarged string of beads. The flowers are carried in mid-summer and are lilac in colour. Callicarpa will grow on a wide range of sites, preferring damp fertile soils. It likes a sunny aspect, not fruiting well in more than moderate shade. They are well sited in shrub and mixed borders, and can be used as specimens. The leaves turn yellow to purple in autumn. Callicarpa can be propagated by seed or by cuttings with a heel in spring.

	SPRING	SUMMER	AUTUMN	WINTER	height 5yrs (m)	height 10yrs (m)	spread 5yrs (m)	spread 10yrs (m)	petal colour	
Callicarpa bodinieri var. *giraldii* 'Profusion'		● ● ●	● 🌰 🌰	🌰	1.2	1.5	1	1.5		Excellent fruiting shrub
C. dichotoma f. *albifructa*		● ● ●	● 🌰 🌰	🌰	1.2	1.5	1	1.5		White fruits
C. japonica 'Leucocarpa'		● ● ●	● 🌰 🌰	🌰	1	1.2	1	1.2		White fruits

● flowering   🌰 harvest

Callistemon
Bottle brush

The bottle brushes are so named because of the way in which the flowers are carried, and because the flowers are primarily a mass of stamens, hence resembling a bottle brush.

The flowers are produced in summer in cylindrical spikes which grow on to produce the next length of foliage. The scientific name is from the Greek *kallos* (beauty) and *stemon* (stamens). The leaves are willow-like, persisting for two years. The shoots tend to be pendulous. The species like a hot sunny situation with freely drained but moisture retentive soil – water during dry periods. They have only a limited cold tolerance and are often killed, or killed back to ground level, by hard winters. In colder regions, they are worth trying beside a sun-facing wall. They can be used in shrub and mixed beds, or as specimen shrubs. Plant out in the spring after the worst of the weather, except in mild districts. The fruits are urn-shaped woody capsules which take a full year to ripen. Propagate either from semi-hardwood or fully ripe cuttings with a heel in summer, or by seed. Seed should be sown into a damp compost.

soil	Plant in well drained, neutral to acid and moderately fertile soil
site	Enjoys plenty of sunshine, as well as moisture at the roots but not in stagnant water
general care	Make sure that the plant is sheltered from cold winds and that it is watered sparingly in the winter
pruning	Shorten tips of new plants to form a bush and remove defective or crowded stems
pests & diseases	No particular problems from pests and disease, however the plant can be susceptible to winter cold

Callistemon citrinus

Callistemon citrinus

	SPRING	SUMMER	AUTUMN	WINTER	height 5yrs (m)	height 10yrs (m)	spread 5yrs (m)	spread 10yrs (m)	petal colour	
Callistemon citrinus		● ●			1.8	2.5	1.5	2.5		Rather tender – use as a conservatory shrub
C. linearis		● ●			1.5	2	1.5	2		Leaves are very narrow – 2.5mm
C. pallidus		● ●			1.5	2	1.5	2		Unusual flower colour
C. salignus		● ●			1.5	2.5	1.5	2.5		Leaves willow-like, can make a tree to 10m

● flowering

Calycanthus & Sinocalycanthus

Allspices

The Allspices are shrubs with curious flowers which are composed of a large number of strap-like sepals and petals in two or several whorls. The flowers are carried over an extended period during summer at the end of short leafy shoots. Florally they are not stunning, but their fragrance is a delight to the olfactory senses. They also attract beetles, which are the main pollinators.

The vegetative parts – leaves, bark and roots, are aromatic, with a fragrance likened either to camphor or cloves if bruised. The bark of *Calycanthus floridus*, the Carolina allspice, has been used as a substitute for cinnamon. Allspices sit well in a shrub bed or as specimen shrubs, perhaps at a corner of two paths where their fragrance can be

Sinocalycanthus chinensis

enjoyed. The foliage turns yellow in autumn. Allspices are not fussy as to soil, although they prefer deep, rich and moist soils. However, they do need a sunny site,

especially to ripen the wood so that they do not suffer twig dieback during the winter. Propagation is either by layers or by seed if produced. The mature bushes may also throw suckers and these can be removed and grown on. The reason for including these two genera together is not dyslexia but because *Sinocalycanthus chinensis* was originally described as a species of Calycanthus and the two genera are very close and of similar horticultural value. They are related to Chimonanthus.

The fruit is a woody capsule, shaped like an upright fig, 2–3cm (1in) in length. The seeds are shiny and dark, as a consequence of being retained in the capsule for some time.

soil	Prefers a soil that is rich in humus, fertile and moisture retentive
site	Sunny position in cooler areas, but in temperate regions shade is tolerated
general care	Easy to cultivate and look after, but may need protection in regions with very severe winters
pruning	No pruning necessary, trim to restrict size or to remove dead or weak branches
pests & diseases	This is an excellent plant to maintain as it is generally trouble-free from pests and diseases

Calycanthus occidentalis

	SPRING	SUMMER	AUTUMN	WINTER	height 5yrs (m)	height 10yrs (m)	spread 5yrs (m)	spread 10yrs (m)	petal colour	
Calycanthus floridus		● ● ●			1.2	2.2	1.2	2.5	▓	Flowers 6–7cm across over several weeks
Sinocalycanthus chinensis		●			1.2	2.2	1.2	2.5	░	Flowers 7cm, nodding

● *flowering*

Camellia

Camellia is a large genus of shrubs worthy of its place in the garden for the showy flowers which are carried over a long period during the winter/spring season and for the bright or glossy evergreen foliage. The genus includes the tea plant and an oil, used in perfumery and cooking, is extracted from the seeds of some species.

The flowers consist of one or more whorls of petals which are united to a large boss of stamens. When the flower is finished, the petals and stamens fall together – these fallen flowers can enhance the display from *Camellia williamsii* as they lie strewn around the parent shrub in large quantities. However, in the inferior *Camellia japonica*, the petals tend to hang around on the bush to the detriment of the whole display. Nowhere is this trait seen to worse effect than with the white flowered forms, such as *Camellia japonica* 'Nobilissima', where frosted petals turn brown. These forms can look stunning at their best, but do require regular dead-heading. The flower buds tend to open in sequence, providing a protracted display.

The flowering season starts in the late autumn and early winter with *Camellia sasanqua* varieties, whose flowering can last into early spring. The *Camellia japonica* and *Camellia williamsii* forms follow in mid-winter, usually producing a succession of blooms from late winter to late spring. The flowers are divided into six classes, with single (one row of 5–8 petals and a prominent boss of stamens), semi-double (two or more rows of petals and prominent boss of stamens), and anemone form (a row of large flat or undulating petals

Camellia japonica 'Lavinia Maggi'

Camellia williamsii 'J.C. Williams'

soil	Flourishes in well drained, deep, moisture retaining soils, but dislikes lime
site	Position in a site that has access to both sun and moderate shade
general care	Add fertilizer and mulch for the best flower production and keep watered in dry weather
pruning	Dead-wood and prune to restrict the size. They can also be coppiced
pests & diseases	*Phytophthora cinnamomi* can cause damage. Scale insects can lead to a sooty mould

Camellia 'Leonard Messel'

Camellia williamsii
'J.C. Williams'

Camellia japonica
'Elegans'

Camellia japonica
'Ruddigore'

and a centre formed from a mass of stamens and petaloids – stamens modified into petal-like structures).

Camellia will make large shrubs over time, but at a steady and rather slow rate. Also, ultimate size is very dependent upon your climate. In mild conditions, expect *Camellia sasanqua* to make a maximum of 4m (13ft), and *Camellia japonica* and *Camellia williamsii* 6m (20ft), but *Camellia japonica* in warmer climes have, over a century, made nearly 15m (50ft).

In the garden, camellias should be used as specimen shrubs, in woodland garden settings and shrub borders where their early flowering season can be enjoyed in comfort. Avoid situations where they will be liable to spring frost damage, particularly the delicate fleshy petals.

Camellias like deep moisture retentive but well drained soils. They dislike lime in the soil, which will show as chlorotic foliage, but as floriferous evergreens are more tolerant of clay and limy soils than Rhododendron; they are happiest on a pH range of 5 through to 7. If the soil is on the alkaline side, treating the bushes with Epsom salts (1 tablespoon per 10 litres/two gallons of water) can assist. Fertilize with a standard fertilizer or use organic mulches. Nitrogen is good for growth but avoid over feeding, or you will only get the evergreen foliage. Phosphorus should be given if there is poor bud set. Camellia are

Camellia leaves are glossy and evergreen

happiest with a light woodland covering overhead, but established bushes will tolerate full sun and flower profusely. Too dense shade can inhibit flower bud set. Small plants can be difficult to get established and using larger sizes (60–75cm/24–30in) in frosty localities can greatly assist. Like most plants, they deeply resent deep planting. Camellia will respond well to being grown in greenhouses and pots.

Camellia can be propagated at almost any time of the year. The main season is to take semi-hardwood cuttings in late summer. These can take the form of either a shoot with several leaves and buds, or of a single node (leaf and bud). Rooting should take from two to three months. They can also be grafted or layered. Seed can be used and is the way to make new clones. Plant out in early spring.

	SPRING	SUMMER	AUTUMN	WINTER	height 5yrs (m)	height 10yrs (m)	spread 5yrs (m)	spread 10yrs (m)	petal colour	
Camellia 'Leonard Messel'	● ● ●			● ● ●	1	2	1	2		Hybrid between *C. reticulata* and *C. williamsii*
C. japonica 'Adolphe Audusson'	● ● ●			● ● ●	1	2	0.8	1.5		Compact vigorous growth
C. japonica 'Elegans'	● ● ●			● ● ●	1	2	1.2	2.5		Large flowers
C. japonica 'Lady Vansittart'	● ● ●			● ●	0.8	1.5	0.8	1.5		Slow growing and bushy
C. japonica 'Lavinia Maggi'	● ● ●			● ● ●	1	2	1	2		White flower with red/pink stripes
C. japonica 'Nobilissima'				● ●	1	2	0.8	1.5		Erect habit and early flowering
C. japonica 'Tricolor'	● ● ●			● ●	0.8	1.5	0.8	1.5		Compact growth
C. sasanqua 'Narumigata'				●	1	2	1	2		Fragrant flowers, excellent against a wall
C. williamsii 'Brigadoon'	● ● ●			●	1	2	1	2		Large, semi-double flowers
C. williamsii 'J.C. Williams'	● ● ●			●	1	2	1	2		Good for training up a semi-shaded wall
C. williamsii 'Jury's Yellow'	● ●			●	1	2	1	2		Narrow and erect with anemone-type flowers
C. williamsii 'St Ewe'	● ●			●	1	2	1	2		Rounded shrub with trumpet-shaped flowers

 flowering

Caragana
Pea-tree

This is a genus of legumes which range from small shrubs to small trees. The generic name is a Latinization of the Mongolian name 'Karaghan', which applies to the species featured here. It is native to Siberia, Mongolia and Manchuria, where the winters are dry and extremely cold but the summers warm. Unlike many shrubs from this part of the world, it does not get caught by spring frosts.

The flowers are produced from buds laid down in the previous year. They are carried singly on long stalks but several are produced from each bud, giving a display of yellow pea-like flowers. The fruit is a cylindric pod. The foliage is pinnate with four to six pairs of leaflets and terminates in a small spine (other species in the genus have spines on the branches). The leaves turn yellow in autumn but are a fresh green in spring when they provide a back-cloth to the flowers. The branches tend to be wand-like, giving the shrub an open habit. It can be trained to make

soil	Well drained, preferably rather barren to moderately fertile soil
site	Prefers a sunny position in the garden, not a plant for any significant shade
general care	A hardy shrub, useful as a windbreak, and more or less looks after itself. Propagate by seed or grafting
pruning	Remove dead and damaged branches; can be hard pruned after flowering
pests & diseases	This is an ideal shrub to grow as it is not generally affected by pests and diseases

Caragana arborescens 'Lobergii'

a small tree but is also suited as a shrub. The growth can be restricted by pruning after flowering (Group 1) (see page 23).

Pea-tree is not a shrub for the best garden soils. It wants full sun but is better on a dry and somewhat barren soil, making it excellent for those gardening on sands. It does demand good drainage.

Propagation is by seed, which is freely produced. It requires patience to break through the waxy covering, which can be accomplished by pouring an equal quantity of boiling water over the seeds and leaving them to soak for some hours, or by scraping though the seed coat with a rasp. Grafting is necessary for 'Lobergii', 'Pendula' and 'Walker'.

	SPRING	SUMMER	AUTUMN	WINTER	height 5yrs (m)	height 10yrs (m)	spread 5yrs (m)	spread 10yrs (m)	petal colour	
Caragana arborescens	●				1.5	2.5	1	1.8		Upright habit
C. arborescens 'Lobergii'	●				1.5	2.5	1	1.8		Leaflets grass-like, feathery appearance
C. arborescens 'Pendula'	●				1	1	1	1.8		Shoots stiffly pendulous
C. arborescens 'Walker'	●				1	1	1	1.5		Hybrid of 'Lobergii' and 'Pendula'

● *flowering*

Carpenteria
Tree anemone

This is a genus of one species related to Deutzia and Philadelphus. It is native to hot, dry, sunny situations in California and has only a limited tolerance to cold weather. It should therefore be sited where it can ripen the wood, and is best for sun-facing borders or against sun-drenched walls. The leaves are evergreen.

The flowers are carried in a terminal cluster of three to five blooms on the new growths in early to mid-summer, and some also singly from the leaf axils. The bark on older shoots is rusty red and exfoliates in thin sheets. The flowers are white, 5–8cm across (2–3in) and fragrant, with a boss of numerous yellow stamens. Good forms are 'Bodnant' and Ladham's Variety', which are worth searching out. They can be propagated by hardwood cuttings in spring or by semi-ripe cuttings in summer. They can be raised from seed, but the resultant plants tend to give poorer flowers with narrow, watery coloured petals.

Carpenteria californica

soil	Well drained and moisture retentive. Caryopteris even tolerates chalky soils
site	Sunny for both plants. Carpenteria likes to be sheltered from cold winds
general care	Carpenteria: mulch in autumn to protect the base in winter. Caryopteris: do not over fertilize
pruning	Carpenteria: after flowering (Group 1). Caryopteris: to basal framework (Group 2)
pests & diseases	Both species of shrubs do not have any problems and are usually trouble-free from pests and diseases

Caryopteris
Bluebeard

This genus is mainly represented in gardens by *Caryopteris clandonensis*, which is a hybrid between the Chinese and Japanese *Caryopteris incana* and the Mongolian *Caryopteris mongolica*.

This has leaves which are grey-green or dull green above and silvery grey on the underside. The flowers are carried in late

Caryopteris clandonensis

summer and early autumn on the current season's growths. They thrive on light and well drained soils of moderate fertility, including those derived from chalk and limestone. They are excellent plants for mixed and shrub borders where they should be located towards the front. The foliage also fits it into a silver theme in a part of the garden. They can be propagated by softwood and semi-hardwood cuttings in summer.

	SPRING	SUMMER	AUTUMN	WINTER	height 5yrs (m)	height 10yrs (m)	spread 5yrs (m)	spread 10yrs (m)	petal colour	
Carpenteria californica		●			1	2	1	2		Fragrant flowers
Caryopteris clandonensis 'Arthur Simmonds'		●	●		0.7	1.5	0.8	1.5		The typical form of the cross
C. clandonensis 'Heavenly Blue'		●	●		0.7	1.5	0.8	1.5		Deeper blue flowers and more compact habit
C. clandonensis 'Kew Blue'		●	●		0.7	1.5	0.8	1.5		Darker blue flowers
C. clandonensis 'Worcester Gold'		●	●		0.7	1.5	0.8	1.5		Golden leaves

● *flowering*

Ceanothus
California lilac

Blue flowers are the order of the day in this American genus, and about the best blues that can be grown. Individually the flowers are quite small but are carried in large clusters, and often masses of clusters – so much so that the display can be almost overwhelming.

There are two main seasons of flowering, in the spring and in late summer or early autumn. The evergreen forms mainly flower in the spring (often with some flowers later in the year), whilst the deciduous ones flower in late summer/autumn. These two flowering habits have different pruning requirements. The evergreen forms are Group 1 – requiring minimal trimming after flowering, whereas the deciduous forms are Group 2 – prune back to within a few centimetres of the previous year's shoots in early spring. In habit the plants range from prostrate or mound forming shrubs to tall upright ones. The mound forms can be used for ground cover whereas the taller ones fit well into a shrub bed or mixed border. In colder districts they may need the shelter of a wall.

They require either full sun or no more than light shade. All species are very tolerant of soils, from acid sands to chalky soils, but demand good drainage. Propagation is by softwood to semi-hardwood cuttings taken in summer.

Ceanothus 'Cascade'

soil	Any soil, provided it is well drained, except shallow soils over chalk	
site	Sunny aspects, especially sun-drenched walls; protect from cold dry winds	
general care	Feed in spring, especially those deciduous forms which have been pruned back hard	
pruning	Deciduous forms pruned as Group 2 in early spring. Little pruning for evergreen forms	
pests & diseases	Can suffer root rot on wet soils, but apart from this, usually trouble-free from pests and diseases	

	SPRING	SUMMER	AUTUMN	WINTER	height 5yrs (m)	height 10yrs (m)	spread 5yrs (m)	spread 10yrs (m)	petal colour	
Ceanothus arboreus 'Trewithen Blue'	● ● ●	● ● ●			2	4	2	4		Can grow to 6–8m. Flowers strongly in spring
C. 'Autumnal Blue'	● ● ●		● ●	● ● ●	1	1.5	1	1.5		Spring flowering less intense than late summer
C. 'Blue Mound'		● ●		● ● ●	0.8	1.2	1	1.5		Evergreen with glossy, undulate leaves
C. 'Burkwoodii'		●	● ● ●	●	0.8	1.2	0.8	1.2		Leaves glossy, densely set
C. 'Cascade'	●	●			1.5	3	1.5	3		Narrow, glossy dark green leaves
C. 'Concha'		●			1.2	2	1.5	2.5		Evergreen
C. 'Italian Skies'	●				1	1.5	1.5	2.5		Evergreen with small, dark green leaves
C. pallidus 'Marie Simon'		● ●	● ● ●		1	1.5	1	1.5		Deciduous
C. 'Puget Blue'	●				1.5	2.5	1.5	2.5		Evergreen dense shrub
C. 'Southmead'	●	●			1	1.5	1	1.5		Evergreen with glossy dark green leaves
C. thyrsiflorus	●				1	2	1	2		Evergreen species, capable of making a tree
C. thyrsiflorus var. *repens*	●				0.3	0.5	1	2		Evergreen prostrate shrub
C. thyrsiflorus 'Skylark'	●	● ● ●			1	2	0.8	1.5		Evergreen, flowers over a long period

● *flowering*

Ceratostigma
Hardy plumbago

The hardy plumbago are noted for their deep blue flowers, which are carried from mid-summer into autumn. In late autumn the foliage turns bronze or red, often whilst the plant is still flowering. They make small shrubs which are usually wider than high.

Locate them at the front of a border or in a small bed beside a low wall, or use them to provide scale to summer bedding schemes. They can also be used to make informal hedges. They tolerate dry, poor soils but are better on more equitable and moist ones provided there is good drainage. They like a warm, sunny site, but if you garden in a cold area they can be treated as herbaceous plants – protect the root system by applying a deep dry mulch in autumn and cut them down to ground level in early spring when they will sprout and flower in summer (Group 2). They can also be given the shelter of a sun-facing wall. In cold seasons in more temperate areas, they may be cut to ground level. They can be propagated by softwood and semi-hardwood cuttings in summer. The rooted plants should be protected over winter in a cold frame or greenhouse, keeping them on the dry side.

Ceratostigma willmottianum

Ceratostigma griffithii

soil	Unfussy, preferring dry, poor soils to those of moderate fertility
site	Sunny but protect from cold winds, such as by planting on the warm side of a wall
general care	Usually takes care of itself once established. Mulch in autumn to protect the root system, though
pruning	Cut down to ground level or to a frame of low branches in spring
pests & diseases	Generally fairly trouble-free from most pests and diseases, but keep protected during harsh winters

	SPRING	SUMMER	AUTUMN	WINTER	height 5yrs (m)	height 10yrs (m)	spread 5yrs (m)	spread 10yrs (m)	petal colour	
Ceratostigma griffithii		● ●	● ● ●		1	1.2	1.5	1.5		Tallest growing species
C. plumbaginoides		● ●	● ● ●		0.4	0.4	0.4	0.6		Use in summer bedding
C. willmottianum		● ●	● ● ●		0.6	1	0.8	1.2		Free-flowering over a long period
C. willmotianum 'Forest Blue'		● ●	● ● ●		0.6	1	0.8	1.2		Free-flowering over a long period

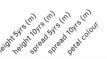 *flowering*

Cestrum

This is a genus related to the tomato. They come from tropical and subtropical parts of South and Central America. They are not fully hardy and may be cut down to ground level in winter. It is sensible to treat them as not being long lived, but notwithstanding this, they are worth their garden space.

The flowers of *Cestrum* 'Newellii' are crimson and this is the showiest form of the genus. *Cestrum nocturnum* has pale green to ivory coloured flowers, whereas *Cestrum parqui* has yellow-green to yellow – and sometimes purple

Cestrum parqui 'Cretan Purple'

soil	Fertile, freely drained soil is preferable, although it tolerates most soil types
site	Enjoys a sheltered position but make sure it is in full to moderate sun
general care	For best results, mulch over winter and take precautionary cuttings. Plant in spring
pruning	To achieve the best from this shrub, cut back old wood that has died over winter
pests & diseases	There are generally no problems from pests and diseases with this vigorous plant

– blooms. In both cases, it is not the flower colour which makes them desirable, but the scent produced after dark. The foliage of Cestrum is vigorous and can be used to add structure to a border. However, if bruised it has an unpleasant odour. They are best located in a sheltered bed beside a wall where the wall will give some protection over winter. This can be enhanced by covering them with a dry mulch for winter, such as matting or prunings from holly and other evergreens. Where old wood remains alive, two or three flushes of flowers may be produced during the subsequent summer, but if regrowth is made from the base, expect only one. They tolerate most soils but are best on fertile, freely drained ones. Propagate them from softwood cuttings in summer; do this as a precautionary measure in case of a hard winter.

Cestrum parqui 'Cretan Purple'

	SPRING	SUMMER	AUTUMN	WINTER	height 5yrs (m)	height 10yrs (m)	spread 5yrs (m)	spread 10yrs (m)	petal colour	
Cestrum 'Newellii'	●	● ● ●			2	2.5	2	2.5	▧	Best flowers, some night scent
C. nocturnum		● ● ●	● ● ●		1.5	2.5	1.5	2.5	☐	Flowers fragrant over night
C. parqui 'Cretan Purple'		● ● ●	●		1.5	2	1.5	2	☐	Leaves narrow, lance-shape

● *flowering*

Chaenomeles

Japonica *or*
Flowering quince

These relatives of the true quince are chiefly grown for their early flowers. These are borne on last year's shoots in clusters of three to six blooms. As they open before the leaves on the bare branches and come in colours from white through to deep red, they provide a strong show at the start of spring.

Frequently flowering quinces are fan- or espalier-trained against a wall. This is an effective way of growing them, although it does require some attention to detail. This involves tying a framework of branches onto wires on a wall; after flowering, shorten each shoot to two or three buds from the base of last year's growth, and periodically tie in new basal growths to replace the framework shoots as these become exhausted. However, they are as effective when grown as free standing shrubs, whether in a border or as an isolated specimen; they make low spreading, dense bushes and require much less attention to pruning in these positions.

The flowering quinces belong to the apple subfamily and the fruits contain many seeds surrounded by a thick fleshy layer. The shoots often have spines. Flowering quinces tolerate a wide range of soils but become chlorotic on shallow chalky ones. They need good drainage. Propagate by semi-hardwood cuttings with a heel in summer or by layering.

Chaenomeles superba

Chaenomeles speciosa 'Nivalis'

soil	Fertile and well drained. Foliage will become chlorotic on shallow, chalky soils
site	This likes to be positioned in a site which offers sun to light shade
general care	When looking after this shrub, be aware of the spines on some shoots, which can be quite vicious
pruning	Wall-trained plants need tying in and shoots shortened after flowering (Group 1)
pests & diseases	Although fairly trouble-free, the plant can be prone to fireblight and attack from scale insects

	SPRING	SUMMER	AUTUMN	WINTER	height 5yrs (m)	height 10yrs (m)	spread 5yrs (m)	spread 10yrs (m)	petal colour	
Chaenomeles cathayensis	flowering		harvest		2	4	1.5	3		Excellent fruiting form
C. speciosa 'Nivalis'	flowering		harvest		1.2	2	1.2	2.5		Large flowers
C. superba 'Crimson and Gold'	flowering		harvest		0.8	1	0.8	2		Spreading habit
C. superba 'Knaphill Scarlet'	flowering		harvest		1	1.5	1.2	2		Spreading habit
C. superba 'Pink Lady'	flowering		harvest		0.8	1.2	1.2	2.5		Spreading habit

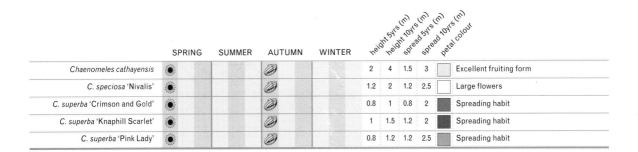

● flowering   🌰 harvest

Choisya
Mexican orange blossom

This is a small group of evergreen shrubs from the highlands of Mexico and south-east USA. They are grown for the very fragrant white flowers. These are carried in axillary clusters at the ends of the shoots in spring to early summer and then again with a lesser flush of blooms in the autumn, and often with a smattering of flowers between these main flushes.

The leaves are generally ternate or trifoliate, that is with three leaflets on a common stalk. The genus is in the orange family (Rutaceae). All members of this family have glands in the leaves which, if crushed, emit a pungent odour. Mexican orange blossom has proved surprisingly hardy. It thrives in sun and shade. In severe winters, it will show some scorch to the foliage but is rarely killed. In the garden, it is good in shrub borders. However, because of the fragrance from the blooms and the extended flowering season, it is particularly effective when located beside an entrance or in a similar setting where these attributes can be enjoyed to their full, such as beneath a window where the aroma can waft up in a breeze. The clone 'Sundance' has young foliage which is a bright yellow in colour; this matures to lime green. 'Aztec Pearl' has leaves with slender three to five

soil	Will tolerate any moderately fertile, well drained soil, including chalky ones
site	For best results, position in a site with sun to moderate shade
general care	Very easy to grow and generally takes care of itself. Propagate from semi-ripe cuttings taken in summer
pruning	Prune young plants to form a bushy framework, then only to remove damaged shoots
pests & diseases	Relatively trouble-free. Pests and diseases do not usually cause any problems

Choisya ternata

Choisya ternata 'Sundance'

leaflets. Mexican orange blossom thrives on a wide range of soil types, including chalky ones. It can be propagated from semi-ripe cuttings taken in summer.

	SPRING	SUMMER	AUTUMN	WINTER	height 5yrs (m)	height 10yrs (m)	spread 5yrs (m)	spread 10yrs (m)	petal colour	
Choisya 'Aztec Pearl'	● ●	● ● ●	● ●		1.2	2.5	1.2	2.5		Leaves with 3–5 narrow leaflets
C. ternata	● ●	● ● ●	● ●		1.2	2.5	1.2	2.5		Fragrant flowers for most of the summer
C. ternata 'Sundance'	● ●	● ● ●	● ●		1.2	2.5	1.2	2.5		New foliage bright yellow

● *flowering*

Cistus
Rock rose

The rock roses have blooms which last for a day, if you are lucky; in fact most open in the morning and drop the petals around mid-afternoon, and only the flowers which open towards the evening may be found the next day. Nevertheless, at 4–10cm (1½–4in) they are large relative to the size of the plants and carried in such numbers that in the early part of summer the shrubs are smothered.

White is the principal colour, followed by pink, but most have petals marked with various blotches. The individual bloom has five wide spreading petals which resemble those of the wild roses and rock roses are native to the maquis areas of the mediterranean region, hence the common name. However, they are also known as sun roses, as their natural habitat is characterized by hot dry and sunny summers and cool winters. Consequently in the garden they require hot, dry and rather barren sites. They fare badly on fertile sites, largely because they grow too fast and soft, and thus are clobbered by even the mildest of winters. They are excellent in rockeries and sun-facing banks and can be grown in containers on patios. The foliage can look attractive, especially that of *Cistus ladanifer* and *Cistus cyprius*. Rock roses are fast growing plants of limited lifespan and are not particularly hardy. It is sensible, therefore, to make annual backups and keep these over winter in a frost-free environment. The simplest method of propagation is softwood or semi-ripe cuttings in summer, but they can also be layered. They tolerate coastal exposure, windy sites and thrive on a wide range of soils provided they are well drained, including shallow chalky ones.

Cistus dansereaui 'Decumbens'

soil	Will perform in well drained, but preferably not very fertile soil
site	A sunny position. They cannot tolerate much shade but will grow in coastal sites
general care	A shrub that is very easy to look after and withstands windy conditions, but unfortunately is short lived
pruning	Remove dead wood and winter damage. Nip out the tips of young plants
pests & diseases	Relatively trouble-free. Pests and diseases do not usually cause any problems

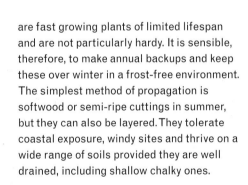

	SPRING	SUMMER	AUTUMN	WINTER	height 5yrs (m)	height 10yrs (m)	spread 5yrs (m)	spread 10yrs (m)	petal colour	
Cistus aguilarii 'Maculatus'		●			0.9	1.2	0.9	1.2		Large flowered hybrid
C. argenteus 'Peggy Sammons'		●			0.7	1	0.7	1		Grey-green leaves
C. cyprius		●			1	2	1	2		Leaves are clammy
C. dansereaui 'Decumbens'		●			0.5	0.6	0.5	0.8		Also listed as *C. lusitanicus*
C. hybridus		●			0.7	1	0.7	1		Also listed as *C. corbariensis*
C. 'Grayswood Pink'		●			0.7	1	0.7	1		Excellent pink flowers
C. ladanifer		●			1	2.5	1	2.5		Leaves gummy with resin
C. laxus 'Snow White'		●			0.7	1	0.7	1		Good white-flowered form
C. purpureus		●			0.7	1	0.7	1		Flowers pinkish with deep red blotches
C. skanbergii		●			0.7	1	0.7	1		Foliage grey-green, flowers small

● *flowering*

Clerodendrum
Chance tree

These shrubs are useful for their flowers which are produced late in the summer as it gives way to autumn. The name Chance tree is a translation of the Greek words *Kleros* (chance) and *dendron* (tree) and was given by Linnaeus.

Clerodendrum bungei is a sub-shrub, regularly cut back to ground level in all but the mildest winters and sprouting from the woody root system to produce the purplish-red blooms; by this time the shoots may be 1–2m (3–6ft) long, and carrying large heart-shaped leaves. It should be placed in a shrub or herbaceous border, or used to fill a space at the base of a wall. *Clerodendrum trichotomum* and its variety *fargesii* are taller growing, with time capable of making 3–6m (10–20ft). The flowers have white petals subtended by the reddish purple calyx with prominent stamens, and open from mid-summer to early autumn. The fruits ripen a month later and are bright blue, about the size of a pea and displayed by the still reddish purple calyx which has become fleshy. This species is useful at the back of a border or as a specimen shrub. Both species have fragrant flowers but the foliage, if bruised, has an unpleasant smell. They like a well drained fertile soil, in sunny positions. They can be propagated by softwood and semi-hardwood cuttings, by root cuttings, by division of suckers and by seed.

Clerodendrum trichotomum

soil	Well drained, fertile and moisture retentive soils; will tolerate chalk sites
site	Prefers a sunny site, but certainly no more than light shade
general care	Feed or mulch to maintain soil fertility; cover root system of *C. bungei* to protect over winter
pruning	Can be pruned as Group 2, as they flower on the current growth
pests & diseases	Relatively trouble-free. Pests and diseases do not usually cause any problems

Clerodendrum bungei

	SPRING	SUMMER	AUTUMN	WINTER	height 5yrs (m)	height 10yrs (m)	spread 5yrs (m)	spread 10yrs (m)	petal colour	
Clerodendrum bungei		● ●			2	2	1.2	2.5	■	Normally cut to ground level in winter
C. trichotomum		● ●	🌰 🌰		1.5	3	1.5	3	☐	Valuable late summer to autumn flowers
C. trichotomum var. *fargesii*		● ●	🌰 🌰		1.5	3	1.5	3	☐	Valuable late summer to autumn flowers

● flowering   🌰 harvest

Clethra

Lily-of-the-valley
tree *or*
White alder *or*
Summer-sweet

Clethra are more demanding in their requirements than most flowering shrubs, but amply reward the extra effort. It is not that the flowers are spectacularly showy – they are pretty but not outstanding – but because of their wonderful spicy fragrance. This is capable of filling the entire garden.

The flowers are carried at the end of the current year's shoots towards the end of summer, at a time when most shrubs have finished flowering. The trusses are erect or spreading racemes or panicles, which consist of many small, white bell-shaped blooms. Some species have attractive peeling bark as an added attraction. The hardy species featured here are deciduous, with the foliage turning red or yellow in autumn in *Clethra barbinervis*, but there are some evergreen species which are less hardy. Their specific requirements are an acidic, preferably humus-rich, moist soil and light to moderate shade and shelter. They are shrubs for the woodland garden, or where the house casts shade for most of the day. If you cannot provide the ideal conditions, arrange a site where the

soil	Moist, humus-rich acid soils that retain moisture; avoid dry and lime or chalky soils
site	Prefers the semi-shade, with the root system at least in shade
general care	To obtain the best results for this shrub, mulch regularly to retain a soil rich in organic matter
pruning	Minimal pruning is required; remove dead wood and defective branches
pests & diseases	This is an ideal shrub to grow as it is not generally affected by pests and diseases

Clethra alnifolia

Clethra alnifolia 'Rosea'

roots at least are in shade. Clethra are not suitable for dry sandy soils, nor for those containing as much as a hint of lime or chalk. They can be grown from seed, and for *Clethra delavayi* this is the best method, or by division of root suckers (*Clethra alnifolia*) or from semi-hardwood cuttings taken with a heel in mid- to late summer.

	SPRING	SUMMER	AUTUMN	WINTER	height 5yrs (m)	height 10yrs (m)	spread 5yrs (m)	spread 10yrs (m)	petal colour	
Clethra alnifolia		● ●	●		0.8	1.2	0.9	1.5		Needs plenty of moisture at the roots
C. alnifolia 'Rosea'		● ●	●		0.8	1.2	0.9	1.5		Needs plenty of moisture at the roots
C. barbinervis		● ●	●		1	2	1	2		Good autumn colour
C. delavayi		● ●	●		1.2	2.5	0.9	2		Best flowering species, slightly tender

 *flowering*

Colutea
Bladder senna

This genus belongs to the legume family, and has pea-shaped flowers. They are yellow and are carried in small racemes on the current year's shoots. The fruits, rather than being the typical legume or pea-pod, are curiously inflated bladders, which can be popped like balloons.

The leaves are pinnate, with nine to thirteen leaflets and may assume yellow tints in autumn. Colutea is a shrub for a mixed or shrub border, or as a curiosity for its bladder fruits. They tolerate most garden soils provided the drainage is good, and require full sun. They are extremely useful for hot inhospitable banks, and for stabilising sandy soils. They can be propagated by seed which, like most legumes, has a waxy layer which needs either to be melted (with an equal quantity of boiling water) or broken by scarifying the seeds; otherwise germination will be slow and erratic. Semi-hardwood cuttings in summer are an alternative method of propagation.

Colutea arborescens

soil	Colutea: any freely drained soil. Convolvulus: prefers well drained and dry soil
site	Colutea likes lots of sun. Convolvulus prefers the sun but also a sheltered site
general care	No special requirements for both plants. Colutea especially is very hardy and tough
pruning	Colutea can be pruned back to old wood in spring (Group 2). None needed for Convolvulus
pests & diseases	Both plants are relatively trouble-free. Pests and diseases do not usually cause any problems

Convolvulus
Shrubby bindweed

Many gardeners would question the sanity of someone advocating planting a bindweed. However, this delightful shrub, *Convolvulus cneorum*, has all the benefits and none of the drawbacks of the congeneric weeds.

Convolvulus cneorum

The foliage is 'evergreen' but due to a covering of silky hairs, it is silver coloured when young, justifying the common name of 'silverbush'. The flowers are funnel-shaped; they are white with a yellow centre when open but are very pale pink in bud, and are carried from late spring through most of the summer. The plant is excellent for rockeries, or at the base of walls. *Convolvulus cneorum* can be tender and is not long lived. It requires a hot, dry and well drained site for best effect. It can be propagated by semi-hardwood cuttings in summer or by seed in spring.

	SPRING	SUMMER	AUTUMN	WINTER	height 5yrs (m)	height 10yrs (m)	spread 5yrs (m)	spread 10yrs (m)	petal colour	
Colutea arborescens		● ● ● 🌾			1.6	3	1.6	3	▨	Very tough, excellent for sandy soils
Convolvulus cneorum	●	● ● ●			0.5	0.9	0.5	0.9	☐	Floriferous shrub, yellow-centred flowers

● flowering   🌾 harvest

Cornus
Dogwood

The shrubby dogwoods are grown for the colour of their twigs more than for any other feature. This colours as it matures in autumn and makes a vivid display towards the end of the winter, from bright crimson in *Cornus alba* 'Sibirica', to yellow to olive-green in *Cornus stolonifera* 'Flaviramea'.

These forms are normally coppiced in early spring just as the new growth is being made, and thus do not display the white flowers or fruits which are carried on two year old shoots. Other forms, especially *Cornus alba* 'Spaethii' with variegated leaves and *Cornus alba* 'Aurea' with leaves suffused with a soft yellow, are grown primarily for their summer foliage. These species all more properly belong to the genus Swida, but in gardens and nursery catalogues will be found under Cornus. Most of these forms are strong growers – perhaps rampant is a better term – and

Cornus alba 'Spaethii'

need careful siting so that they do not swamp other plants. They thrive on heavy wet sites, but will grow on a wide range of soils, including shallow chalk or limy soils. They are useful wherever winter twig colour or summer foliage is required. They look good beside a large pond where the colour of the winter stems can be reflected in the water, or as an isolated plant in a lawn. They are easily propagated from 20cm (8in) lengths of stem inserted as hardwood cuttings.

soil	Relatively unfussy, grows in any soil, but especially good on heavy wet sites
site	Prefers a position in the sun with a certain amount of moderate shade
general care	Very easy to cultivate. Feed and mulch to achieve the most vigorous shoots with best winter colour
pruning	Coppice to within 10cm (4in) of ground level in late winter or early spring
pests & diseases	Relatively trouble-free. Pests and diseases do not usually cause any problems

Cornus stolonifera 'Flaviramea'

	SPRING	SUMMER	AUTUMN	WINTER	height 5yrs (m)	height 10yrs (m)	spread 5yrs (m)	spread 10yrs (m)	petal colour	
Cornus alba 'Aurea'		●			1.5	2.5	1.5	1.5		Leaves soft yellow-green
C. alba 'Elegantissima'		●			1.5	2.5	1.5	1.5		Leaves mottled and margined with white
C. alba 'Sibirica'		●			1.5	2.5	1.5	1.5		Stems vivid crimson in winter
C. alba 'Sibirica Variegata'		●			1.5	2.5	1.5	1.5		Leaves variegated; shoots strongly coloured
C. alba 'Spaethii'		●			1.5	2.5	1.5	1.5		Leaves conspicuously gold variegated
C. sanguinea		●			1.5	2.5	1.5	1.5		Native dogwood, stems green and red
C. stolonifera 'Flaviramea'		●			1.5	2.5	1.5	1.5		Stems yellow to olive-green, fruits white
C. stolonifera 'Kelseyi'		●			0.3	0.5	0.3	0.3		Stems yellow-green with red tips

● *flowering*

Corylopsis

Flowering hazel

These deciduous shrubs have flowers which are primrose yellow and highly fragrant and give a wonderful aroma to the garden. The flowers open in late winter or early spring and hang down on short pendulous racemes from the bare leafless branches.

The leaves resemble the foliage of the true hazel, but Corylopsis is in the family Hamamelidaceae, along with large shrubs such as Hamamelis and trees like Parrotia and Liquidambar. *Corylopsis sinensis* 'Spring Purple' has new foliage plum-purple in colour which adds a dimension to the floral display.

This shrub is ideally sited as part of the woodland garden, or in a shrub border, as it likes some shade and also to be sheltered from cold dry winds. *Corylopsis pauciflora* has the blooms in few flowered racemes but they are carried in large numbers and make a stronger and slightly earlier floral display than *Corylopsis sinensis*. It requires a position nearer the house, perhaps as a wall shrub, or in a mixed or shrub border. It is just a little tender for using as an isolated specimen shrub, except in very mild gardens.

Corylopsis does best on moisture retentive soils which are fertile and acidic to neutral. *Corylopsis pauciflora* will tolerate a

soil	Fertile, well drained neutral to acid soil; *C. pauciflora* will grow on deep, chalky soils
site	Prefers light to moderate shade and shelter from the cold winds
general care	Care and maintenance is quite low. Mulch to conserve moisture and water during dry spells
pruning	Minimal pruning required only to remove dead wood and broken branches
pests & diseases	Relatively trouble-free. Pests and diseases do not usually cause any problems

Corylopsis pauciflora

Corylopsis sinensis

moderately deep chalk soil, although on shallow chalk soils it will become chlorotic, but *Corylopsis sinensis* and the other species in the genus will not tolerate these conditions. Corylopsis can be propagated from the shiny black seeds or from softwood or semi-hardwood cuttings in summer. They can also be layered.

	SPRING	SUMMER	AUTUMN	WINTER	height 5yrs (m)	height 10yrs (m)	spread 5yrs (m)	spread 10yrs (m)	petal colour	
Corylopsis pauciflora	●				●	1.2	2	1.2	2		Smaller growing than *C. sinensis*
C. sinensis 'Spring Purple'	●				●	1.5	3	1.5	3		New foliage plum-purple colour

● flowering

Cotoneaster

The Cotoneaster considered here are the smaller growing forms; the taller forms can make trees and are included in the companion volume in this series of books, *Trees & Shrubs*. They can be attractive in flower, and some (such as *Cotoneaster horizontalis*) with minute flowers can buzz with bees. However, think of them as berried treasure for autumn features and treat the flowers as a bonus.

Cotoneaster is mainly a genus of evergreen shrubs, but a few are deciduous and these species produce excellent autumn colour from the dying foliage. They have lots of uses in the garden, apart from the obvious colour of their flowers and fruits. As berrying plants, they provide winter food for many birds.

Cotoneaster are also useful in the shrub bed, as evergreen screens and can

soil	Will tolerate most types of soil, but grows best in well drained conditions
site	Sun to moderate shade is preferred – good trained up a fence or over a wall
general care	Easy to accommodate. Appreciates a good mulching and feed to keep the plant vigorous
pruning	No pruning is necessary, but by all means trim back to keep to size
pests & diseases	They can get fireblight. Also susceptible to honey fungus, silver leaf and various insects

Cotoneaster horizontalis

make effective informal hedges. Some, such as *Cotoneaster horizontalis*, are excellent if trained against a wall or to dangle over a fence.

Cotoneaster grow in almost any well drained soil, including chalky ones and acidic sands. Propagation is by cuttings, semi-hardwood taken in summer, or from seed.

	SPRING	SUMMER	AUTUMN	WINTER	height 5yrs (m)	height 10yrs (m)	spread 5yrs (m)	spread 10yrs (m)	petal colour	
Cotoneaster atropurpureus 'Variegatus'	●		harvest harvest harvest		0.5	16	0.5	1	▨	Leaves edged white and turning pink in autumn
C. bullatus		●	harvest harvest		1.2	2.5	1.2	2.5	▨	Excellent autumn colour. Fruit red
C. conspicuus 'Decorus'		●	harvest harvest harvest harvest		0.4	0.6	1	2	☐	Fruit red. Evergreen shrub
C. dammeri 'Major'		●	harvest		0.1	0.1	1	2.5	▨	Evergreen, prostrate ground cover
C. franchetii		● ●	harvest harvest		1.2	2.5	1.2	2.5	▨	Evergreen shrub, fruit orange to light red
C. horizontalis	●		harvest harvest		0.5	1	1	2.5	▨	Can be trained up a wall, otherwise a mound
C. 'Hybridus Pendulus'		●	harvest harvest		0.1	0.2	1.5	3	☐	Fruit bright red. Prostrate evergreen shrub
C. microphyllus	●		harvest harvest		0.2	0.4	0.8	1.2	☐	Prostrate shrub, fruit large, dull carmine
C. procumbens 'Queen of Carpets'	●		harvest harvest		0.1	0.2	1	2	☐	Prostrate, evergreen shrub
C. simonsii	●		harvest harvest		1	1.5	1	1.5	▨	Erect branched shrub, used for informal hedges
C. suecicus 'Coral Beauty'		●	harvest harvest		0.3	0.5	1	2	☐	Fruit coral red, semi-evergreen ground cover
C. suecicus 'Skogholm'		●	harvest harvest		0.3	0.5	1	2	☐	Fruit red, sparse; semi-evergreen ground cover

● *flowering*   ▱ *harvest*

Cytisus & Chamaecytisus

Brooms

The brooms are very floriferous members of the legume family. The previous year's branches will be wreathed in pea-like flowers in early spring. Brooms make excellent shrubs for the mixed border and can be used on hot dry banks. The lower growing forms which develop mound-shaped habits can look particularly effective when allowed to flop over a low wall.

The leaves are transient and most photosynthesis is carried out by the green shoots (except for *Cytisus battandieri*). *Chamaecytisus purpureus* has been included in Cytisus in the past and it is convenient to consider it here, as the cultural requirements are similar.

The brooms will grow on a wide range of soils but must have good drainage. By nature they are plants from hot dry and sunny sites. They will not tolerate more than light shade and ideally want full sun. They resent root disturbance and should be planted out into their final positions from pots.

Brooms are fast growing but not long lived shrubs. Also, they do not respond to hard trimming and cannot be coppiced. They can be raised from seed sown in spring, but cuttings make a more reliable method to propagate selected forms.

Cytisus 'Lena'

Cytisus praecox 'Warminster'

soil	Any well drained soil, preferably moderate fertility for best floral displays
site	Enjoys a position with plenty of sun and is happy in hot, dry sites
general care	Removing growing pods or legumes will stop the plant putting effort into seed production
pruning	Trim after flowering, but never cut into old wood if you need regrowth
pests & diseases	Relatively trouble-free. Pests and diseases do not usually affect this shrub

	SPRING	SUMMER	AUTUMN	WINTER	height 5yrs (m)	height 10yrs (m)	spread 5yrs (m)	spread 10yrs (m)	petal colour	
Chamaecytisus purpureus	●				0.4	0.5	0.4	0.6		Low growing deciduous shrub
Cytisus battandieri		●			2	4	1.5	3		Leaves large and silky haired, trifoliate
C. 'Hollandia'	●	●			0.7	1.5	0.7	1.5		Flowers cream and dark pink
C. 'Lena'	●	●			0.7	1	0.7	1		Flowers yellow with red
C. kewensis	●				0.3	0.3	1	2		Low growing, good over rocks or walls
C. praecox 'Allgold'	●				0.7	1.2	0.7	1.2		Dark yellow flowers
C. praecox 'Warminster'	●				0.6	1	0.8	1.2		Flowers can be malodorous
C. scoparius	●	●			1.5	2.5	1	2		Vigorous shrub
C. 'Windlesham Ruby'	●	●			1.5	2	1.5	2		Arching shoots, bushy plant
Cytisus 'Zeelandia'	●	●			1.5	2	1.5	2		Arching shoots on a bushy plant

● *flowering*

Daphne

The flowers of most Daphne are intensely fragrant and can waft over a large part of the garden. They are mainly white to mauvy-purple in colour, but yellow and yellow-green flowers also occur. They like well drained soils which are from slightly acidic to slightly alkaline, thus generally tolerating some lime in the soil; however, there are some exceptions, including *Daphne retusa* and *Daphne tangutica* of the species listed here.

The foliage is usually evergreen, but *Daphne mezereum* is deciduous, as are forms of *Daphne bholua* and *Daphne burkwoodii*. The foliage can be a feature, such as in *Daphne odora* 'Aureo Marginata', where the leaves have white, yellow or cream margins. In the garden, the more vigorous sorts, such as *Daphne mezereum* and *Daphne laureola*, can be sited in light shade but they all prefer a bright, sunny situation. They are suited to mixed borders, on rockeries and as specimen plants in tubs. The berries and foliage are poisonous. They can be propagated by seed sown as soon as it is ripe; it may take longer than one year to germinate. Cuttings of semi-hardwood can be taken in summer and rooted in a closed frame. The suckering forms can be divided and grown on until well rooted. They can also be grafted in late winter – cut off the top of a pencil thick (or thinner) seedling about 2cm (1in) above pot level, make a vertical cut down through the centre of the stem, make two cuts on a scion and place it in this cut so that the cambiums meet, and gently tie; put in a closed warm frame and callusing should take 2–3 weeks. When planting grafted stock, always place the graft union 5cm (2in) below the soil surface to encourage scion rooting.

Daphne burkwoodii 'Astrid'

soil	Well drained soils, lightly acidic to lightly alkaline for most species
site	A preferable position is in the sun, or with some dappled shade
general care	Plant grafted shrubs so that the union is below soil level to encourage scion rooting. Keep the soil moist
pruning	No pruning is required for this particular plant, except to trim to size
pests & diseases	Viruses can cause mottling of foliage – burn affected plants and buy new virus-free stock

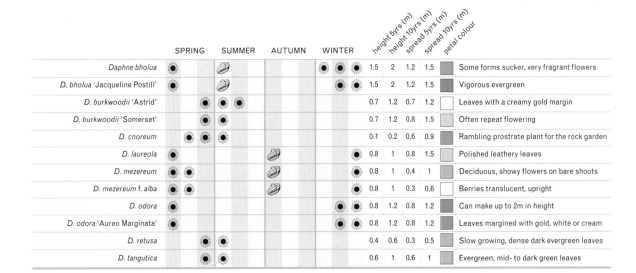

	SPRING	SUMMER	AUTUMN	WINTER	height 5yrs (m)	height 10yrs (m)	spread 5yrs (m)	spread 10yrs (m)	petal colour	
Daphne bholua	●	◎		● ● ●	1.5	2	1.2	1.5		Some forms sucker, very fragrant flowers
D. bholua 'Jacqueline Postill'	●	◎		● ●	1.5	2	1.2	1.5		Vigorous evergreen
D. burkwoodii 'Astrid'	● ● ●	●			0.7	1.2	0.7	1.2		Leaves with a creamy gold margin
D. burkwoodii 'Somerset'	● ●	●			0.7	1.2	0.8	1.5		Often repeat flowering
D. cnoreum	● ● ●	●			0.1	0.2	0.6	0.9		Rambling prostrate plant for the rock garden
D. laureola	●		◎	●	0.8	1	0.8	1.5		Polished leathery leaves
D. mezereum	● ●		◎	●	0.8	1	0.4	1		Deciduous, showy flowers on bare shoots
D. mezereum f. *alba*	● ●		◎	●	0.8	1	0.3	0.6		Berries translucent, upright
D. odora	●			● ● ●	0.8	1.2	0.8	1.2		Can make up to 2m in height
D. odora 'Aureo Marginata'	●			● ●	0.8	1.2	0.8	1.2		Leaves margined with gold, white or cream
D. retusa	● ●	●			0.4	0.6	0.3	0.5		Slow growing, dense dark evergreen leaves
D. tangutica	● ●	●			0.6	1	0.6	1		Evergreen, mid- to dark green leaves

● *flowering*   ◎ *harvest*

Desfontainea

The glossy holly-like leaves of this plant look quite ordinary, except that they are in opposite pairs. Until it flowers, there is nothing to suggest that this plant is anything special, let alone outstanding.

Once Desfontainea produces its flowers, however, you know you have something truly worthwhile. 5cm (2in) long tubes of vermilion and orient red sit on a bush only a metre or less high (3ft). This is a choice shrub which likes half shade in a sheltered spot. It thrives on cool moist soils, not liking shallow chalk soils. Propagate by seed sown on the surface of a tray, or hardwood cuttings taken at the end of summer and kept in a cold frame over winter.

Desfontainea spinosa

soil	Moisture retentive, but well drained for both. Desfontainea dislikes shallow, chalky soils.
site	Desfontainea: sheltered, with some shade. Deutzia: hot sun can bleach flowers
general care	For Desfontainea, little care is needed. For Deutzia add mulch to keep the soil moist to perform well
pruning	Desfontainea: prune in spring to retain shape. Deutzia: take off 3-year-old shoots (Group 1)
pests & diseases	Both plants are relatively trouble-free. Pests and diseases do not usually cause any problems

Deutzia

These are flowering shrubs of the first order, with fragrant flowers which are borne in spring or early summer from buds on last summer's growths.

Deutzia 'Strawberry Fields'

The individual flowers are around 1cm (½in) wide but are carried in clusters, often rising above the arching shoots, and are showy. The genus has star-shaped hairs on all the parts, and in the ten stamens with winged stalks.

All the forms featured here are deciduous but some Chinese species are evergreen. They are suitable for a sheltered spot in half shade, or for an open sunny border.

	SPRING	SUMMER	AUTUMN	WINTER	height 5yrs (m)	height 10yrs (m)	spread 5yrs (m)	spread 10yrs (m)	petal colour	
Desfontainia spinosa		● ● ● ● ● ●			0.7	1.2	0.5	0.9		Spiny leaves, flowers can be 9cm
Deutzia crenata 'Nikko'	● ●				1.5	2	1.5	2		Autumn colour – burgundy
D. elegantissima 'Rosealind'		●			1.2	1.5	0.9	1.2		Upright bush
D. gracilis	● ●	●			1.2	1.5	0.9	1.2		Susceptible to late spring frosts
D. hybrida 'Magicien'		●			1.2	1.5		0.2		Flowers pink and white
D. hybrida 'Mont Rose'		●			1.2	1.5	0.9	1.2		Petals crimped, anthers gold, upright habit
D. ningpoensis		● ●			1.2	1.8	1.2	1.8		Flowers white with pink tinge
D. rosea	●	●			0.8	0.9	0.8	1		Low shrub with branches that arc
D. scabra 'Candidissima'		● ●			1	1.8	0.9	1.5		Upright habit, flowers double
D. scabra 'Plena'		● ●			1	1.8	0.9	1.5		Also called 'Flore Pleno' and 'Rosea Plena'
D. scabra 'Pride of Rochester'		● ●			1	1.8	0.9	1.5		Double white flowers
D. 'Strawberry Fields'		●			1.2	1.5	0.9	1.2		Flowers pink

● *flowering*

Escallonia

These evergreen shrubs are valued for their late flowering, at the end of summer and into autumn. The funnel-shaped flowers are carried at the ends of the current season's shoots; in those that flower in summer the flowering shoots are from buds laid down in last year's wood, but in the late flowering forms, the flowers terminate the current season's wood. The flowers range in colour from white to deep pink.

The foliage of many Escallonia is aromatic if bruised, and in all forms is glossy green. They are excellent for coastal sites and milder areas. In the garden they can be used as specimen shrubs, in shrub beds, or on a wall. They also make

Escallonia 'Pride of Donard'

excellent hedges and windbreaks. Plant in a sheltered position in full sun, or no more than light shade. They like deep, well drained and moisture retentive soils but do not need fertile ones – in fact they

will make better garden plants on less fertile sandy loams. Most will tolerate shallow chalk soils and medium to heavy clay soils. They can be propagated by seeds and by most forms of cuttings – softwood in early summer, semi-hardwood in later summer and hardwood cuttings in a frame in autumn. They do not need pruning.

soil	Very tolerant plant, happy in most types from sandy loams to chalky soils
site	Sun or light shade is the best for these shrubs, but most need shelter
general care	Although very little care is needed, a good mulch will retain moisture, especially in the summer
pruning	Summer flowers after flowering (Group 1); autumn forms in spring (Group 2)
pests & diseases	Relatively trouble free. Pests and diseases do not usually cause any problems

Escallonia rubra var. macrantha

	SPRING	SUMMER	AUTUMN	WINTER	height 5yrs (m)	height 10yrs (m)	spread 5yrs (m)	spread 10yrs (m)	petal colour	
Escallonia 'Apple Blossom'		● ●			1.2	1.5	1.2	1.5		Flowers chalice-shaped
E. 'C. F. Ball'		● ● ● ●			1.5	2.5	1.2	2		Upright habit
E. 'Donard Radiance'		● ● ●			1	1.5	1	1.5		Saucer-shaped flowers
E. 'Donard Seedling'		● ●			1.5	2.5	1.2	2		Hardier than most
E. 'Edensis'		● ●			1	2	1.5	2.5		Arching stems, hardier than most
E. laevis 'Gold Brian'		●			1	1.2	1	1.2		Light yellow-green foliage
E. laevis 'Gold Ellen'		●			1.5	1.2	1	1.2		Bright gold foliage with a green slash
E. laevis 'Langleyensis'		● ● ●			1.5	2.5	2	3		Arching habit
E. 'Peach Blossom'		● ●			1.2	1.5	1.2	1.5		Chalice-shaped flowers
E. 'Red Dream'		●			0.7	1	0.7	1		Flowers red
E. 'Red Elf'		● ● ● ● ●			1.5	2.5	1.2	2		Tubular flowers
E. rubra 'Crimson Spire'		● ● ●			1.5	2.5	1.5	2.5		Good for hedges and coastal sites
E. rubra var. macrantha		● ● ●			1.5	2.5	1.5	2.5		Vigorous – can grow up to 4m

● *flowering*

Euonymus
Spindle

The spindles are, basically, florally challenged. The flowers are important – otherwise there would be none of the attractive fruits which play their part in making autumn interesting, but which are not the reason for planting them. *Euonymus alatus* is a wonderful low growing shrub whose twigs have curious corky flanges, and whose autumn colour is a brilliant crimson-pink.

Euonymus fortunei and *Euonymus japonicus* are evergreen shrubs with coloured foliage. The fruits are capsules which hang down from the branches; they open to reveal the orange-red coated seeds which dangle from long threads until birds eat them. *Euonymus alatus* can be used in a shrub border, or in some prominent spot where its full autumn and winter glory can be appreciated. *Euonymus fortunei* forms are mainly low ground cover plants, for the front of borders and as an understorey to larger shrubs. *Euonymus japonicus* will make an effective screen, or can be sited to provide the evergreen backcloth to a shrub or mixed border; its fruits ripen late, from around mid- to late winter.

Spindles like all well drained soils and thrive on dry sites. They can be propagated by seed or by semi-hardwood cuttings in summer for *Euonymus alatus* and ripe cuttings in a cold frame for the evergreen species.

Euonymus 'Emerald 'n' Gold'

Euonymus fortunei 'Blondy'

soil	Any well drained soil, tolerant of dry and chalky conditions
site	Sun to shade, with the evergreen sorts tolerating quite dense shade
general care	This is a great plant to cultivate as minimal attention is required to maintain growth
pruning	Only prune back to restrict growth and remove damaged shoots
pests & diseases	*Euonymus japonicus* can be prone to mildew, but otherwise there are no particular problems

	SPRING	SUMMER	AUTUMN	WINTER	height 5yrs (m)	height 10yrs (m)	spread 5yrs (m)	spread 10yrs (m)	petal colour	
E. alatus		●	🌰		0.8	1.2	1	1.5	▦	Brilliant autumn colour and corky twigs
E. alatus 'Compactus'		●			0.5	0.7	0.8	1.2	▦	Small form of the species
E. fortunei 'Blondy'		●			0.3	0.5	0.3	0.6	▦	Leaves large yellow with dark green margin
E. fortunei 'Emerald Gaiety'		●			0.3	0.5	0.3	0.6	▦	Leaves with a white margin, pink in winter
E. fortunei 'Emerald 'n' Gold'		●			0.3	0.5	0.3	0.6	▦	Leaves deep green with a bright gold margin
E. fortunei 'Harlequin'		●			0.3	0.5	0.8	1.5	▦	Leaves with white variegations, trailing shrub
E. fortunei 'Sunspot'		●			0.3	0.5	0.3	0.6	▦	Leaves with central golden blotch
E. japonicus 'Aureus'		●		🌰	1	2	0.6	1.2	▦	Leaves green on margin, bright yellow centre
E. japonicus 'Microphyllus Albovariegatus'		●		🌰	0.4	0.6	0.4	0.7	▦	Narrow leaves varied with white
E. japonicus 'Ovatus Aureus'		● ● ●		🌰	1	2	0.6	1.2	▦	Broad yellow margin and paler green centre

● flowering   🌰 harvest

Exochorda
Pearlbush

Pure white flowers in mid- to late spring are the reason for planting these shrubs. They should be sited in full sun so that the brightness of the blooms will dazzle, or beside a pond where their glory can be reflected. *Exochorda giraldii* var. *wilsonii* is excellent as a larger plant towards the back of a shrub border, or as a specimen shrub.

Exochorda macrantha 'The Bride' makes a mound of flowers and foliage. This plant can be used as glorified ground cover; if trained onto a single stem, it makes a cascade of arching, drooping branches. The flowers are produced with the fresh green new foliage in small erect or spreading racemes, often from every bud set along last year's erect or

soil	Flourishes in fertile, well drained soils, including chalky ones
site	Enjoys a position in the sun but can also tolerate light shade
general care	Although very little care is needed, a good mulch in the spring will bring out the best results
pruning	Remove shaded, weak and damaged shoots after flowering
pests & diseases	Relatively trouble free. Pests and diseases do not usually cause any problems

Exochorda macrantha 'The Bride'

arching branches. They have five paper white toothed petals and are faintly scented. The genus is related to Spiraea but differs in the large furrowed capsule which contains flattened winged seeds.

Exochorda thrive on a wide range of well drained soils. They are good for deep chalk soils but inclined to become chlorotic on shallow chalky sites. Ideally, site them in full sun but they will take dappled shade.

They can be propagated by seed or from softwood cuttings taken in early summer, but both methods have drawbacks – seed because the genus is promiscuous and the selected forms will not breed true, and cuttings because they can be slow – or difficult – to root and grow away. Layering is more effective where only the occasional plant is required.

	SPRING	SUMMER	AUTUMN	WINTER	height 5yrs (m)	height 10yrs (m)	spread 5yrs (m)	spread 10yrs (m)	petal colour	
Exochorda giraldii var. *wilsonii*	●●				1.5	2.5	1	2	☐	Vigorous, large shrub
E. macrantha 'The Bride'	●●				1	1.5	1.2	2.5	☐	Mound forming; train as weeping specimen

● flowering

Forsythia

These shrubs are valued for the bright yellow bell-shaped flowers which are carried in large numbers on the bare branches in late winter or early spring. The best flowering is on two year old stems, where there are lots of lateral shoots giving masses of flower buds, with each bud producing from one to four or even five flowers.

Forsythia are normally grown as isolated specimen shrubs or in mixed beds or as part of screening used to define different areas of the garden. They can, however, be very effective as hedges, where provided the hedge is carefully clipped so that the flower buds remain, the bare boughs will be wreathed in yellow. Pruning of specimen shrubs should involve the removal of older shoots immediately flowering has finished to maintain an open branch structure.

Forsythia prefer a sunny aspect, but will grow in light or dappled shade. In denser shade, they will not flower as well. Flowering on these plants appears to be more prolific in colder areas; the reason is that the flowers have a winter cold requirement and once this is met, all the blooms will develop. In milder areas, this requirement is not met as well, so flowering tends to be less concentrated and thus less effective, even if the plant is in flower for longer.

Forsythia are very adaptable in terms of the soil they require, growing on almost anything apart from bogs. They are gross feeders and do best on well drained and fertile soils, tolerating lime or chalk very well. They are easily propagated by cuttings, either semi-hardwood cuttings in summer, or even easier, 30cm (1ft) long hardwood cuttings from mid-autumn to mid-winter, inserted in the ground outside. Some will naturally layer themselves around the garden, especially *Forsythia suspensa*.

Forsythia 'Beatrix Farrand'

soil	Any garden soil, tolerates chalk very well and prefers plenty of nutrients
site	The best position for this shrub is a sunny spot with light shade
general care	Although not much maintenance is required, feed and mulch to gain best flowering
pruning	After flowering, remove older shoots; maintain a crown with 1–3 year old stems
pests & diseases	Relatively trouble free. Pests and diseases do not usually cause any problems

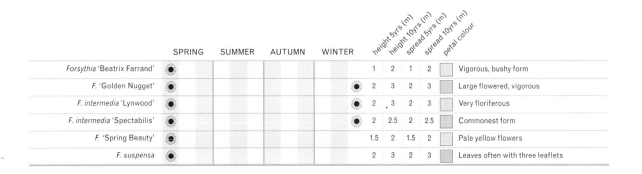

	SPRING	SUMMER	AUTUMN	WINTER	height 5yrs (m)	height 10yrs (m)	spread 5yrs (m)	spread 10yrs (m)	petal colour	
Forsythia 'Beatrix Farrand'	●				1	2	1	2		Vigorous, bushy form
F. 'Golden Nugget'	●			●	2	3	2	3		Large flowered, vigorous
F. intermedia 'Lynwood'	●			●	2	3	2	3		Very floriferous
F. intermedia 'Spectabilis'	●			●	2	2.5	2	2.5		Commonest form
F. 'Spring Beauty'	●				1.5	2	1.5	2		Pale yellow flowers
F. suspensa	●				2	3	2	3		Leaves often with three leaflets

● *flowering*

Fothergilla
Witch alder

These shrubs are characterized by white bottle-brush flowers terminating short branches in spring. The flowers are carried with the new leaves in *Fothergilla major*, so that they develop whilst the leaves are still fresh glossy green with their indented veins.

In *Fothergilla gardenii* the flowers are carried in advance of the leaves on the bare shoots. The flowers are showy, yet like several other members of the Hamamelidaceae (they are related to Hamamelis) they lack petals, the normal form of colour in flowers. Instead, the display is formed from the massed stamens. These have white or pinkish white stalks (filaments) and yellow anthers, appearing predominantly white when viewed as a cluster. The flowers are also attractively fragrant.

For autumn colour, these are amongst the best of all garden shrubs, turning crimson or orange-yellow. The genus requires a lime-free soil; they grow best on soils which are light, moist and rich but reasonably freely drained. They are shrubs for light woodland or woodland edges, tolerating light shade to full sun (which gives the best autumn colour). They are suited to a woodland garden area, not having perhaps enough flower for more formal shrub beds. Ideally, site them where the autumn colour will be strongest, not just in full sun but where the sun will light up the shrub from behind. The forms can be propagated by semi-hardwood cuttings taken in mid-summer, with bottom heat assisting rooting. They can be raised by layering and by seed.

soil	Grows best in lime-free, rich soil, but light and freely-drained conditions
site	Enjoys a position in the sun but can also tolerate light shade
general care	Appreciates a good mulch once or twice a year to maintain a high, organic material content in the soil
pruning	Pruning is not essential for this shrub, unless for containing its growth
pests & diseases	Relatively trouble free. Pests and diseases do not usually cause any problems

Fothergilla gardenii

	SPRING	SUMMER	AUTUMN	WINTER	height 5yrs (m)	height 10yrs (m)	spread 5yrs (m)	spread 10yrs (m)	petal colour	
Fothergilla gardenii	●				0.6	1	0.6	1		Flowers before the leaves
F. gardenii 'Blue Mist'	●				0.6	1	0.6	1		Leaves frosty blue-green during summer
F. major	●				0.8	1.5	0.8	1.5		Ultimately may grow to 2–3m
F. major 'Monticola Group'	●				0.7	1.2	0.8	1.5		More spreading than the typical form

 *flowering*

Fuchsia

Fuchsia is a large genus from South America and New Zealand with about a hundred species. However, in cultivation over 8,000 hybrids and cultivars have been produced. The majority of Fuchsia are deciduous shrubs, but some are perennials and many will remain in leaf in mild winters.

The beauty of the Fuchsia flower is in the combination of the calyx and the corolla. The flowers are pendulous and have a tubular calyx which ends in the four lobes of the sepals. The whole calyx is brightly coloured and the sepals usually reflexed. Inside the sepals are the four erect or spreading petals with the stamens and style poking out prominently. The petals are often a contrasting colour to the sepals. Flowers are produced in a continuous succession from early summer until autumn, making them one of the most floriferous of all shrubs. The fruit is a fleshy berry which forms at the base of the calyx tube. It often ripens to a maroon colour and contains many small seeds.

Fuchsia magellanica

Species Fuchsia

These shrubs generally have rather small flowers with strong colour contrasts. They range in size from *Fuchsia excorticata*, which will make a small tree in mild areas, to *Fuchsia magellanica*, a showy shrub 1–4m (3–13ft) in height which can be used for hedging in milder gardens. It is one of the hardiest of the species and has given rise to a large number of forms. These species should be used in shrub borders. They can be propagated by softwood or semi-hardwood cuttings in spring or summer, or by seed.

soil	Fuchsias are tolerant of most soil types, as long as it is well drained
site	Enjoys a sunny position, but can also tolerate light shade
general care	In cold climates they will be cut back by hard winters; give the plant a generous mulch to protect it
pruning	Remove any damaged shoots; can be hard pruned to ground level in spring
pests & diseases	Susceptible to vine weevil, grey mould, aphids and other common pests and diseases

Hybrid Fuchsia

These are hybrids of several species and have been selected for their colourful flowers. The flowers can be up to 10cm (4in) across at the sepals, such as in 'Dancing Flame'. They are generally less hardy than species such as *Fuchsia magellanica*. However, they are very easily raised from cuttings, either softwood in spring or semi-hardwood in

Fuchsia 'Marinka'

Fuchsia 'Celia Smedley'

Fuchsia 'Dark Eyes'

Fuchsia 'Harry Grey'

Fuchsia 'Snowcap'

Fuchsia 'Swingtime'

Flowering Shrubs

summer, so plants can be over wintered in a greenhouse. When planting them in a shrub border, they will be hardier if planted 5–7cm (2–3in) below the natural soil surface and deeply mulched, at least in autumn. This should enable the base of the plant to survive most winters. When regrowth starts in the spring, protect from slugs and remove excess winter protection. If winter cold has not pruned them to ground level, they can be trimmed in spring and will make a strong show from early summer onwards. Some of the forms have a prostrate or weeping habit, making them excellent for hanging baskets, or to tumble over a wall.

Fuchsias can be used in a variety of ways. In mild areas they make excellent hedges; in cold areas they can be kept over winter in a shed or outbuilding and cuttings can be taken in spring to fill beds or for use in hanging baskets.

	SPRING	SUMMER	AUTUMN	WINTER	height 5yrs (m)	height 10yrs (m)	spread 5yrs (m)	spread 10yrs (m)	petal colour	
[SPECIES] *Fuchsia arborescens*		●			1.2	2	1	1.7		Tender species with evergreen leaves
F. excorticata		●			1.5	3	1.5	2.5		Can make a large tree in mild gardens
F. magellanica		● ● ●	● ●		1.2	1.8	1.2	1.8		Hardy, moisture loving shrub
F. magellanica var. *gracilis* 'Aurea'		● ● ●	● ●		1.2	1.8	1.2	1.8		Leaves golden-yellow
F. magellanica var. *gracilis* 'Variegata'		● ● ●	● ●		1.2	1.8	1.2	1.8		Leaves green with a creamy-yellow
F. magellanica var. *molinae*		● ● ●	● ●		1.2	1.8	1.2	1.8		Flowers pale
F. magellanica var. *molinae* 'Sharpitor'		● ● ●	● ●		1.2	1.8	1.2	1.8		Leaves margined grey-green
F. microphylla		● ● ●	● ●		0.7	1.2	0.7	1.2		Small slender leaves
F. procumbens		● ● ●	● ●		0.1	0.15	0.8	1.2		Trailing species
[HYBRID] *F.* 'Alice Hoffman'		● ● ●	● ● ●		0.6m	0.6m	0.6m	0.6m		Leaves bronze-green
F. 'Autumnale'		●	● ● ●		0.3m	0.3m	0.6m	0.6m		Leaves green and yellow, maturing to dark red
F. 'Blue Satin'		● ● ●	● ● ●		0.6m	0.6m	0.6m	0.6m		Flowers white with violet-blue petals
F. 'Celia Smedley'		● ● ●	● ● ●		0.6m	0.6m	0.6m	0.6m		Very free-flowering
F. 'Dark Eyes'		● ● ●	● ● ●		0.6m	0.6m	0.6m	0.6m		Medium, double flowers that last well
F. 'Happy Wedding Day'		● ● ●	● ● ●		0.6m	0.6m	0.6m	0.6m		White flowers
F. 'Harry Grey'		● ● ●	● ● ●		0.6m	0.6m	0.6m	0.6m		Tube pink with white sepals and tepals
F. 'Marinka'		● ● ●	● ● ●		0.3m	0.3m	0.6m	0.6m		Trailing shrub with bright red flowers
F. 'Phyllis'		● ● ●	● ● ●		0.9m	1.5m	0.6m	0.9m		Hardy shrub with small to medium flowers
F. 'Rufus'		● ● ●	● ● ●		0.75	0.75	0.6m	0.6m		Single red flowers, early
F. 'Snowcap'		● ● ●	● ● ●		0.3m	0.3m	0.3m	0.3m		Summer bedding, not hardy
F. 'Swingtime'		● ● ●	● ● ●		0.6m	0.6m	0.6m	0.75		Leaves with red veins
F. 'Thalia'		● ● ●	● ●		0.6m	0.6m	0.9m	0.9m		Upright
F. 'Winston Churchill'		● ● ●	● ● ●		0.6m	0.6m	0.75	0.75		Double

 flowering

F

Gaultheria

These are low shrubs with glossy small evergreen leaves and relatively large juicy berries. They tolerate shade, but are quite happy in full sun provided they are kept suitably moist at the roots. They like freely draining acidic sands with plenty of organic matter, but most soils which are neither limy nor boggy suit them well.

The flowers are quaint, rather than showy, but give rise to the berries. In *Gaultheria shallon* these are dark purple, whereas in *Gaultheria mucronata* they range from marble white to red. These forms make excellent ground cover, spreading and suckering to fill the space. Many Gaultheria are either male or female, so it is necessary to plant at least one male for every 8–10 female plants; however, some are hermaphrodite (i.e. both sexes), but even with these you will get a better set of berries from planting two or more clones together. Apart from their use as ground cover in shady parts of the garden, gaultherias can be used with heathers, or at the front of shrub beds.

Propagate by semi-hardwood cuttings in summer, by division of layers or by seed. The latter is exceedingly fine and should only be scattered over the surface of damp compost and then kept in a light place but not in direct sunlight. The genus Pernettya used to be kept as distinct from Gaultheria, and *Gaultheria mucronata* may be found in nursery catalogues as *Pernettya mucronata*. Also, the hybrid between *Gaultheria mucronata* and *Gaultheria shallon* may be listed as *Gaulnettya wisleyensis*, rather than as *Gaultheria wisleyensis*.

Gaultheria mucronata 'Signaal'

Gaultheria wisleyensis 'Wisley Pearl'

soil	Likes acidic, freely drained rich soils; avoid lime or chalky soils
site	Enjoys a position in the sun but can also tolerate light shade
general care	Does not need a great deal of care, but mulch to maintain an acidic soil, rich in organic matter
pruning	Clip to restrict height or spread, but at the expense of flowers or fruits for one year
pests & diseases	Relatively trouble free. Pests and diseases do not usually cause any problems

	SPRING	SUMMER	AUTUMN	WINTER	height 5yrs (m)	height 10yrs (m)	spread 5yrs (m)	spread 10yrs (m)	petal colour	
Gaultheria mucronata	● ●		🍂 🍂 🍂	🍂	0.4	0.6	0.5	1		Good ground cover
G. mucronata 'Bell's Seedling'	● ●		🍂 🍂		0.4	0.6	0.5	1		Berries crimson, hermaphrodite form
G. mucronata 'Crimsonia'	● ●		🍂 🍂 🍂		0.4	0.6	0.5	1		Berries carmine red, to 1.4cm (½in)
G. mucronata 'Signaal'	● ●		🍂 🍂 🍂		0.4	0.6	0.5	1		Dark pink berries last most of winter
G. shallon	● ●		🍂		0.4	0.6	0.5	1		Excellent suckering groundcover
G. wisleyensis 'Wisley Pearl'	●		🍂		0.5	1	0.5	1		Berries oxblood red

● flowering   🍂 harvest

Genista
Brooms

These shrubs have yellow pea-like flowers and are closely related to Cytisus. They are mainly small to medium shrubs, although *Genista aetnensis* is distinctly tree-like. Some have spines, but of these species listed only *Genista hispanica*, appropriately named as Spanish gorse, is really spiny.

The leaves of this plant are rather small and transient. Photosynthesis is largely carried out by the green shoots. This indicates that they are species from hot dry climates, tolerating summers of low rainfall. In the garden, genistas should be located in the hottest parts, in full sun. They can suffer from early autumn frosts, especially after cool wet autumns which trick the plant into continuing growth late in the year; normally this kills branches rather than whole plants. For this reason, avoid planting them on rich soils, and as an extra precaution grow half-hardy species in a cool greenhouse.

Genista hispanica can be very effective when planted en masse – in late spring or

soil	Any well drained soil, preferably of low to medium nutritional status
site	The warmest place in the garden as this plant likes as much sun as it can get
general care	This shrub is very easy to cultivate as it is tolerant of fairly poor and dry conditions
pruning	Clip to restrict size; regrowth only from green shoots. These do not tolerate hard pruning
pests & diseases	Relatively trouble free. Pests and diseases do not usually cause any problems

Genista tenera 'Golden Shower'

early summer it will be smothered by the blooms. *Genista lydia* is a shrub for the rock garden or tumbling over a low wall. *Genista pilosa* and *Genista tenera* are spreading shrubs which will attain 0.6m (2ft) in height but wider in spread.

The important aspect of the soil for these plants is that it is freely drained; with this requirement satisfied, they will tolerate acidic to limy soils.

Genista can be propagated by semi-hardwood cuttings in late summer, rooted in a very sandy medium, or by seed. They deeply resent root disturbance and should be planted out straight from pots, and as small as possible.

	SPRING	SUMMER	AUTUMN	WINTER	height 5yrs (m)	height 10yrs (m)	spread 5yrs (m)	spread 10yrs (m)	petal colour	
Genista hispanica	● ●				0.3	0.5	0.3	0.5		Spiny, dense mounds of interlocking branches
G. lydia	● ●				0.3	0.5	0.3	0.5		Arching, prostrate habit
G. pilosa 'Vancouver Gold'	●				0.3	0.4	0.3	0.4		Mound-forming habit
G. tenera 'Golden Shower'		● ● ●	●		0.5	1	0.5	1		Graceful shrub with spreading habit
G. tinctoria 'Flore Pleno'		● ● ●	●		0.2	0.3	0.2	0.3		Procumbent shrub; flowers double, floriferous

● *flowering*

Grevillea
Spider flower

This is a large genus of mainly tender trees and shrubs from Australia and adjacent territories. The genus belong to the Protea family (Proteaceae) which are major components of the southern hemisphere flora.

The chief character of this family is the flower. This does not have separate calyx (sepals) and corolla (petals) as found in most broadleaved trees and shrubs; instead the two are combined into a calyx-tube. At the bud stage this has four more or less united valvate segments, which become free as the flower opens. This gives the flowers their characteristic 'spider' appearance, superficially resembling the flowers of climbing honeysuckle or woodbine (*Lonicera periclymenum*). They are also nectar-rich,

Grevillea 'Canberra Gem'

Grevillea rosmarinifolia

soil	Well drained, rich soils of moderate fertility – avoid soils high in phosphorus
site	A sheltered position except in very mild areas. Enjoys sun to light shade
general care	Avoid using fertilizer, as this plant family is generally adapted to soils low in phosphorus
pruning	Clip after flowering if you need to keep to a restricted size or shape
pests & diseases	Relatively trouble free. Pests and diseases do not usually cause any problems

attracting nectar-feeding birds. In cool temperate climates we can grow only a small selection. The three plants featured here are amongst the hardiest of their kind and are desirable garden plants for their evergreen needle-like leaves and terminal clusters of flowers – deep rosy-red in *Grevillea rosmarinifolia*, waxy reddish pink in *Grevillea* 'Canberra Gem' and yellow in *Grevillea juniperina* f. *sulphurea*. The flowers can be produced at almost any time of year, but are mainly carried in spring to summer.

	SPRING	SUMMER	AUTUMN	WINTER	height 5yrs (m)	height 10yrs (m)	spread 5yrs (m)	spread 10yrs (m)	petal colour	
Grevillea 'Canberra Gem'	●	● ● ● ●			1	1.8	1	1.8	■	Hybrid of *G. juniperina* and *G. rosmarinifolia*
G. juniperina f. *sulphurea*	●	● ● ● ●			1	1.8	1	1.8	□	Also known as *G. sulphurea*
G. rosmarinifolia		● ● ●			1	1.5	1	1.5	■	Just summer flowering

● flowering

Hebe
Shrubby
veronica

These shrubs are mainly New Zealander in origin, but also occur in Australia and South America, including one species on the Falkland Islands. They are grown for the flowers and the evergreen foliage. The flowers are in terminal or axillary clusters, with four petals joined at the base into a tube. They are mainly white, especially in New Zealand, but cultivated Hebe include pink, blue, purple and red.

The leaves come in two main forms; either closely addressed onto the shoot, like the foliage of cypresses (Cupressus) (these being known as 'whipcord' hebes) or much larger and lanceolate – in the table these are described as 'large' but are rarely as much as 5cm (2in).

Some forms of Hebe have a purple colour to the leaves, especially the undersides, whilst some of the whipcord forms are khaki or yellow over winter. The leaves are always in opposite pairs. The genus does not form resting buds, but the terminal pair of leaves normally stand erect, covering the immature leaves. In the garden the smaller growing forms are especially useful on rockeries and at the front of shrub borders. The larger growing kinds can also be used in borders

Hebe 'Red Edge'

or as specimen plants. They can also be used for hedging, but if you choose them for this purpose do take great care over pruning. Some will re-grow if severely pruned, but others are unlikely to make satisfactory regrowth from hard pruning.

soil	Relatively unfussy. Likes any well drained soil, including chalky ones
site	Enjoys a position in the sun, preferably with protection from cold winds
general care	Fairly easy to cultivate and manage. Mulch and feed, especially on light, unfertile soils
pruning	Limit *H. salicifolia* to trimming into leafy shoots; others can be cut back in spring
pests & diseases	Can be prone to phytophthora root rot, especially on poorly drained soils

Hebe recurva

Hebe 'Margret'

Always trim lightly into live foliage, rather than more severely into bare wood. Generally, spring pruning is best for these plants; it also allows them to be tidied if there is any winter damage to clear away and to flower later in the summer.

Hebe are tolerant of salt spray and coastal conditions, and also atmospheric pollution. Some forms are absolutely hardy but others may be damaged by winter cold. This is especially a problem with cold drying winds and on poorly drained soils. They will grow on a wide range of soils, including chalky ones. They like full sun, and are not shrubs for shady sites. They are easily propagated from semi-hardwood cuttings taken at the end of the summer. These should be kept over winter in a cold frame and potted-on in spring. The whipcord Hebe should be kept dry over winter, otherwise they are inclined to rot at the base. Seed can also be used for propagation, but as these plants hybridize very readily you will be unlikely to produce something just like the parent, especially if that is a cultivar.

Hebe are easily transplanted, and can even be moved in flower to fill gaps in bedding schemes.

H

Flowering Shrubs

	SPRING	SUMMER	AUTUMN	WINTER	height 5yrs (m)	height 10yrs (m)	spread 5yrs (m)	spread 10yrs (m)	petal colour	
Hebe albicans		● ●			0.4	0.6	0.5	0.8		Compact and mound-forming whipcord species
Hebe armstrongii	●	● ● ●			0.3	0.5	0.3	0.5		Whipcord species, olive-green foliage
Hebe 'Autumn Glory'		● ●	● ● ●	●	0.4	0.6	0.6	0.9		Leaves large, dark green with red margin
Hebe carnosula		●			0.15	0.25	0.2	0.3		Low growing, spreading
Hebe cupressoides		● ●			0.6	0.6	1	1		Whipcord species, foliage glaucous mid-green
Hebe 'Emerald Green'		● ●			0.15	0.25	0.15	0.25		Bright, shiny green foliage
Hebe franciscana 'Blue Gem'		● ● ●	● ● ●		0.8	1.2	0.8	1.2		Leaves large, light to mid-green
Hebe hulkeana	●	●			1	1.5	1	1.5		Open growing upright shrub, leaves – red margin
Hebe 'Margret'		● ●	●		0.3	0.5	0.3	0.5		Rich, green leaves
Hebe odora 'New Zealand Gold'	●	●			0.2	0.3	0.2	0.3		Yellow stems and glossy dark green leaves
Hebe rakaiensis		● ●			0.6	1	0.8	1.2		Leaves glossy bright green
Hebe recurva		● ● ●			0.4	0.6	0.5	0.7		Compact shrub
Hebe 'Red Edge'		● ● ●			0.3	0.4	0.4	0.6		Leaves grey-green, veined red when young
Hebe salicifolia		● ● ●			1.2	2	1.2	2		Leaves to 12cm, flowers fragrant
Hebe topiaria		● ● ●			0.4	0.6	0.5	0.8		Dome-shaped, dense, leaves glossy grey-green
Hebe vernicosa		● ●			0.4	0.6	0.7	1		Glossy grey-green leaves, dense rounded bush

● *flowering*

Helianthemum
Sun rose

Like their close relatives the rock roses, the sun roses have large showy blooms (relative to the size of the plant) but each flower lasts less than a day. However, because the blooms are carried in such profusion, the bushes appear smothered in flowers.

Most flowers open in the morning, and close and wither around lunchtime. However, on dull days, there are few blooms. The main flowering period is late spring to early summer, but a smattering of blooms are often borne later in the summer. There are a hundred or so species from the Mediterranean regions, although a few of these are annual herbaceous plants. The common forms are a number of garden hybrids involving several different species.

Sun roses are small shrubs with evergreen leaves, mainly in pairs. They thrive in the hottest sunniest sites, preferring sun-

soil	Relatively unfussy. Can tolerate any well drained soil type
site	Hot and sunny sites only – they dislike dull days, let alone shade!
general care	Short lived, so expect to replace every few years. In cold areas, protect with a loose mulch of bracken
pruning	Trim after flowering to restrict spread. This may give a second flush of blooms
pests & diseases	Relatively trouble free. Pests and diseases do not usually cause any problems

Helianthemum 'Ben Macdhui'

facing slopes for extra light and warmth. They need good drainage and will not tolerate waterlogging at the roots. They tolerate acidic to limy soils. Sun roses are ideal plants for rockeries, and can be used as the low shrubs at the front of a mixed border. In the wild they occur on rocky sites, and this makes them excellent for draping over low walls. They are fast growing and short lived plants. It is sensible, therefore, to propagate replacements, keeping them over winter in a cold frame. Softwood cuttings in early summer will root with some bottom heat, and semi-hardwood cuttings should root in late summer.

	SPRING	SUMMER	AUTUMN	WINTER	height 5yrs (m)	height 10yrs (m)	spread 5yrs (m)	spread 10yrs (m)	petal colour	
Helianthemum 'Beech Park Red'	●	● ●			0.4	0.4	0.5	0.5	■	Good red form
H. 'Ben Fhada'	●	● ●			0.4	0.4	0.5	0.5	▨	Leaves grey-green
H. 'Ben Macdhui'	●	● ●			0.4	0.4	0.5	0.5	■	Leaves dark green
H. 'Mrs C.W. Earle'	●	● ●			0.4	0.4	0.5	0.5	■	Leaves dark green
H. 'Rhodanthe Carneum'	●	● ●			0.4	0.4	0.5	0.5	▨	Leaves silvery grey
H. 'Wisley Primrose'	●	● ●			0.5	0.5	0.5	0.5	□	Light grey-green

● *flowering*

Helichrysum
Everlasting
flower

This genus is best known for providing the 'everlasting' flowers, which are cut and dried for flower arrangements. These are predominantly plucked from the perennial forms, although there is no reason why the flowers of the shrub forms should not be dried, by hanging upside down over a gentle heat source out of direct sunlight.

This genus includes a number of shrubby forms. At one time, the species of Ozothamnus were also included in Helichrysum and this may persist in some nursery catalogues. They are also useful for their silvery-grey foliage; in practice, *Helichysum splendidum* is more splendid for this feature than for the flowers. These shrubs require a sheltered and well drained situation in full sun. They will neither cope with shade nor with wet at the roots, and some species benefit from being covered by a pane of glass over winter just to divert rainfall away from the roots. In cold conditions, they can be mulched with a light covering of bracken over winter. Propagate by semi-hardwood cuttings taken with a heel of older wood in summer.

Helichrysum splendidum

soil	Both like well drained soil. Holodiscus: moist, fertile with high organic content
site	Helichrysum: prefers a mix of sun and shelter. Holodiscus: Sun and moderate shade
general care	Helichrysum: in temperate areas, protect with loose mulch of bracken. Holodiscus: mulch to keep organic content
pruning	Helichrysum: hard prune (Group 2) mid-spring. Holodiscus: after flowering
pests & diseases	Both plants are relatively trouble-free. Pests and diseases do not usually cause any problems

Holodiscus
Ocean spray

The flowers are small and cup-shaped, but are carried in clusters up to 30cm (1ft) long at the ends of the arching shoots in mid-summer and give the feel of ocean spray sweeping the plant.

Holodiscus discolor

Holodiscus thrives on moist and fertile, well drained soils, and should not be allowed to become dry in summer. Ocean spray is ideal as a large plant in mixed shrub borders, as a specimen shrub and in a light woodland setting. It can be propagated by seed, which should be sown as soon as it is ripe. Cuttings can be difficult to root; take semi-hardwood cuttings with a heel of older wood in summer.

	SPRING	SUMMER	AUTUMN	WINTER	height 5yrs (m)	height 10yrs (m)	spread 5yrs (m)	spread 10yrs (m)	petal colour	
Helichrysum italicum		● ● ●	● ●		0.5	0.6	0.7	1		Foliage silver-grey to yellow-green;
H. italicum ssp. *serotimum*		● ● ●	● ●		0.3	0.4	0.5	0.7		Foliage intensely aromatic, the 'curry plant'
H. 'Schwefelicht'		● ● ●			0.9	0.3	0.9	0.3		Herbaceous. Really should be cut
H. splendidum		●	● ●		0.8	1.2	0.8	1.2		White woolly stems, silver grey leaves
Holodiscus discolor		●			1.5	2.5	1.5	2.5		Leaves grey-green above, white hairy beneath

● *flowering*

Hydrangea

This is a large genus containing very many excellent garden plants. These can be divided into shrubby species and climbers. Only the shrubby species are addressed here; for the climbing species, see _Clematis & Climbers_ in this series of books.

Shrubby Hydrangea include species which grow to less than a metre (3ft), to species such as _Hydrangea heteromalla_ which I have seen grown as a tree to a height of 13m (40ft) in the Himalayas. However, in terms of cultivation the conditions are not as favourable for growth in most countries, and we do not have a hundred or so years to wait, so even _Hydrangea heteromalla_ is unlikely to exceed 4m (13ft) in your garden.

Hydrangea are mainly grown for their flowers, which are carried in large heads. In the normal wild forms, the flowerheads contain two types of flowers. Around the perimeter of the truss are a small number of sterile flowers, or ray-flowers. These are large and flat, with three to five petal-like sepals, which are usually white. The purpose of these flowers is to attract insects to the many fertile flowers in the centre of the truss. The fertile flowers do not have sepals but have four or five very small white, pink or blue petals. The fertile flowers are not so showy, but give a haze of colour within the ray-flowers. The shrubs with this flower type are known as 'Lace-cap' Hydrangea.

Many garden forms have been selected to be more overtly showy. These forms have all the fertile flowers replaced by sterile ray-flowers and give a more rounded flower. This flower type is particularly prevalent amongst the garden forms of _Hydrangea macrophylla_, where they are known as 'Hortensia' Hydrangea or 'mopheads'.

The genus is perfectly happy on both acidic and alkaline soils, but inclined to become

Hydrangea quercifolia 'Snow Flake'

soil	Any moist soil. Flower colour can be determined by acidity/alkalinity
site	Full sun for smaller forms; most benefit from light shade in woodland garden
general care	Relatively easy to cultivate and maintain. Make sure the soil is kept moist and well mulched
pruning	Remove defecting branches. Some can be hard pruned in spring to above base of stem
pests & diseases	Unfortunately, hydrangeas are prone to mildew and most other common diseases

chlorotic on shallow chalk soils. However, the colour of the ray-flowers is dependent upon whether aluminium is available to the flowers, and the ability of the individual cultivar to

Hydrangea aspera Villosa Group

_H.m._ 'Generale Vicomtesse de Vibraye'

Hydrangea 'Preziosa'

utilize it. Aluminium gives intense blue to the flowers but it is only fully available on acidic soils with a pH between 4.5 & 5.5. Above these pH levels, the availability of aluminium drops and the flowers become pink. By a pH of 7.4 (alkaline) the flowers may be a deep pink in some clones.

In the garden, Hydrangea can be used in shrub or mixed beds, as specimen plants and in light woodland. *Hydrangea aspera* forms like woodland shelter and are not suited to full sun. Other hydrangeas will like these conditions but will also tolerate full sun.

Most hydrangeas should be pruned only after flowering (Group 1). Generally, pruning should only consist of the removal of crowded and weaker shoots. However,

species which flower late in the year, especially *Hydrangea paniculata*, but also *Hydrangea arborescens* and *Hydrangea quercifolia*, can be hard pruned in spring and will produce fewer but larger flowers in late summer/autumn.

Hydrangea can be propagated by seed. This is very fine and should be shaken out of the capsules onto a moist compost. Cover with a sheet of newspaper and a pane of glass. After a few days, the minute seedlings will emerge and the paper and glass should be removed. Water at this stage by soaking, not by overhead spray. Slugs find young Hydrangea particularly palatable.

Hydrangea heteromalla

	SPRING	SUMMER	AUTUMN	WINTER	height 5yrs (m)	height 10yrs (m)	spread 5yrs (m)	spread 10yrs (m)	petal colour	
Hydrangea arborescens 'Grandiflora'		✳ ✳ ✳			1.2	1.5	1.2	1.5		Flower heads large, inclined to flop over
H. aspera ssp. *sargentiana*		✳ ✳			1.2	1.8	1	1.5		Will withstand chalky soils better than most
H. aspera Villosa Group		✳ ✳			1.2	1.5	1.2	1.5		Lacecap type flowers
H. heteromalla		✳ ✳			1	1	2	2		Can make a small tree
H. macrophylla 'Ayesha'		✳ ✳			0.5	0.9	0.6	1		Hortensia
H. m. 'Generale Vicomtesse de Vibraye'		✳ ✳			0.5	0.9	0.6	1		Hortensia, hardy and good blue on acid soils
H. macrophylla 'Hamburg'		✳ ✳			0.6	1	0.6	1		Hortensia
H. macrophylla 'King George'		✳ ✳			0.5	0.9	0.6	1		Hortensia, ray flowers large
H. macrophylla 'Mariesii Perfecta'		✳ ✳			0.5	0.9	0.6	1		Lacecap, also known as 'Blue Wave'
H. macrophylla 'White Wave'		✳ ✳			0.5	0.9	0.6	1		Lacecap, free-flowering
H. paniculata 'Grandiflora'		✳ ✳	✳		1.2	1.5	1.2	1.5		Large heads of ray-flowers
H. paniculata 'Unique'		✳ ✳	✳		1.2	1.5	1.2	1.5		Large ray-flowers
H. 'Preziosa'		✳	✳		1.2	1.5	1.2	1.5		Upright shrub
H. quercifolia 'Snow Flake'		✳ ✳	✳		1.2	2	1.2	2.5		Scalloped leaves

✳ *flowering*

Hypericum
St John's wort

This genus contains a large number of shrubs and herbaceous plants. They all have yellow, rather cup-shaped, flowers which have a central boss of many stamens and five large petals.

Hypericum 'Hidcote' is remarkable for the length of time during which the flowers almost hide the foliage; it is a garden hybrid which is sterile and thus does not put any energy into forming fruits and seeds. It makes an excellent shrub for a mixed border, as a specimen and also for informal hedges. The flowers are produced on the current year's growth and thus it can be hard pruned in the spring (Group 2). Another hybrid is *Hypericum inodorum* 'Elstead'. The flowers, whilst attractive enough in their way, are not the main feature of this plant – the fruits are brilliant salmon-red as they mature. This is a medium shrub for the mixed or shrub border, which is inclined to seed itself around the garden. The other two forms

soil	Likes any well drained garden soil, and will tolerate chalky soils
site	Prefers a position where there is sun as well as light shade
general care	Generally very easy to look after and cultivate as it does not require much maintenance
pruning	*H.* 'Hidcote' can be hard pruned in spring (Group 2). Others better lightly pruned
pests & diseases	Hypericum rust can damage some forms, especially *H. calycinum* and *H. inodorum* 'Elstead'

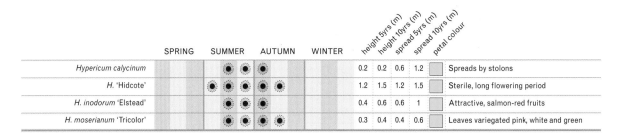

Hypericum moserianum 'Tricolor'

listed here are basically ground cover plants. *Hypericum calycinum* makes a low shrub which spreads by suckering and has relatively enormous golden flowers. It is good for areas of dry shade. *Hypericum moserianum* 'Tricolor' is a hybrid of *Hypericum calycinum*, especially grown for the leaves which are prettily variegated pink, white and green.

These shrubs thrive on a wide range of soils, and are especially good on chalky ones. They will tolerate some shade but flower much better in full sunlight. They can be easily propagated from semi-hardwood cuttings in summer.

These plants do not generally suffer from pests and diseases, although Hypericum rust can trouble some varieties.

	SPRING	SUMMER	AUTUMN	WINTER	height 5yrs (m)	height 10yrs (m)	spread 5yrs (m)	spread 10yrs (m)	petal colour	
Hypericum calycinum		● ● ●			0.2	0.2	0.6	1.2		Spreads by stolons
H. 'Hidcote'		● ● ●	● ●		1.2	1.5	1.2	1.5		Sterile, long flowering period
H. inodorum 'Elstead'		● ●	●		0.4	0.6	0.6	1		Attractive, salmon-red fruits
H. moserianum 'Tricolor'		● ● ●	● ●		0.3	0.4	0.4	0.6		Leaves variegated pink, white and green

● *flowering*

Ilex
Holly

Most hollies are large shrubs or tall trees. However, the forms of the varieties discussed here make much smaller shrubs.

Ilex crenata is mainly grown for the small dense foliage. It makes a narrow upright shrub with glossy green leaves less than 2cm (¾in) in length. The fruits are crowded in female plants, and are curiously black. *Ilex meserveae* is a hybrid between *Ilex aquifolium*, the common holly of Europe, and *Ilex rugosa* from Japan and adjacent islands. The hybrid was raised in an attempt to get a hardier plant than *Ilex aquifolium* for cold winters in New York state. The result is a number of clones, grown primarily for the colour of their foliage. The glossy blue-green is an unusual foliage colour and has proved very useful in the garden.

The blue hollies are better suited to sites which experience a continental climate, with hard dry winters. These hollies can be used in shrub beds and in a woodland garden. They will tolerate quite dense shade but will be slow to flower in these settings. They can be propagated by seed, but may take two or more years to germinate. Hardwood cuttings in late summer and autumn will root readily in a cold frame. Seed can also be used, but the seeds may take two or three years to germinate.

Ilex aquifolium 'Ferox Argentea'

Ilex meserveae 'Blue Angel'

Ilex crenata 'Golden Gem'

soil	Will tolerate most types of soil, but grows best in well drained conditions
site	Prefers a position where there is sun as well as light shade
general care	Will thrive with a good mulch. Plant from containers or in late spring and water initially
pruning	Prune after flowering. Hedges can be trimmed just before they come into leaf
pests & diseases	Leaf miners can be a problem, eating the middle part of the leaf blade, so keep a close watch

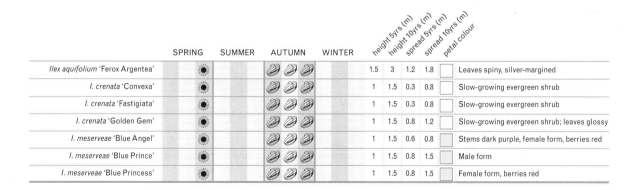

	SPRING	SUMMER	AUTUMN	WINTER	height 5yrs (m)	height 10yrs (m)	spread 5yrs (m)	spread 10yrs (m)	petal colour	
Ilex aquifolium 'Ferox Argentea'	●		🌰🌰🌰		1.5	3	1.2	1.8		Leaves spiny, silver-margined
I. crenata 'Convexa'	●		🌰🌰🌰		1	1.5	0.3	0.8		Slow-growing evergreen shrub
I. crenata 'Fastigiata'	●		🌰🌰🌰		1	1.5	0.3	0.8		Slow-growing evergreen shrub
I. crenata 'Golden Gem'	●		🌰🌰🌰		1	1.5	0.8	1.2		Slow-growing evergreen shrub; leaves glossy
I. meserveae 'Blue Angel'	●		🌰🌰🌰		1	1.5	0.6	0.8		Stems dark purple, female form, berries red
I. meserveae 'Blue Prince'	●		🌰🌰🌰		1	1.5	0.8	1.5		Male form
I. meserveae 'Blue Princess'	●		🌰🌰🌰		1	1.5	0.8	1.5		Female form, berries red

● flowering   🌰 harvest

Illicium
Anise tree

This genus has flowers with many strap-like petals which give rise to the curious star-shaped fruit.

Illicium anisatum makes an evergreen bush and is useful in milder areas in shrub beds. The flowers are yellow-green, maturing to creamy white. They are not as strongly fragrant as some species in the genus. However, the bark, wood and leaves are aromatic if bruised. The species like a site in light woodland but also thrive in full to moderate sun. They will tolerate only a little lime in the soil and are best on well drained acidic to neutral soils. Propagate by cuttings taken before they are fully ripe in late summer, or by layering.

Illicium anisatum

Indigofera

This genus of legumes was historically grown for indigo dye, and this gives them their Latin name (*-fera* translating as bearing, hence indigo-bearing). However, artificial dyes have ruled since the 1870s and today we can appreciate the beauty of the flowers and foliage for their own sake.

Indigofera heterantha

soil	Indigofera: any soil. Illicium: moisture retentive acidic to neutral soils of good fertility
site	Illicium: sun to light or dappled shade. Indigofera: likes the sun
general care	For both plants, mulch to maintain high organic matter (Illicium) and protect base of stems (Indigofera)
pruning	Illicium: minimal to control size. Indigofera: cut to ground level for vigorous shoots
pests & diseases	Both plants are relatively trouble-free. Pests and diseases do not usually cause any problems

The flowers are carried in dense racemes in the leaf axils of the current season's growths. They are pea-like and some are shades of pink. Indigofera thrive on almost all well drained soils, from acidic sands to chalky soils. They tend to be rather winter tender, as except in hot sunny climates the wood does not fully ripen. However, the base is usually untouched and will sprout and flower the next year. Propagate them either from seed or from semi-hardwood cuttings in summer.

	SPRING	SUMMER	AUTUMN	WINTER	height 5yrs (m)	height 10yrs (m)	spread 5yrs (m)	spread 10yrs (m)	petal colour	
Illicium anisatum	● ● ●				1.2	2.5	1.2	2.5	☐	Grown for the unusual and fragrant flowers
Indigofera amblyantha		● ● ●	●		1.5	1.5	1.5	1.5	▨	Leaves pinnate, fresh green
I. heterantha		● ● ●	●		0.9	1.2	0.9	1.2	▨	Neat foliage. Will grow taller if sheltered by wall

● *flowering*

Jasminum
Jasmine

The jasmines straddle the boundary between climbers and shrubs. The climbers make delightful plants, often with fragrant flowers, but are beyond the scope of this book.

The commonest of the shrubby species shows this uncertainty as to whether the plant is a climber or a shrub – *Jasminum nudiflorum* has branches which are rambling and wand-like. It can be grown as a free-standing shrub, but the wiry stems are better displayed against a wall. The flowers are bright yellow and produced throughout winter. *Jasminum humile* is purely a shrub, with pinnate deciduous leaves set on arching shoots. The flowers are carried in summer at the end of short shoots from buds on last year's shoots; always yellow, in some forms they are fragrant, and are followed by black berries. *Jasminum parkeri* is evergreen and makes a low shrub. It is suited to the rock garden, but can be very effective if planted at the top of a wall where it will make a tumbling curtain of foliage. It also has yellow flowers, albeit tiny ones carried in early summer and followed by translucent white berries.

These shrubs will thrive on a wide range of soil types; provided it is well drained, they will flourish, but they prefer moist, well drained and fertile soil. Jasmines can be propagated by semi-hardwood cuttings in summer, by seed and by layering.

soil	Any well drained, preferably moisture retentive and fertile soil
site	Flourishes well in the sun or, at the very most, light shade
general care	Not much care and attention needed, apart from occasional mulching to maintain a fertile soil
pruning	Remove older shoots after flowering, especially from wall-trained specimens
pests & diseases	Occasionally aphids can be a problem, but apart from that, generally trouble-free from pests and diseases

Jasminum humile

	SPRING	SUMMER	AUTUMN	WINTER	height 5yrs (m)	height 10yrs (m)	spread 5yrs (m)	spread 10yrs (m)	petal colour	
Jasminum humile		● ●	🌰 🌰		1	1.8	1	1.5	☐	Semi-evergreen, with green bark on twigs
J. nudiflorum				● ● ●	1.5	2.5	2	3	☐	Flowers on bare branches
J. parkeri		● ● ● ●	🌰		0.2	0.3	0.4	0.8	☐	Evergreen, greenish-white fruit

● flowering   🌰 harvest

Kalmia

Calico bush *or*
Mountain laurel

Kalmia are close relatives of Rhododendron and have similar, open saucer-shaped flowers. These are predominantly pink and are carried in showy clusters in late spring and early summer when they swamp the foliage.

The flowers of Kalmia have an odd mechanism for spreading the pollen. The ten stamens are bent backwards so that there is a kink in the filament (stalk) and the anther fits into a cavity in the petals. When ripe, any stimulus on the kink in the filament will result in a shower of pollen.

The foliage is evergreen and is poisonous to stock. In the garden, kalmias are wonderful for the apex of a corner where two beds meet, so that the flowers can be appreciated from two directions, as specimen plants and in shrub beds. Kalmias can also be used to make informal and very colourful hedges. They are shrubs for full sun to light shade for the aerial parts. The roots are happiest in moist to boggy conditions. Like their Rhododendron relatives, kalmias dislike lime in the soil. The fruit of these plants is a dry, flat capsule which turns brown when ripe.

Kalmia latifolia 'Pink Charm'

soil	Does well in acidic soils with a high capacity for holding water, and bogs
site	Although they like boggy conditions, these plants are definitely sun lovers
general care	It is important that these plants are kept moist during dry periods and are given a mulch annually
pruning	Can be coppiced to re-invigorate bush – best spaced over 2–3 years
pests & diseases	Relatively trouble free. Pests and diseases do not usually cause any problems

Propagation can be by seed – this is very fine and should be sparingly scattered over damp compost which is watered from below (by standing in a bowl). The selected forms can be propagated by semi-hardwood cuttings taken in summer. Layering can also be used.

Flowering Shrubs

	SPRING	SUMMER	AUTUMN	WINTER	height 5yrs (m)	height 10yrs (m)	spread 5yrs (m)	spread 10yrs (m)	petal colour	
Kalmia angustifolia f. *rubra*		● ●			0.5	0.6	0.8	1.2		Narrow leaves
K. latifolia	●	● ●			1	2	1	2		Only likes acidic soils. Can make 3m
K. latifolia 'Pink Charm'	●	● ●			1	2	1	2		Red buds opening to pale pink flowers

● *flowering*

Kerria & Rhodotypos

Jews mallow

These two shrubs are closely related and share many characteristics, which is why Rhodotypos has been brought forward in the alphabetical organisation of this book. This similarity is less evident in *Kerria japonica* 'Pleniflora', the commonest form.

In this form the yellow flowers are fully double, with lots of petals and flowers 3cm (1¼in) across. 'Pleniflora' is also unusual in being a much more vigorous plant than typical Kerria, with stouter erect shoots and suckering freely. The green stems provide a valuable interest feature over winter.

Typical Kerria is mainly represented by the variegated clone 'Picta', whose leaves have a broad but irregular band of white. It makes an arching shrub. It does, however, bear typical flowers, with five spreading petals, which are carried intermittently throughout the summer. It is less vigorous than 'Pleniflora'. Like Kerria, Rhodotypos has the flowers at the end of short shoots which grow from last year's wood. The differences are that in Rhodotypos there are only four petals and these are white, giving a flower up to 5cm (2in) across. Another

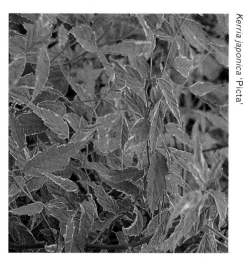

Kerria japonica 'Picta'

Rhodotypos scandens

character by which the two can be separated is that in Kerria the leaves are alternate along the shoot whereas in Rhodotypos they are in opposite pairs.

Both shrubs thrive on a wide range of soils, preferring well drained soils which do not dry out in summer. They are excellent for shrub and mixed borders and are often planted against walls. They are easily propagated by soft to semi-hardwood cuttings in summer. Suckers of 'Pleniflora' can also be separated and grown on to form new plants.

soil	Prefers well drained moisture retentive soils of moderate to good fertility
site	Sun to dappled shade; some mid-day shade will help prolong the flowers
general care	Generally a relatively easy shrub to cultivate and take care of in the garden
pruning	Remove older stems after flowering. Cut back to ground level in late winter
pests & diseases	Relatively trouble-free. Pests and diseases do not usually cause any problems

	SPRING	SUMMER	AUTUMN	WINTER	height 5yrs (m)	height 10yrs (m)	spread 5yrs (m)	spread 10yrs (m)	petal colour	
Kerria japonica 'Picta'	● ●	● ●			0.9	1.5	1	1.8		Leaves variegated, single flowers
K. japonica 'Pleniflora'	● ●	●			1.2	2	1	2		Double flowers
Rhodotypos scandens		● ●	●		1.2	1.5	1.2	1.5		White flowers with four petals

● *flowering*

Kolkwitzia & Dipelta
Beauty bushes

Kolkwitzia is the more common of these two very similar genera in gardens, but both are worthy of their place. They are related to the honeysuckles (Lonicera) and their chief attribute is in the flowers – large numbers of tubular bell-shaped flowers in late spring or early summer on short shoots from last year's growth.

The flowers are carried in pairs on Kolkwitzia and are a clear pink. In Dipelta there may be up to half a dozen fragrant pale pink blooms with a yellow throat. Both genera like full sun but will tolerate light shade for part of the day. They make excellent specimen plants, or as the 'body' to a mixed or shrub border. The bark is light brown and flakes off in thin sheets. Kolkwitzia tends to be more spreading with arching branches whilst Dipelta is more upright in habit and better suited to the rear of the border; with time Dipelta will make a taller bush. Dipelta produces curious fruits, in which two of the four bracts beneath the flower expand to produce wings to the fruit.

soil	Any well drained and moderately fertile soil, including chalk soils
site	Likes full sun but will tolerate light shade for part of the day
general care	Not a great deal of care needed, except mulching to maintain soil fertility and conserve moisture
pruning	Hard pruning not needed. May be pruned to remove old shoots after flowering
pests & diseases	Relatively trouble free. Pests and diseases do not usually cause any problems

Kolkwitzia amabilis 'Pink Cloud'

Kolkwitzia and Dipelta will happily grow on chalk soils but are equally at home on any fertile, well drained loam. They are easily propagated from semi-hardwood cuttings in summer. Seed is also an option, especially for Dipelta, whilst Kolkwitzia may form suckers, which can be removed and grown-on.

	SPRING	SUMMER	AUTUMN	WINTER	height 5yrs (m)	height 10yrs (m)	spread 5yrs (m)	spread 10yrs (m)	petal colour	
Kolkwitzia amabilis 'Pink Cloud'	● ● ●				1.5	2.5	1.5	3		Massed flowers on arching branches
Dipelta floribunda	●	●			1.5	2.5	1.2	2		More upright, can make 6m with time
D. ventricosa	●	●			1.5	2.5	1.5	2.5		Pitcher-shaped bells

● *flowering*

Lavandula
Lavender

These shrubs owe their name to lavender water, which is made using the oil distilled from the foliage and flowers; with '*lavo*' being the Latin for 'I wash'. Lavenders can be grown both for the flowers, which are usually some shade of blue or purple, as well as for the aromatic foliage.

The flowers are in erect spikes carried on long stalks above the level of the foliage. They can be cut and dried, as pot-pourri; treated in this manner, the flowers should be cut before they are fully open and when dried will retain their fragrance for many years.

Lavenders have grey-green foliage and make excellent low hedges. They should be clipped in spring to keep them in shape and given a light tidy-up after flowering has finished. They are not long lived and unlikely to last ten years as good shrubs; older plants become distinctly leggy and are much less attractive. If young plants are reduced at age three or four, they may last some more years, but generally propagate new ones from softwood to semi-hardwood cuttings in summer and expect to replace them every few years. Lavenders are excellent on chalky soils, but this is more a matter of drainage than needing alkaline conditions. Avoid soils or positions which become wet or waterlogged in winter. They like coastal conditions. However, whatever position you give them, they demand full sun.

Lavandula angustifolia 'Hidcote'

Lavandula 'Marshwood'

soil	Well drained soil but very tolerant of hot, dry, acidic or chalky sites
site	Lavender enjoys plenty of sunshine with no shade, if at all possible
general care	Plan on replacing them every 5–10 years as they tend to become woody and straggly-looking
pruning	Clip them regularly to shape or to remove spent flowerheads
pests & diseases	Relatively trouble free. Pests and diseases do not usually cause any problems

	SPRING	SUMMER	AUTUMN	WINTER	height 5yrs (m)	height 10yrs (m)	spread 5yrs (m)	spread 10yrs (m)	petal colour	
Lavandula angustifolia		●			0.6	0.6	0.7	0.8		Grey-green leaves
L. angustifolia 'Hidcote'		●			0.6	0.6	0.7	0.8		Grey-green leaves
L. angustifolia 'Hidcote Pink'		●			0.6	0.6	0.7	0.8		Grey-green leaves
L. angustifolia 'Munstead'		●			0.4	0.5	0.5	0.6		Green leaves
L. angustifolia 'Rosea'		●			0.6	0.6	0.7	0.8		Narrow green leaves
L. 'Helmsdale'		●			0.6	0.6	0.7	0.8		Grey-green leaves, burgundy-purple flowers
L. 'Marshwood'		●			0.6	0.6	0.7	0.8		Grey-green leaves, purple-pink flowers
L. stoechas 'Kew Red'		●			0.6	0.6	0.7	0.8		Flower spikes have coloured bracts at tip
L. stoechas ssp. *pedunculata*		●			0.6	0.6	0.7	0.8		Flower spikes have coloured bracts at tip
L. viridis		●			0.6	0.8	0.7	0.8		Green leaves

● *flowering*

L

Flowering Shrubs

Lavandula angustifolia 'Hidcote'

Lavatera
Tree mallow

The term 'flowering machines' might aptly describe these shrubs. They produce masses of large mallow-type flowers (with the stamens set as a ring around the style) in the few short years that they live.

The flowers have five spreading petals which are textured. They are produced from early summer into the autumn from the axils of leaves along the shoots. The leaves are palmately lobed and some variant of dark to grey-green.

Most tree mallows do not see their fifth summer, having expended all their energy in growth, flowers and fruits. Either because or notwithstanding this, they make excellent if ephemeral garden shrubs. They can be used in beds or borders but are at their best as specimen shrubs in grass areas or in other prominent locations. They tolerate a wide range of site, provided the soil is well drained, and are especially good on chalky sites and in coastal areas. They are best on soils of limited fertility – if the soil is too fertile, there is likely to be excess foliage and fewer flowers. They are not fully hardy, and are best with some side shelter. However, they need full sunlight, which can make giving them shelter tricky.

Take cuttings each year and keep these in a cold frame over winter. Lavatera will root as softwood cuttings taken in late spring.

Lavatera maritima var. bicolor

Lavatera 'Bredon Springs'

soil	Unfussy. Prefers well drained soils, including chalky ones
site	Full sun but with shelter from cold winds; good for coastal sites
general care	Relatively easy to maintain and look after. Take annual cuttings from these plants as they are short lived
pruning	None needed except to trim back to size and shape if necessary
pests & diseases	Relatively trouble free. Pests and diseases do not usually cause any problems

	SPRING	SUMMER	AUTUMN	WINTER	height 5yrs (m)	height 10yrs (m)	spread 5yrs (m)	spread 10yrs (m)	petal colour	
Lavatera arborea 'Variegata'	●	● ● ●	● ●		3	3	1.5	1.5		Flowers funnel-shaped; evergreen foliage
L. 'Barnsley'	●	● ● ●	● ●		2	2	2	2		Semi-evergreen
L. 'Bredon Springs'	●	● ● ●	● ●		2	2	2	2		Semi-evergreen
L. 'Burgundy Wine'	●	● ● ●	● ●		2	2	2	2		Semi-evergreen
L. maritima var. bicolor		●	● ●		1.5	1.5	1	1		Evergreen
L. 'Rosea'	●	● ● ●	● ●		2	2	2	2		Semi-evergreen
L. thuringiaca 'Ice Cool'	●	● ● ●	● ●		1.5	1.5	1.5	1.5		Pure white flowers

● *flowering*

Leptospermum

Tea tree

These shrubs are related to the myrtles (Myrtus) and like them have rather small but glossy and aromatic foliage. Leptospermums are not reliably hardy in cold districts and in these districts are best planted against a wall; however, they are excellent for coastal settings and milder areas, where they are capable of making quite large shrubs.

In most gardens, however, leptospermums are unlikely to exceed 2–3m (6–10ft) in height and spread. They look good in a mixed or shrub border and in mild or coastal areas can make very effective informal hedges.

The flowers are carried in large numbers, completely smothering the foliage. Each flower has five spreading petals, although double forms exist (see 'Red Damask'). The flowers are usually 1.5–2cm across (¾in), but some forms have larger or smaller flowers. In the wild the species have white flowers but the cultivated forms include pinks and reds, such as 'Red Damask' (with very double flowers of a deep red colour and which are

soil	Neutral to acidic soils, tolerating both wet and dry situations
site	For best results, site in the full sun or on a sun-drenched wall
general care	Does not like root disturbance; plant out from pot-grown stock, not from an open ground nursery
pruning	Does not tolerate severe pruning when mature, so restrict trimming to shoot tips
pests & diseases	Relatively trouble free. Pests and diseases do not usually cause any problems

Leptospermum scoparium 'Red Damask'

long lasting), or 'Keatleyi' (with soft pink waxy petals and large flowers). The flowering stems can be cut and will last for some time in a vase of water. They tolerate a wide range of soil types, including both wet and dry sites. They need an acidic to neutral soil, not thriving on chalky soils. They can be propagated from both softwood and semi-hardwood cuttings in summer. The very fine seeds can be sown onto the top of damp compost and watered by plunging their container into water and allowing it to soak up.

	SPRING	SUMMER	AUTUMN	WINTER	height 5yrs (m)	height 10yrs (m)	spread 5yrs (m)	spread 10yrs (m)	petal colour	
Leptospermum lanigerum	●	● ●			1.5	2.5	1	1.5	☐	Can make 3–5m
L. rupestre	●	● ●			0.35	0.5	0.8	1.2	☐	Prostrate shrub
L. scoparium 'Keatleyi'	●	● ●			1.5	2.5	1	1.5	▨	Flowers to 2.5cm across
L. scoparium 'Kiwi'	●	● ●			0.6	1	0.6	1	■	New foliage purple tinted
L. scoparium 'Nichollsii'	●	● ●			1.5	2.5	1.2	2.5	■	Foliage purple-tinted
L. scoparium 'Nichollsii Nanum'	●	● ●			0.2	0.2	0.3	0.3	▨	Dwarf form
L. scoparium 'Red Damask'	●	● ●			1.5	2.5	1	1.5	■	Dark green leaves. Double form

● *flowering*

Lespedeza
Bush clover

This genus is mainly represented in gardens by *Lespedeza thunbergii*. It lies somewhere between a shrub and a herbaceous perennial.

There is a woody rootstock at the base; however, the growths are pithy and last only for the one year, dying back over winter. The stems may make 1.2m (4ft) to 2.4m (8ft) in height and form a bush 3m (10ft) across. It flowers on the new growths at the end of the summer. Lespedeza needs a warm situation, or there is a risk that the flowers will not develop before it is cut down by autumn frost. The flowers are produced in numerous racemes 15cm (6in) in length from the upper parts of the shoots which are bowed down by their weight. The flowers are pea-like and rosy-purple. The leaves are trifoliate but it only starts into growth late in the spring. Lespedeza thrives on well drained fertile soils. It can be propagated by semi-hardwood cuttings.

Lespedeza thunbergii

Leucothoë

These evergreen shrubs are grown for the fragrant white flowers and glossy foliage. The flowers, which are white and bell-shaped, are carried in late spring and hang down from each leaf axil on the arching branches.

The foliage of 'Rainbow' is variegated with a mixture of cream, yellow and pink on the green leaves. That of 'Scarletta' is deep red-purple when young, ageing to green during the summer and then bronze in winter.

These shrubs need an acidic soil, preferably rich in organic matter. They like partial shade and will grow in boggy conditions. This is especially important if they are grown in full sun, where the soil may need to be watered to keep it suitably moist. Propagate by semi-hardwood cuttings in summer.

Leucothoë walterii 'Rainbow'

soil	Lespedeza: fertile well drained soils. Leucothoë: acidic, fertile, preferably moist
site	Lespedeza: full sun. Leucothoë: likes light to moderate shade
general care	Lespedeza: late in leafing in the spring. Leucothoë: mulch to maintain organic matter content of the soil
pruning	Lespedeza: Cut back to ground level in spring. Leucothoë: none needed
pests & diseases	Both plants are relatively trouble-free. Pests and diseases do not usually cause any problems

Leucothoë fontanesiana 'Rainbow'

	SPRING	SUMMER	AUTUMN	WINTER	height 5yrs (m)	height 10yrs (m)	spread 5yrs (m)	spread 10yrs (m)	petal colour	
Lespedeza thunbergii		● ● ●			1.5	2	1.5	2	▨	Semi-woody; better in hot sunny seasons
Leucothoë walterii 'Rainbow'	●				1	1.5	1.5	2	☐	Leaves green with cream, yellow, pink mottling
L. walterii 'Scarletta'	●				1	1.5	1.5	2	☐	New foliage red-purple, ageing to dark green

● *flowering*

Leycesteria

Himalayan honeysuckle

Leycesteria are suckering, deciduous shrubs with hollow, cane-like stems. The flowers of *Leycesteria formosa* are in pendulous spikes. They have white flowers which show the relationship with the true honeysuckle (Lonicera).

The main colour in *Leycesteria formosa*, however, is provided by the bracts; these are claret red and persist until the shiny reddish purple berry has ripened and been eaten. The berries contain masses of small seeds; they are a favourite food for pheasants and the species has become naturalized in many areas as a consequence of their being planted in pheasantries.

soil	Enjoys well drained fertile soils, including chalky ones
site	Prefers a situation with sun as well as moderate shade
general care	The hollow stems may be cut back by frost but general care is fairly minimal for this plant
pruning	Remove older stems, but if cut down as Group 2, will flower by autumn
pests & diseases	Relatively trouble-free. Pests and diseases do not usually cause any problems

Leycesteria formosa

The species *Leycesteria crocothyrsos* has yellow flowers. Unfortunately, *Leycesteria crocothyrsos* is rather tender and can only reliably be grown in mild areas, or as a conservatory shrub.

Both species have thick and pithy sea-green shoots, which are hollow in the centre, and greyish green leaves. They thrive on all soils, including chalky ones, except those of poor drainage.

In the garden, Leycesteria are useful in light woodland, at the back of a border or beneath a large tree. The flowers and fruits develop stronger colours when the plants are grown in full sun. They can be propagated by seed (the birds do this very well, eating the seeds and passing them on elsewhere, thus widely dispersing the plant) and by semi-hardwood cuttings in summer.

Flowering Shrubs

L

	SPRING	SUMMER	AUTUMN	WINTER	height 5yrs (m)	height 10yrs (m)	spread 5yrs (m)	spread 10yrs (m)	petal colour	
Leycesteria formosa		● ● ● ● ●	● 🌰🌰		1.5	2	1.5	2	☐	Shiny purple berries; green stems
L. crocothyrsos	●	● ● ● ●	🌰🌰		1.5	2	1.5	2	☐	Only for mild or protected sites

● *flowering*   🌰 *harvest*

93

Lonicera
Shrubby honeysuckle

Woodbine (*Lonicera periclymenum*) is the archetypal honeysuckle, a climbing plant with terminal heads of tubular fragrant flowers. Honeysuckles like woodbine, however, only represent a small part of this large genus of some 200 species. The ones featured here are all shrubby species and actually represent the predominant part of the genus.

The shrubby honeysuckles have flowers in pairs carried from each leaf axil along a shoot. (As the leaves are in opposite pairs, this means that there are two pairs of flowers at each node.) The flowers can be a showy rose-pink in species such as *Lonicera tartarica* 'Hack's Red', but are more usually some form of cream or yellow. *Lonicera fragrantissima* is especially valuable in carrying its fragrant flowers on the bare branches during late winter and spring . The fruits are berries which are turquoise in *Lonicera nitida* (but rather lost amongst the foliage) to red such as *Lonicera fragrantissima*, or even translucent white in other species.

Shrubby honeysuckles are useful in shrub or mixed borders. *Lonicera pileata* is extremely good as ground cover or beneath larger shrubs. *Lonicera nitida* can make neat hedges, but does require frequent clipping to keep it neat. The form 'Baggesen's Gold' has yellow leaves which stay yellow-green through winter. They all thrive on a wide range of soils, including chalky ones but require good drainage. They can be propagated by semi-hardwood cuttings in summer and by hardwood cuttings taken in late autumn.

Lonicera fragrantissima

Lonicera nitida 'Baggesen's Gold'

soil	Well drained soils, including chalky ones of moderate fertility	
site	Prefers a situation with sun as well as moderate shade	
general care	Easy to cultivate apart from mulching in spring to control weeds and keep the soil moist	
pruning	Remove older shoots after flowering. For hedges, trim 3–4 times during the summer	
pests & diseases	Aphids can cause distortion of leaves, but generally trouble-free from pests and diseases	

	SPRING	SUMMER	AUTUMN	WINTER	height 5yrs (m)	height 10yrs (m)	spread 5yrs (m)	spread 10yrs (m)	petal colour	
Lonicera fragrantissima	●		🌰	●	1.2	2	1.5	2.5	☐	Fragrant flowers
L. pileata		●	🌰		0.5	1	1	1.5	☐	Small flowers; violet translucent berries
L. nitida 'Baggesen's Gold'		●			1	2	1	1.5	☐	Shiny evergreen leaves
L. tartarica 'Hack's Red'	●	●	🌰		1.5	3	1	2	▨	Deciduous

● flowering   🌰 harvest

Lupinus
Tree lupin

The lupins are mainly herbaceous plants associated with the perennial border. However, the genus includes a number of shrubs, of which the following species is the most reliable.

Lupinus arboreus quickly grows to 1.5–2m in height (5–7ft) and almost as quickly dies of old age. However, it makes an excellent shrub both as a filler and for its yellow racemes of flowers which are carried over a long period through the summer. It thrives on coastal exposure.

Lupinus will fix atmospheric nitrogen to make nitrogen fertilizers, and can be used to add nitrogen to soils of low fertility. It will grow on any well drained soil. It can be propagated from seed, which is freely set, or from semi-hardwood cuttings taken in summer.

Lupinus arboreus

Magnolia

Magnolias are mainly trees or large shrubs, with some species attaining 30m (100ft) or more. These species and forms are discussed in *Trees & Shrubs*, also in this series of books. However, the forms of the Star magnolia (*Magnolia stellata*) will flower from a small size and better fits within the definition of flowering shrubs.

Magnolia stellata 'Royal Star'

The flowers are carried on the bare branches in early spring, and consist of twelve to eighteen strap-like 'tepals'. This is the name used when it is impossible to determine whether the floral part is a sepal (from the calyx) or petal (from the corolla). The flowers are fragrant with white or pink-flushed tepals. It will grow on any well drained soil, including some chalk, but thrives best in a deep fertile one. The flowers are easily damaged by spring frosts and the plant should be given a sheltered site.

soil	Lupinus: well drained soils. Magnolia: any well drained but not shallow chalk	
site	Lupinus: sun to light shade. Magnolia: dappled shade or full sun	
general care	Lupinus: short lived, usually only 5 years; add nitrogen to the soil. Magnolia: mulch and avoid disturbing root system	
pruning	Lupinus: none required. Magnolia: prune to restrict or reshape after flowering	
pests & diseases	Both plants are relatively trouble-free. Pests and diseases do not usually cause any problems	

	SPRING	SUMMER	AUTUMN	WINTER	height 5yrs (m)	height 10yrs (m)	spread 5yrs (m)	spread 10yrs (m)	petal colour	
Lupinus arboreus	●	● ● ●			2	2	2	2		Leaves with 7–11 grey-green leaflets, evergreen
Magnolia stellata	● ●		harvest		0.8	1.5	1	1.5		Spreading habit
M. stellata 'Royal Star'	● ●		harvest		0.8	1.5	1	1.5		Large flowers with 25–30 tepals
M. stellata 'Waterlily'	● ●		harvest		0.8	1.5	1	1.5		Up to 32 tepals

● flowering   ✎ harvest

Mahonia
Oregon grape

Mahonia is closely related to Berberis, sharing the yellow wood and yellow cup-shaped flowers. The obvious differences are that the leaves in Mahonia are always evergreen and pinnate, whereas they are sometimes deciduous and always simple in Berberis.

Mahonia shoots never bear the sharp spines which are found in all Berberis, although the leaves in some forms are spiny, especially in the taller growing forms. The smaller growing Mahonia are useful for their bright yellow flowers in late winter or spring. The fruits ripen to black but with a dense violet waxy bloom. They are edible and can be used to make jellies and other conserves. The Oregon grapes sit well in the shrub bed and mixed border. They tolerate a fair degree of shade as well as growing happily in full sun. They can be used as underplanting for larger shrubs or trees, and are especially good in this role in providing a foil of bronzed evergreen foliage against which the flowers of shrubs which bloom on their bare

soil	Unfussy plant. At home in any garden soil including chalky ones
site	Prefers a situation with sun as well as moderate shade
general care	Inclined to become straggly. Can be propagated by semi-hardwood cuttings in the summer
pruning	No particular pruning is required, except to resize and reshape
pests & diseases	Relatively trouble-free. Pests and diseases do not usually cause any problems

boughs can be displayed. They thrive on a wide range of soils including chalky ones. The bushes tend to become rather straggly but they respond to trimming. They can be propagated by semi-hardwood cuttings in summer. The seed can be cleaned out of the juicy part and sown in spring. Suckers can also be removed from established bushes and potted on until well rooted.

Mahonia aquifolium 'Apollo'

Mahonia aquifolium flowers

	SPRING	SUMMER	AUTUMN	WINTER	height 5yrs (m)	height 10yrs (m)	spread 5yrs (m)	spread 10yrs (m)	petal colour	
Mahonia aquifolium	● ●		🌰 🌰	●	0.6	1	0.8	1.2		Leaves become bronzed over winter
M. aquifolium 'Apollo'	● ●		🌰 🌰	●	0.6	1	0.8	1.2		Leaves deep green with reddish stalks
M. wagneri 'Pinnacle'	● ●		🌰 🌰	●	0.8	1	0.8	1.2		Upright habit

● flowering   🌰 harvest

Flowering Shrubs

M

Myrtus
Myrtle

Myrtle is valued for the flowers which are carried singly in the axils of the leaves, mainly in mid- to late summer. The flowers are fragrant, 2cm (¾in) across and have five rounded white petals and a conspicuous cluster of stamens which protrude from the centre of the flower. The ancient world held myrtle sacred to the Goddess of Love and sprigs of it have been used for bridal wreaths and garlands since then.

The flowers are more freely carried during hot sunny summers and it is a shrub for sunny sites, not for any shade. The fruit is a purplish black berry. The leaves are aromatic and glossy. Myrtle is not fully hardy; in cold districts it should be sited with the protection of a sun-facing wall and trained as an espalier. However, in milder gardens, it makes an excellent shrub for the aromatic leaves and late summer flowers. It can also be used to make hedges, withstanding trimming and still flowering. It is also at home in shrub beds and will complement the herbaceous plants in a mixed border. It is very tolerant of soils provided they are well drained, and is at home on those derived from chalk and limestone. Myrtle can be propagated from semi-hardwood cuttings in summer and hardwood cuttings in late autumn. It can also be grown from seed and by layering.

Myrtus communis

Myrtus communis ssp. *tarentina*

soil	Can tolerate any well drained soil types, including chalk
site	This shrub prefers any sunny position – does not like shade particularly
general care	Not much general care and maintenance is required. Remove any winter cold damage in spring
pruning	No pruning needed – responds to clipping; flowers on current season's shoots
pests & diseases	Relatively trouble-free. Pests and diseases do not usually cause any problems

	SPRING	SUMMER	AUTUMN	WINTER	height 5yrs (m)	height 10yrs (m)	spread 5yrs (m)	spread 10yrs (m)	petal colour	
Myrtus communis		● ● ●	🌰		1.2	2	1.2	2	☐	Evergreen aromatic foliage
M. communis 'Variegata'		● ● ●	🌰		1.2	2	1.2	2	☐	Leaves grey-green, narrow, cream margin
M. communis ssp. *tarentina*		● ● ●	🌰		1	1.5	1	1.5	☐	Fruits white, leaves smaller, hairy

● flowering   🌰 harvest

M

Flowering Shrubs

Nandina
Heavenly bamboo

A bamboo it is not, but it really is a heavenly plant. It doesn't sound quite so romantic though when you learn that it belongs to the same family as Berberis! The habit of growth is this plant's greatest asset.

The similarity to bamboo comes from the erect stems; these may rise to 2m (7ft) without branching but support the doubly or trebly pinnate leaves. These are green but open as an attractive purplish or pinky red; they persist into the second year but turn reddish purple in autumn. The flowers are carried in erect panicles at the top of the stems, which are 8–40cm (3–16in) in length. The white flowers have prominent yellow

soil	This plant grows best if planted in fertile, well drained soils
site	Prefers sun, but will tolerate very light shade
general care	Not much care and maintenance needed. Mulch to maintain a humus-rich soil
pruning	Remove older stems from ground level to maintain bamboo-like appearance
pests & diseases	Relatively trouble-free. Pests and diseases do not usually cause any problems

Nandina domestica

anthers. The fruits ripen in the autumn, usually to red, but other colours are known.

Nandina can be used in all the 'normal' locations for shrubs, but is perhaps best when planted as a focal point, such as in a raised bed beside the front door. It will thrive with moderate care in containers and can make an interesting patio shrub. It also does well in indoor planters if placed in well lit positions and adequately provisioned. It likes fertile and well drained soils but ones rich in organic matter. It needs summer heat to be seen at its best, which is one reason why it makes a good patio plant, as patios are often sited in sun traps. It should be protected from cold and dry winds. Propagation is best effected by seed, which can be slow to germinate and grow away. Cuttings of short pieces of a young stem with only one leaf can be taken in summer, but these are slow to root.

	SPRING	SUMMER	AUTUMN	WINTER	height 5yrs (m)	height 10yrs (m)	spread 5yrs (m)	spread 10yrs (m)	petal colour	
Nandina domestica		●	🍂		0.8	1.8	0.6	1.5	☐	May flower at any time, but most in mid-summer
N. domestica 'Firepower'					0.3	0.45	0.4	0.6	☐	Dwarf form, summer foliage yellow-green

● flowering	🍂 harvest

Flowering Shrubs

N

Neillia

This combines an arching habit, neat foliage and racemes of pink, tubular flowers in one attractive shrub.

The foliage is neatly cut, and often three-lobed, being a fresh green when the flowers are carried; the shoots tend to zig-zag. The flowers are in slender racemes up to 15cm (6in) in length and may contain sixty small blooms. Neillia makes a good specimen shrub, either on its own, in a shrub border or in a light woodland setting. It will grow in either sun or light shade. Pruning of the commonest species should include removal of older stems to maintain a young branch structure. However, one species, *Neillia thrysiflora*, flowers on the new wood and this species alone can be pruned as Group 2. Neillia can be propagated by softwood and semi-hardwood cuttings in summer, by removal of suckers and from seed.

Oemleria
Oso berry

This suckering deciduous shrub has been called Osmaronia in the past. It is desirable for its almond-scented flowers in late winter or early spring.

The flowers are carried on pendent racemes and have a flowering currant-like appearance. There are separate male and female plants, with the flowers on male bushes being more freely borne. However,

Neillia thibetica

soil	Neillia: dislikes waterlogged and dry soils. Oemleria: dry to wet, avoid chalky soils
site	Neillia: sun to dappled shade. Oemleria: light to moderate shade
general care	Neillia: mulch to maintain a moist soil in summer. Oemleria: mulch to ensure organic matter and moisture
pruning	Neillia: after flowering to maintain neat branching. Oemleria: remove older shoots
pests & diseases	Both plants are relatively trouble-free. Pests and diseases do not usually cause any problems

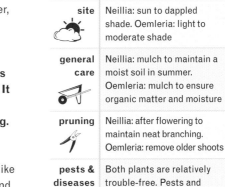
Oemleria cerasiformis

those on female plants are followed by the black fruits like a plum or sloe. The leaves are early harbingers of spring, expanding soon after the flowers. Oso berry is not happy on thin chalky soils but is otherwise tolerant of soil and site conditions. It can be propagated from ripe seed, from suckers and from semi-hardwood cuttings taken in summer.

	SPRING	SUMMER	AUTUMN	WINTER	height 5yrs (m)	height 10yrs (m)	spread 5yrs (m)	spread 10yrs (m)	petal colour	
Neillia thibetica	●	●			1	1.8	1	1.8	▨	Attractive but not flamboyant
Oemleria cerasiformis	●	🌰		●	1	2	1	2.5	☐	Early into leaf

● flowering   🌰 harvest

Olearia
Daisy bush

The Daisy bushes have small, daisy-style flowerheads, comprising a number of showy white sterile flowers around the perimeter of a cluster of small fertile flowers. They are especially useful for carrying the flowers, which can be strongly honey-scented, in late summer.

Olearia make evergreen shrubs useful for sunny borders and are especially good on maritime sites. Some will also take urban pollution. The leaves are aromatic when crushed in some species, such as *Olearia macrodonta*. Daisy bushes respond well to trimming and old bushes can be cut down to near ground level and will break to reform a crown. They can be very effective when used in hedges, with *Olearia macrodonta* being particularly good in this role. The main use of Olearia in the garden, though, is in shrub beds.

The hardiness of the many species differs and the more tender ones should be given a sheltered site. Daisy bushes need full sunlight, not really liking any shade (although they will put up with a little). They thrive on a wide range of soils, provided they are freely drained, including chalky soils.

Daisy bushes are usually propagated by semi-hardwood cuttings in summer. They can also be raised from seed, but this is likely to produce hybrids. Young plants are tender and should be grown over winter in a sheltered environment.

Olearia macrodonta

soil	Freely drained soils, including acid sands and alkaline chalky soils
site	Prefers sun, but make sure it has no more than light shade
general care	Winter damage may occur to tender forms; wait for new growth to establish in spring before removing damage
pruning	Prune back after flowering; can also be coppiced to rejuvenate
pests & diseases	Relatively trouble-free. Pests and diseases do not usually cause any problems

	SPRING	SUMMER	AUTUMN	WINTER	height 5yrs (m)	height 10yrs (m)	spread 5yrs (m)	spread 10yrs (m)	petal colour	
Olearia macrodonta		● ● ●			1.2	2.5	1.2	2.5	☐	Leaves coarsely toothed, musk scent if crushed
O. nummulariifolia		●			1	1.5	1	1.5	☐	Leaves small and thick, yellow-green
O. paniculata				● ●	1.5	3	1.5	3	☐	Bright olive-green leaves; flowers fragrant
O. phlogoppa	● ●				1	1.5	1	1.5	☐	Leaves aromatic
O. stellulata	●				1.5	2.5	1.5	2.5	☐	Leaves yellow-hairy beneath
O. 'Waikariensis'		● ●			1	2	1	2	☐	Leaves sea-green above, white on underside

● *flowering*

Osmanthus

These are evergreen shrubs grown for the rich fragrance of their white, tubular flowers. The best flowering Osmanthus is *O. delavayi*, which has pure white flowers in terminal and axillary clusters – all of which cover the shrubs in mid-spring.

The leaves are stiff, leathery and glossy green, to no more than 2.5cm (1in) in length. It makes a small tree in mild areas, to 6m (20ft), but in most regions it is no more than 4m (13ft) in height even after 30–40 years. Nearly as good is its hybrid with *Osmanthus decorus*, viz *Osmanthus burkwoodii*. This is very similar and of equal garden merit, with slightly larger leaves. *Osmanthus decorus*

has larger leaves still, to 5–12cm (2–5in) and makes a tough evergreen shrub. The larger leaves give it a more open habit compared to the dense leafy aspect of *Osmanthus delavayi* with its masses of small leaves.

These three species have oval fruits which ripen blue-black or reddish purple in early autumn. The other common species in cultivation is *Osmanthus heterophyllus*. This

Osmanthus heterophyllus 'Variegatus'

soil	Well drained neutral to acidic; chalk for *O. delavayi* and *O. burkwoodii*
site	This plant performs best in a position with sun to light shade
general care	No particular maintenance programme required. Needs to be sheltered from cold winds, however
pruning	No hard pruning required but very tolerant of clipping for shaping and resizing
pests & diseases	Scale insects can be a problem, but not really affected by any other pests or diseases

flowers in the autumn. They are similarly sweetly scented but visually less showy. Propagate by semi-hardwood cuttings in summer with some bottom heat.

	SPRING	SUMMER	AUTUMN	WINTER	height 5yrs (m)	height 10yrs (m)	spread 5yrs (m)	spread 10yrs (m)	petal colour	
Osmanthus burkwoodii	●		🌰		1.2	2	1.2	2	☐	Also called *Osmarea burkwoodii*, leaves 2.5–5cm
O. decorus	●		🌰		1	1.5	1	1.5	☐	Also called *Phillyrea decorus*; leaves 5–12cm
O. delavayi	●		🌰		1.5	2.5	1.2	2	☐	Excellent evergreen flowering shrub
O. heterophyllus			● ●		1.2	2.5	1.2	2.5	☐	Holly-like leaves
O. heterophyllus 'Goshiki'			● ●		1.2	2.5	1.2	2.5	☐	Bronze-tinged leaves when young
O. heterophyllus 'Gulftide'			● ●		1.2	2.5	1.2	2.5	☐	Spiny leaves; twisted or lobed, dense bush
O. heterophyllus 'Purpureus'			● ●		1.2	2.5	1.2	2.5	☐	New foliage strongly purple
O. heterophyllus 'Variegatus'			● ●		1.2	2.5	1.2	2.5	☐	Leaves with a creamy-white margin

● flowering   🌰 harvest

Ozothamnus
Kerosene bush

These are southern hemisphere relatives of Helichrysum and often included in that genus. The majority of species are not frost hardy but the two featured here should survive in all but the coldest and most exposed gardens.

Their value lies in the heath-like evergreen foliage, which gives densely branched erect or rounded bushes, and in the showy daisy-style flowers with white disc-florets. In *Ozothamnus ledifolius* the leaves and shoots are covered by a sweetly aromatic yellowish exudate, which is flammable, especially in hot sunny weather, and has given the plant the common name of Kerosene bush.

Ozothamnus rosmarinifolius is particularly showy for about ten days before the flowers open. This is because of the bracts which surround the flowers in bud; they are crimson-red in colour before giving way to the white flowers.

Ozothamnus flowers are honey-scented, and the seed heads of *Ozothamnus ledifolius* continue to emit a honey scent. The species of Ozothamnus are useful for a shrub or mixed border and can be associated with heathers and dwarf conifers. They require full sun, and are not suitable for shady sites. However, they are better with shelter from cold dry winds. They thrive on a wide range of soils provided they have good drainage.

Ozothamnus rosmarinifolius grows on moist, fertile sites but still needs good drainage. They can be propagated by semi-hardwood cuttings in late summer.

Ozothamnus rosmarinifolius 'Silver Jubilee'

Ozothamnus ledifolius

soil	This plant is relatively unfussy, growing in any well drained soil type
site	Prefers a sheltered, sunny position, but without any shade
general care	They need side shelter from cold winds in the winter months and mulch to protect the roots
pruning	None needed but they can be cut back in spring before growth commences
pests & diseases	Relatively trouble-free. Pests and diseases do not usually cause any problems

	SPRING	SUMMER	AUTUMN	WINTER	height 5yrs (m)	height 10yrs (m)	spread 5yrs (m)	spread 10yrs (m)	petal colour	
Ozothamnus ledifolius		● ●			0.7	1	0.7	1		Densely branched leafy habit
O. rosmarinifolius		● ●			1	1.5	1	1.5		Buds are showy red before the white flowers
O. rosmarinifolius 'Silver Jubilee'		● ●			1	1.5	1	1.5		Leaves silver-grey

● *flowering*

Paeonia
Paeony

This genus comprises many species of herbaceous perennials, but the section named 'Moutan' consists of shrubs. They are grown for their very showy flowers in late spring or early summer as well as for their deeply dissected leaves.

The most outstanding species is *Paeonia suffruticosa*. These make a stiffly branched and rather gaunt shrub to about 1.5m (5ft). At the end of the new growth it carries flowers which may be 30cm (12in) across in some forms. Most garden varieties have some or all of the stamens converted into petals and thus are double. Single wild forms have recently been reclassified as *Paeonia rockii* and *Paeonia ostii*, but these are rare in garden centres where Japanese selections are usually offered as very small plants. The new foliage is often pink coloured. At this stage the foliage is frost tender and as it includes the flowers, it is worth making an effort to protect it. Siting the plant with overhead shelter can assist, but make a framework over which hessian can be strung on frosty nights, removing it in the morning

Paeonia ludlowii

Paeonia suffruticosa subsp. *rockii* (fruit)

soil	Prefers any well drained soil, from neutral to slightly lime
site	For best results, position in a sunny site with a touch of light shade
general care	Plant grafted paeonies with the union 5–8cm (2–3in) below ground; mulch and plant in the spring
pruning	No pruning required, except for reshaping or cutting back purposes
pests & diseases	Relatively trouble-free. Pests and diseases do not usually cause any problems

and whenever the weather is wet and windy. Once hardened, the protection can be removed until next spring. *Paeonia delavayi* is a suckering shrub. Some types are more like subshrubs, flowering from underground shoots, but other forms make shrubs to 1.5m (5ft). The flowers are all shades of maroon to yellow. *Paeonia ludlowii* is a yellow-flowered shrub to 3–4m (10–13ft). They thrive on all well drained soils, including clays and chalks. Propagation is by removing suckers (*Paeonia delavayi*), by grafting onto herbaceous rootstocks or by seed. The seeds send out a root in response to warmth, but do not throw out a shoot until after a winter's cool period, so germination is in the second spring.

	SPRING	SUMMER	AUTUMN	WINTER	height 5yrs (m)	height 10yrs (m)	spread 5yrs (m)	spread 10yrs (m)	petal colour
Paeonia delavayi	●		🍂		1	1.5	1	1.5	▦ Suckering shrub
Paeonia ludlowii	●		🍂		1.2	1.8	1.2	1.8	☐ Vigorous shrub
Paeonia rockii	●	●	🍂		1	1.5	1	1.5	☐ Large double flowers, frost tender in spring
Paeonia suffruticosa	●	●	🍂		1	1.5	1	1.5	☐ Semi-double white flowers, maroon bases

● flowering   🍂 harvest

Perovskia

This deciduous species is more of a sub-shrub in cultivation than a proper shrub, forming a woody base but effectively making its flowering growth from the current season's growth at the base.

Perovskia needs to be pruned as a Group 2 shrub (see page 24), cutting back to ground level in spring each year. The annual growths are cut back in winter months to a woody base. The plant is a member of the mint family and the leaves have a sage-like smell. *Perovskia atriplicifolia* has grey-green leaves, but in *P. a.* 'Blue Spire' they are more silvery-grey, set on grey-white stems. The flowers are the typical mint family flower, two-lipped with the upper lip having four lobes and the lower lip entire. They are carried in panicles which are 17–30cm (9–12in) in length and contain a number of flowering spikes 5–12cm (2–5in). Individually, the flowers are small, but in mass their violet-purple colour creates an effective display. The flowers are set off against the white powder-like down which clothes the stem. In the garden it is a useful plant, making a splash of colour in late summer and into early autumn. However, a single plant is too small to achieve this and a planting of half a dozen or so over an area of 2–5 square metres (yards) is desirable. Fortunately, it is easily propagated from softwood cuttings in early summer when the new shoots are 5–8cm (2–3in) long. It requires full sun, preferably in as hot and sunny a site as possible. It will thrive on gravels and chalk, requiring very good drainage, but will fail on waterlogged or poorly drained soils. It is also excellent in coastal situations.

Perovskia atriplicifolia 'Blue Spire'

soil	Tolerates any well drained soil, including gravel, sand and chalk
site	Prefers as much sun as possible – much less effective in any shade
general care	Tends to partially die back to ground level over winter; mulch annually to maintain moisture and soil content
pruning	Cut back to just above ground level, as per Group 2 pruning instructions
pests & diseases	Relatively trouble-free. Pests and diseases do not usually cause any problems

	SPRING	SUMMER	AUTUMN	WINTER	height 5yrs (m)	height 10yrs (m)	spread 5yrs (m)	spread 10yrs (m)	petal colour	
Perovskia atriplicifolia		● ●	●		0.9	1	0.9	1		Deciduous shrub, can make 1.5m
P. atriplicifolia 'Blue Spire'		● ●	●		0.9	1	0.9	1		Larger flowering panicles; erect habit to 1m

● *flowering*

Flowering Shrubs

P

Philadelphus
Mock orange

These shrubs are closely related to Deutzia, although their petals and sepals appear in fours, not fives, and they have simple hairs. They are all deciduous shrubs, generally larger than Deutzia and some can qualify as small trees. Their attraction is in the masses of very pleasantly fragrant white flowers which smother the bushes in early to mid-summer.

Philadelphus 'Virginal'

The flowering season on any individual bush lasts for about three weeks, but by choosing different forms this can be extended to perhaps six weeks. The flowers are produced on short leafy shoots on the wood laid down in the previous year. The double-flowered forms tend to have less

soil	Well drained soils of low to good fertility; happy on thin soils overlying chalk
site	Sun or some shade, but flowering is poorer as the shade increases
general care	Not a great deal of care and maintenance required. However, mulch and feed on poor soils
pruning	Prune to remove 2–3 year old wood after flowering (Group 1 pruning)
pests & diseases	Relatively trouble-free. Pests and diseases do not usually cause any problems

Philadelphus 'Belle Etoile'

fragrance than the single-flowered types, which have contrasting yellow stamens.

The greatest profusion of flowers comes when there are side branches on the stems. Therefore, prune so that there is a rotation of one, two and three year old shoots, and remove the three year old ones immediately after flowering is finished. Philadelphus are excellent in shrubberies and when used to make informal hedging or screening, and can be sited as an isolated shrub in a sea of lawn. They need full sun to light shade. They are propagated by softwood or semi-hardwood cuttings in early summer.

	SPRING	SUMMER	AUTUMN	WINTER	height 5yrs (m)	height 10yrs (m)	spread 5yrs (m)	spread 10yrs (m)	petal colour	
Philadelphus 'Beauclerk'		● ●			1.2	2	1.2	2		Single flowers, cup-shaped with a pink centre
P. 'Belle Etoile'		● ●			0.8	1.2	1.5	2.5		Flowers fragrant, single, pale purple centre
P. coronarius 'Aureus'		● ●			1.2	2	1.2	2		Leaves bright yellow, duller after mid-summer
P. microphyllus		● ●			0.7	1	0.7	1		Pure white, very fragrant single flowers
P. 'Sybille'		● ●			0.8	1.2	1.2	2		Single flowers, fragrant, with purple centre
P. 'Virginal'		● ●			1.5	3	1.2	2.5		Double flowers, fragrant, to 5cm across

● *flowering*

Phlomis
Jerusalem Sage

This genus has the typical two-lopped flowers of the mint family or Labiatae. Most species are herbs, but there are a few shrubby species including the following three, which are all evergreen.

The shrubby Phlomis are grown for their combination of attractive flowers and foliage. The flowers are clustered into whorls along the erect stems; they are tubular with a hooded upper lip and resemble the flowers of dead nettle. In *Phlomis fruticosa* or Jerusalem sage, the flowers are bright yellow and the foliage grey-green. It makes a shrub to a metre (3ft).

Phlomis chrysophylla also has yellow flowers and is a similar sized shrub; the leaves have a golden-green tinge due to a covering of hairs but are not golden as in the Latin name (*chryso* = golden, *phylla* = leaves), except in dried samples. *Phlomis*

soil	Enjoys very freely drained soils, whether acidic or alkaline
site	Likes to be situated in the full sun, preferably in a hot, dry setting
general care	These plants are short-lived shrubs, so propagate from them and regularly replant to keep them going
pruning	Does not really need any specialist pruning apart from trimming after flowering
pests & diseases	Relatively trouble-free from most pests and diseases. Leafhoppers can be a problem, however

Phlomis fruticosa

italica is much smaller, rarely exceeding 0.3m (1ft) but the flowers are pink or pale lilac.

These three shrubs are suitable for a warm sunny and sheltered spot. They will not take kindly to shade nor to cold dry winds in winter. In the garden they are excellent as part of a mixed border or at the front of a shrub border. They can also be located in a dry, hot sun-drenched area beside the house, as they tolerate dry soils. In cold areas or exposed gardens, they should be sited beside a wall for protection. They need perfect drainage, and are inclined to rot off if there is a hint of waterlogging at the roots. They are easily propagated from softwood cuttings in summer. They can also be raised from seed sown in spring.

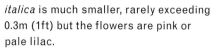

	SPRING	SUMMER	AUTUMN	WINTER	height 5yrs (m)	height 10yrs (m)	spread 5yrs (m)	spread 10yrs (m)	petal colour	
Phlomis chrysophylla		●			0.8	1	0.8	1.2		Flowers along shoots in early summer
P. fruticosa		● ●			0.8	1	0.8	1.2		Grey-green leaves which are mildly scented
P. italica		●			0.25	0.3	0.4	0.6		Subshrub, leaves and stems silvery hairy

 flowering

Flowering Shrubs

P

Physocarpus

This genus of deciduous shrubs is related to **N**eillia and is in the Spiraea part of the Rosaceae. The most widely cultivated is *Physocarpus opulifolius*, but others including *Physocarpus malvaceus* are grown for their hemispherical trusses of predominantly white flowers (often with a hint of pink) in late spring or early summer and their smooth peeling bark.

The leaves are usually three-lobed. In *Physocarpus opulifolius* 'Luteus' they are a bright golden-yellow when they first emerge, although they soon age to normal green. *Physocarpus opulifolius* 'Dart's Gold' is a seedling of 'Luteus'; it makes a compact shrub and the golden colour of the new foliage is much longer lasting. *Physocarpus opulifolius* 'Diabolo' has reddish purple, almost black leaves. These shrubs are excellent for providing variation in foliage colour in a shrub bed. They like moist soils but are generally tolerant; however, they become chlorotic on shallow chalky soils. They are readily propagated by softwood cuttings in summer.

Physocarpus opulifolius 'Diabolo'

Physocarpus opulifolius 'Diabolo'

soil	Physocarpus: moist/acidic, but also drier soils. Piptanthus: acidic/alkaline, well drained
site	Physocarpus: sun to light shade. Piptanthus: prefers the sun
general care	Physocarpus: none required. Piptanthus: provide shelter from cold winds; resents root disturbance; short lived
pruning	Physocarpus: remove 2–3 year old shoots after flowering. Piptanthus: remove old shoots
pests & diseases	Both plants are relatively trouble-free. Pests and diseases do not usually cause them any problems

Piptanthus

This genus has pea-like flowers in erect terminal racemes and fresh green trifoliate leaves.

Piptanthus nepalensis

It is a fast growing but rather short lived shrub. It is excellent for a border or on a sheltered side of the house. It must have good light to flower well. It thrives in any well drained soil, including chalky soils. As a legume, it will fix atmospheric nitrogen to make nitrogen fertilizer and thus is useful for barren sites. It is easily propagated by seed. This should be collected when ripe and stored dry, otherwise it will rot. Germination is hastened if the seed is abrased or the wax coat removed. It can also be propagated by semi-hardwood cuttings in summer, taken with a basal heel.

	SPRING	SUMMER	AUTUMN	WINTER	height 5yrs (m)	height 10yrs (m)	spread 5yrs (m)	spread 10yrs (m)	petal colour	
Physocarpus malvaceus	●	●			1	2	1.2	2.5		Spreading shrub with green, lobed leaves
P. opulifolius 'Dart's Gold'		●			1	2	1.2	2.5		Leaves bright yellow when new
P. opulifolius 'Diabolo'		●			1.5	2.5	1.8	3		Leaves reddish purple, dark and almost black
P. opulifolius 'Luteus'		●			1.5	3	2	5		New leaves are bright golden yellow
Piptanthus nepalensis	●				1.5	2.5	1.5	2.5		Evergreen, leaves trifoliate, good wall shrub

● flowering   🥜 harvest

Pieris

Lily of the valley flowers are only part of the display shown by Pieris species but the usually white bell-shaped blooms in spreading panicles can smother the foliage when they open in the spring.

Pieris 'Forest Flame'

The flowers are formed at the end of the growth in the previous autumn and exposed over winter at the bud stage. They slowly enlarge over winter, providing both hope for spring and frustration at the time taken! However, the best display is from the new foliage. In cultivars like 'Forest Flame' and 'Wakehurst' the new foliage is vivid red, passing through pink and creamy-white before settling on green. When a large bush flushes it is quite stunning.

Unfortunately, there are two drawbacks with these plants. Most serious is that they must have an acidic soil, with a pH of below 6 to look at their best. If your soil is above neutral (pH 6.5), choose *Photinia fraseri* 'Red Robin' instead. The other drawback is that the new foliage is tender to late spring frosts. If caught by frost, the plant will send out another flush of new foliage but it is never quite as good. Site these plants so that they avoid frost pockets and are unlikely to get very wet before frosty nights.

Pieris 'Firecrest'

Pieris 'Flaming Silver'

soil	Prefers acidic soils and other humus rich but well drained soils
site	Plant in a position that can provide sun or even just a light shade
general care	Mulch with an acidic leaf mould and protect the plant from cold, dry winds and spring frost
pruning	None, but can be coppiced or progressively reduced to reshape and restrict
pests & diseases	Relatively trouble-free. Pests and diseases do not usually cause any problems

	SPRING	SUMMER	AUTUMN	WINTER	height 5yrs (m)	height 10yrs (m)	spread 5yrs (m)	spread 10yrs (m)	petal colour	
Pieris 'Firecrest'	● ●				0.8	1.5	0.5	1	☐	Bright red new leaves
P. 'Flaming Silver'	● ●				0.5	1	0.5	1	☐	Leaves edged white but few flowers
P. 'Forest Flame'	● ●				0.8	1.5	0.5	1	☐	New foliage red, turning to dark green
P. formosana var. forrestii 'Wakehurst'	● ●				0.8	1.5	0.5	1.2	☐	Leaves brilliant red, crimson-pink then to green
P. japonica 'Flamingo'	● ●			●	0.8	1.2	0.5	1	■	Deepest of the pink flowered forms
P. japonica 'Little Heath'	● ●				0.3	0.6	0.3	0.6	☐	Leaves small, pink-flushed when young
P. japonica 'Little Heath Green'	● ●				0.3	0.5	0.3	0.5	☐	Sport of 'Little Heath', for the rock garden
P. japonica 'Purity'	● ●			●	0.6	1	0.6	1	☐	Pale green foliage contrasts with white flowers

 *flowering*

Pieris 'Firecrest'

Potentilla

Shrubby cinquefoils

The shrubby cinquefoils are a small group of plants in what is otherwise an enormous genus, of perhaps as many as 500 species. These plants are usually listed in horticulture as forms of *Potentilla fruticosa*, but botanically they actually belong to a cluster of related species.

Potentilla 'Abbotswood'

Here the cultivars are listed alphabetically, with botanical species in the text notes. They are grown for the single flowers which have five widely spreading petals and emulate the beauty of dog rose and other species roses. They make small bushes and are very attractive for the length of their flowering season, starting in late spring and often still having a few blooms out in late autumn. In the garden they are excellent as informal hedges, requiring very little in the way of maintenance. They can also be used as ground cover where their arching habit, foliage and flowers combine.

Potentillas thrive on a wide range of soils, from moist to well drained and from acidic to chalky. They are tough and hardy. They flower better in full sun but some, especially the red flowered forms, tend to be bleached by the sun and are better coloured in light shade. Rich soils can give rise to too much foliage at the expense of flower colour. The leaves have five or seven leaflets, in some forms being silky hairy and thus silver coloured. They are deciduous and usually turn yellow or red. They can be propagated by softwood cuttings in summer. The species can be raised by seed.

Potentilla 'Katherine Dykes'

soil	Any soil ranging from moist to well-drained, acidic or alkaline
site	Sun to moderate shade; flowers best in sun but some will be bleached
general care	Very easy plants to cultivate, as minimal general care and maintenance is required
pruning	Trim hedges in spring, otherwise only prune to restrict or reshape
pests & diseases	Relatively trouble-free. Pests and diseases do not usually cause any problems

Potentilla 'Princess'

Flowering Shrubs

	SPRING	SUMMER	AUTUMN	WINTER	height 5yrs (m)	height 10yrs (m)	spread 5yrs (m)	spread 10yrs (m)	petal colour	
Potentilla 'Abbotswood'	●	●●●	●●●		0.5	0.75	0.8	1.2	☐	Leaves dark blue-green. Form of *P. davurica*
P. 'Abbotswood Silver'	●	●●●	●●●		0.5	0.75	0.8	1.2	☐	Leaves with a narrow, creamy-white margin
P. 'Beesii'		●●	●●●		0.6	1	0.6	1	▧	Golden flowers, silvery foliage. Form of *P. arbuscula*
P. 'Elizabeth'	●	●●●	●●●		0.6	1	1	1.2	▧	Domed-shaped bush
P. 'Goldfinger'	●	●●●	●●●		0.5	0.8	0.6	0.8	▧	Blue-green leaves, pink shoots, large flowers
P. 'Katherine Dykes'		●●	●●		0.8	1	1.5	1.5	▧	Will make 2m in height
P. Marian Red Robin ('Marrob')	●	●●●	●●●		0.6	1	1	1.5	■	Intense red-flowered form
P. 'Primrose Beauty'	●	●●●	●●●		0.6	0.8	1	1.5	▧	Leaves grey-green
P. 'Princess'	●	●●●	●●●		0.4	0.6	0.8	1	☐	Flowers sometimes with extra petals
P. 'Red Ace'	●	●●●	●●●		0.6	1	1	1.5	▧	Bright green foliage; flowers fade in full sun
P. 'Sunset'	●	●●●	●●●		0.6	1	0.8	1	■	Best in partial shade
P. 'Vilmoriniana'	●	●●●	●●●		1	2	0.8	1.5	☐	Erect habit to 2m. Very silvery leaves

● *flowering*

Prunus
Cherries

Most cherries are small trees, a few even large ones, and these are featured in _Trees & Shrubs_, also in this series of books. The four shrubs described here only grow to a maximum of 2m (7ft) and thus make excellent plants for shrub and mixed borders.

The most floriferous is _Prunus tenella_ 'Fire Hill'. This is related to the almond (_Prunus dulcis_) and makes suckering shrubs to 1.5m (5ft). The stems are erect and last year's growths are covered in spring in dark pink or rose-red flowers. No garden is too small to be without this plant, which can be used in a number of roles, such as to provide a contrast to a heather bed. _Prunus cistena_ also flowers in spring, but here the flowers are white. The chief attraction of this hybrid is in the foliage, which is crimson when it first flushes, then ageing to bronze-red. The fruit is occasionally produced and is a dark purple cherry. _Prunus cistena_ makes an excellent hedge if you want one of this foliage colour. _Prunus glandulosa_ 'Alba Plena' has choice white flowers which contain numerous petals. It blooms a little later, towards the end of spring. The wood of _Prunus glandulosa_ needs a hot sunny spot to become more fully ripened. For this reason, it is best when planted against a sun-drenched wall; it will grow if sited in the open but there is likely to be some dieback of twigs. They thrive on a wide range of freely drained soils, including chalky sites. Prunus are best propagated by semi-hardwood cuttings in summer or by layering.

Prunus cistena

Prunus laurocerasus 'Otto Luyken'

soil	Reasonable to well drained soils, from acidic sands to clays to chalky sites
site	Particularly enjoys being planted in a sunny position in the garden
general care	The sunnier the spot, the better the wood ripens – this is especially important for _P. glandulosa_
pruning	Can be cut back to 2–3 buds at the base of last year's shoots after flowering
pests & diseases	Aphids can be a problem, especially black fly. Also silver leaf, honey fungus and blossom wilt

	SPRING	SUMMER	AUTUMN	WINTER	height 5yrs (m)	height 10yrs (m)	spread 5yrs (m)	spread 10yrs (m)	petal colour	
Prunus cistena	●				0.8	1.2	0.6	1	▨	Suckering, floriferous shrub
P. glandulosa 'Alba Plena'		●			0.8	1.2	0.7	1.2	□	Double flowers; excellent as a wall shrub
P. laurocerasus 'Otto Luyken'	●	●	✎		0.7	1.2	0.7	1.2	□	Erect habit
P. tenella 'Fire Hill'	●				0.6	1	0.6	1.2	▨	Good growing above ground cover

● _flowering_   ✎ _harvest_

Punica
Pomegranate

Pomegranate is a delicious fruit, but it rarely ripens in cool conditions.

However, the flowers are visually as delectable; they are tubular bells 2.5–4cm (1–1⅛in) in length and carried singly or in pairs at the ends of short leafy shoots in late summer or early autumn. The corolla is orange-scarlet and showy. The fruit is formed but will only ripen after a particularly long and hot summer followed by an autumn under cooler conditions.

   This shrub is hardy for the average winter but does so much better when planted against a sunny wall. Preferably grow the plants in a greenhouse until they are three or four years old, as they become hardier with age. Punica will grow on any well drained soil. Propagation is by seeds, semi-hardwood cuttings in summer, or by layers.

Rhaphiolepis

This genus is in the apple subfamily. They have leathery evergreen leaves which are often bronze when new. The flowers are in white or rose-pink and carried at the ends of new growth.

Punica granatum var. nana

soil	Punica: well drained soils. Rhaphiolepis: well drained, fertile and even chalky
site	Both plants enjoy lots of sun, preferably at the base of a sun-drenched wall
general care	Punica: mulch to protect roots to survive a hard winter. Rhaphiolepis: give shelter from cold, dry winter winds
pruning	Punica: remove old branches in spring/late summer. Rhaphiolepis: none needed
pests & diseases	Both plants are relatively trouble-free. Pests and diseases do not usually cause them any problems

The time of flowering is rather dependent upon the weather, generally in spring or early summer but sometimes before winter is out. The fruits are pear-shaped and blue-black. They make good shrubs, either for borders or against walls. They thrive on well drained soils, doing better in fertile sites and really needing a sunny spot. They can be propagated by semi-hardwood cuttings in summer.

Rhaphiolepis delacourii

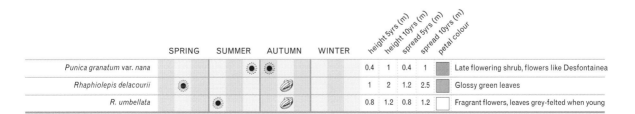

	SPRING	SUMMER	AUTUMN	WINTER	height 5yrs (m)	height 10yrs (m)	spread 5yrs (m)	spread 10yrs (m)	petal colour	
Punica granatum var. nana		●	●		0.4	1	0.4	1		Late flowering shrub, flowers like Desfontainea
Rhaphiolepis delacourii	●		🌰		1	2	1.2	2.5		Glossy green leaves
R. umbellata		●	🌰		0.8	1.2	0.8	1.2		Fragrant flowers, leaves grey-felted when young

● flowering   🌰 harvest

Rhododendron

Azaleas *or*
Alpine roses

This genus is one of the largest of all groups of flowering plants, with some 800 or so species plus countless thousands of hybrids. These plants are enormously popular and are employed ubiquitously in gardens for any number of different purposes. This is quite surprising in so far as rhododendrons cannot be grown just anywhere; they will fail in alkaline soils and ideally need acid soil in order to thrive. We only have sufficient space to cover a small selection of rhododendrons in this book. The majority of rhododendrons are hardy in most conditions. The genus is distributed across the cooler parts of the northern hemisphere, but extending south through Indonesia with two species making it into northern Australia.

As stated above, a basic requirement of this genus is for an acidic soil. The best advice is to garden within the limitations of your soil. Recently, a hybrid rootstock has become available which will allow the Hymenanthes group to be grown on neutral soils and heavier clays. All Rhododendron can be propagated by layering or by grafting onto related rootstocks. They can also be propagated by cuttings. All species have very fibrous root systems and are easily moved.

Four basic groups of Rhododendron are discussed here: deciduous azaleas; evergreen azaleas; alpine roses; and hymenanthes. Each group has its own distinctive characteristics and preferences.

soil	These plants grow best in acidic soils, preferably rich in organic matter
site	The most preferable position is in sun to light shade
general care	Mulch to maintain organic matter in soil and feed with ericaceous fertilizer mix to maintain acidic soil conditions
pruning	None except to remove dead branches. Trim evergreen azaleas after flowering
pests & diseases	Bud blast can kill flower buds; powdery mildew can affect 'Alpine rose' types; vine weevil damaging to all

Deciduous azalea

Rhododendron 'Daviesii'

This group of plants are spectacular when the bushes are smothered by scores of large, very showy flowers – made all the more spectacular because the bushes are bare of leaves.

Deciduous azalea also tend to have fragrant flowers. The flowering season of this group of Rhododendron ranges from mid-spring to mid-summer, but the peak period is late spring.

The deciduous azalea generally give excellent autumn colour. They are majestic when located in beds or large drifts of mixed colours, but even a single plant in full bloom will enlighten the dankest border.

	SPRING	SUMMER	AUTUMN	WINTER	height 5yrs (m)	height 10yrs (m)	spread 5yrs (m)	spread 10yrs (m)	petal colour	
Rhododendron 'Berryrose'	●				1	1.8	1	1.8		Good autumn colour; foliage coppery after flowers
R. 'Daviesii'	●	●			0.9	1.5	1	1.8		Fragrant flowers
R. 'Homebush'	●	●			1	1.5	1	1.5		Flowers in pompon trusses, good autumn colour
R. 'Klondyke'	●	●			1	1.8	1	1.8		Copper foliage after flowers, good autumn colour
R. *luteum*	●				1	1.8	1	1.8		Fragrant flowers, good autumn colour
R. 'Persil'	●				1	1.5	1	1.5		Clear white colour
R. 'Strawberry Ice'	●				1	1.8	1	1.8		Flowers deep pink in bud

● *flowering*

Evergreen azalea

The evergreen azaleas are extremely floriferous and established bushes are hidden by the mass of flowers, giving strong and startling colour to a border. They can also be used in patio pots. They will thrive in full sun and are better here than in light shade provided they are kept moist (but not sodden) at the roots. They like shelter from cold winds in winter, but most of the forms generally offered are fully hardy. However, like most of us, they do prefer a warm and sunny climate!

The flowering period is mainly in mid- to late spring. The flowers are usually single, but some of the forms, known as 'hose-in-hose' varieties, are double, with a second flower inserted into the corolla of the main flower. The foliage is rather small and out of flower they are just small-leafed evergreen bushes. The majority of evergreen azaleas will slowly make bushes to 1.2m (4ft) or so, over thirty years. However, they can be trimmed immediately after flowering to restrict their height growth without affecting next year's blooming. They are propagated from semi-hardwood cuttings in mid-summer and most will root in six to eight weeks. Harden them off in the frame and pot on in the second autumn.

Rhododendron 'Addy Wery'

	SPRING	SUMMER	AUTUMN	WINTER	height 5yrs (m)	height 10yrs (m)	spread 5yrs (m)	spread 10yrs (m)	petal colour	
Rhododendron 'Addy Wery'	● ●				0.5	0.8	0.6	1	■	Glossy foliage
R. 'Amoenum'	●				0.5	0.8	0.6	1	■	Often listed as *R. obtusatum* 'Amoenum'
R. 'Blaauw's Pink'	●				0.5	0.8	0.6	1	□	Hose-in-hose flowers
R. 'Blue Danube'	● ●				0.5	0.8	0.6	1	▨	Blue-violet flowers
R. 'Colyer'	● ●				0.5	0.8	0.6	1	□	White flowers
R. 'Hino-crimson'	● ●				0.5	1	0.6	1	▨	Glossy foliage turns bronze in winter
R. 'Hinode-giri'	● ●				0.5	0.8	0.6	1	▨	Compact, with bright crimson flowers
R. 'Hino-mayo'	● ●				0.5	1	0.6	1	▨	Compact, clear pink flowers
R. 'Kirin'	● ●				0.5	0.8	0.6	1	▨	Hose-in-hose flowers
R. 'Lemur'	● ●				0.2	0.3	0.6	1	▨	Prostrate habit
R. 'Orange Beauty'	●				0.5	0.8	0.6	1	▨	Good autumn colour but needs shade
R. 'Palestrina'	● ●				0.5	0.8	0.6	1	□	Faint ray of green in flowers
R. 'Rosebud'	●				0.5	0.8	0.6	1	▨	Spreading habit
R. 'Squirrel'	●	●			0.4	0.6	0.6	1	▨	Long lasting flowers
R. 'Vuyk's Rosyred'	●				0.5	0.8	0.6	1	▨	Glossy foliage colours in autumn
R. 'Vuyk's Scarlet'	● ●				0.5	0.8	0.6	1	▨	Glossy foliage in autumn, forms dense mound

● *flowering*

Alpine roses

Deeply committed Rhododendron fans will recognize this group as being the lepidote species and hybrids of section Rhododendron. The type species in the genus belongs to this section and to call them 'alpine roses' is more attractive than 'lepidote (or scaly) Rhododendron'. The generic name is from the Greek rose-tree. Also, most of the species in this group are moorland plants, from most of the high mountains of Asia and occupying the same habit as *Calluna vulgaris* in the uplands of Britain.

This group of Rhododendron species are mainly low shrubs, rarely making a metre (3ft) in height in thirty years (although there are some taller species which are detailed in *Trees & Shrubs*, also in this series of books). They have small leaves which are glaucous blue in a number of forms, and often turn bronze over winter. The flowers are often lavender blue but also yellow, white or pink. The forms make excellent low shrubs, either for peat beds, for rock gardens or in drifts, especially on acidic sandy soils with suitable irrigation. They can be propagated by cuttings at most times of the year but are most reliable from cuttings in late winter and rooted with heat from beneath.

Rhododendron 'Sapphire'

Flowering Shrubs

	SPRING	SUMMER	AUTUMN	WINTER	height 5yrs (m)	height 10yrs (m)	spread 5yrs (m)	spread 10yrs (m)	petal colour	
Rhododendron 'Blue Diamond'	● ● ●				0.5	0.8	0.6	0.9		Saucer-shaped flowers, colour deeper with age
R. 'Blue Peter'	● ●				0.6	0.9	0.5	0.8		Flowers with maroon spots and white throat
R. calostrotum 'Gigha'	● ●				0.2	0.4	0.2	0.4		Saucer-shaped flowers, foliage silver-grey
R. 'Chikor'	● ●				0.4	0.5	0.4	0.6		Needs good drainage
R. fastigiatum	● ●				0.5	0.7	0.5	0.7		Funnel-shaped flowers, sea-green leaves
R. 'Fragrantissimum'	● ●				0.7	1	0.7	1		Fragrant flowers, good as conservatory plant
R. impeditum	● ●				0.15	0.2	0.15	0.2		Funnel-shaped flowers, good for rock garden
R. lepidostylum	● ●				0.4	0.7	0.5	0.8		Grown for bright, glaucous blue-green foliage
R. pemakoense	● ●				0.2	0.3	0.3	0.5		Protect funnel-shaped flowers from frost
R. 'Pink Drift'	● ●				0.2	0.4	0.3	0.4		Aromatic foliage, for the rock garden
R. 'Princess Anne'	● ●				0.4	0.6	0.4	0.6		Good winter foliage, new growth bronzy-red
R. 'Ptarmigan'	● ●				0.4	0.6	0.4	0.6		Drought tolerant, dark foliage
R. 'Sapphire'	● ●				0.3	0.6	0.3	0.6		Glossy green leaves
R. 'Snipe'	●				0.3	0.6	0.3	0.6		Flowers shaded pale violet and purple

● *flowering*

Hymenanthes

These make attractive flowering bushes which can be used in tubs on patios, or in shrub beds or in collections. Unlike the 'Alpine rose' group, these are mainly derived from species which occur in mixed shrubberies or light woodland, although a few are found on moorland. They will grow in full sun provided they are given adequate soil moisture, but are happier with light shade. The leaves tend to be much larger and can be attractive in their own right – two of the species listed here are good examples: in *Rhododendron williamsianum* the leaves are heart-shaped and rather glaucous blue-green, but the new foliage is bronze, whereas in *Rhododendron yakushimanum* the

new foliage is silvery and the mature leaves have a dense brown wool covering the undersides; this character is inherited by some of its hybrids, such as 'Hydon Dawn'.

'Cunningham's White' is a smaller growing 'Hardy Hybrid' and is also tolerant of neutral soils. It is frequently used as a rootstock where these plants need propagating by grafting. However, most can be struck from cuttings, taken in late winter.

	SPRING	SUMMER	AUTUMN	WINTER	height 5yrs (m)	height 10yrs (m)	spread 5yrs (m)	spread 10yrs (m)	petal colour	
Rhododendron 'Anna Rose Whitney'	●	●			0.8	1.5	0.8	1.5		Flowers funnel-shaped
R. 'Baden-Baden'	●	●			0.2	0.3	0.4	0.6		Glossy leaves
R. 'Bow Bells'	● ●				0.5	0.8	0.5	0.8		Bell-shaped nodding flowers, leaves coppery
R. 'Carmen'	●	●			0.2	0.3	0.4	0.6		Bell-shaped flowers
R. 'Christmas Cheer'	●				0.8	1.5	0.8	1.5		For Christmas opening, bring into conservatory
R. 'Cunningham's White'	●				0.8	1.5	0.8	1.5		Tolerant of windy sites, slightly alkaline soils
R. 'Doc'	●				0.5	0.8	0.5	0.8		Flowers with frilly margins
R. 'Dopey'	●	●			0.5	0.8	0.5	0.8		Long lasting blooms
R. 'Elizabeth'	●				0.5	0.8	0.5	0.8		Funnel-shaped flowers; full sun or light shade
R. 'Golden Torch'	●	●			0.5	0.8	0.5	0.8		Compact habit
R. 'Grumpy'	●	●			0.5	0.8	0.5	0.8		Foliage with a woolly indumentum
R. 'Hotei'	●				0.8	1.5	0.8	1.5		Compact habit, best in partial shade
R. 'Hummingbird'	●				0.5	0.8	0.5	0.8		Flowers wide bell-shaped, half nodding
R. 'Morning Cloud'	●	●			0.5	0.8	0.5	0.8		Creamy-buff woolly indumentum
R. 'Percy Wiseman'	●				0.7	1.2	0.7	1.2		Very floriferous
R. 'Scarlet Wonder'	●	●			0.5	0.8	0.5	0.8		Dense foliage, trumpet-shaped flowers
R. 'Sneezy'	●				0.5	0.8	0.5	0.8		Upright habit
R. 'Surrey Heath'	●				0.5	0.8	0.5	0.8		Fading flowers give a two-tone effect
R. 'Unique'	● ●				0.8	1.5	0.8	1.5		Compact and dense habit
R. williamsianum	●				0.5	0.8	0.5	0.8		Bell-shaped flowers, blue-green foliage
R. yakushimanum	●				0.3m	0.5	0.3	0.5		Silvery leaves mature to deep glossy green

● *flowering*

Flowering Shrubs

Ribes
Flowering currant

The genus Ribes includes the currants – black, red and white – and the gooseberries, but here we are interested in the sorts grown for the beauty of their flower, not their fruit, and which are generally without spines.

Foremost amongst the flowering currants is *Ribes sanguineum*. It is an excellent shrub which flowers with, or just in advance of, the new foliage in spring. The colourful flowers hang down from the branches when they first open but turn up as they expand. The foliage has a typical, somewhat pungent currant scent. It can be used as a hedging plant, trimmed immediately after flowering, or in shrub beds.

Ribes alpinum, and its yellow-green form 'Aureum', has yellow-green flowers of modest beauty. However, it is one of the best shrubs for dry shady spots. *Ribes odoratum* has clove-scented flowers in spring which are golden-yellow, and also gives good autumn colour. However, the choicest species is *Ribes speciosum*. This semi-evergreen shrub has fuchsia-like rich red flowers which hang down from last year's branches in spring. It needs wall protection except in mild gardens but is well worth the space. Ribes thrive on a wide range of soils. They are easily propagated by softwood or semi-hardwood cuttings in summer or hardwood cuttings in autumn and rooted outside.

soil	Relatively unfussy. Likes any reasonable, well drained garden soil
site	Sun, or light shade; *Ribes alpinum* will flourish in fairly deep shade
general care	Very easy but some species have separate male and female plants. The fruits are all edible
pruning	Remove older shoots after flowering (Group 1). Can be coppiced to reshape
pests & diseases	Can get the pests and diseases associated with fruiting currants, so keep a watchful eye

Ribes speciosum

Ribes sanguineum 'Pulborough Scarlet'

Ribes sanguineum 'Pulborough Scarlet'

	SPRING	SUMMER	AUTUMN	WINTER	height 5yrs (m)	height 10yrs (m)	spread 5yrs (m)	spread 10yrs (m)	petal colour	
Ribes alpinum	☀		harvest		1	1.5	1	1.5		Separate male and female plants
R. alpinum 'Aureum'	☀		harvest		1	1.5	1	1.5		New leaves yellow, later pale yellow-green
R. gordonianum	☀ ☀		harvest		1	1.5	1	1.5		Suitable for tough sites
R. laurifolium	☀		harvest	☀	0.6	0.9	0.6	0.9		Evergreen; females – edible red/black currants
R. odoratum	☀ ☀		harvest		1	1.5	1	1.5		Clove scented flowers – useful in wild borders
R. sanguineum 'Brocklebankii'	☀		harvest		0.8	1.2	0.8	1.2		For golden yellow leaves, hard prune in winter
R. sanguineum 'King Edwards VII'	☀		harvest		0.8	1	0.8	1		Good flowering currant
R. sanguineum 'Pulborough Scarlet'	☀		harvest		1	1.8	1	1.8		Flowers dark red with white centres
R. speciosum	☀ ☀		harvest		1	2	1	2		Bell shaped flowers from old shoots

☀ flowering   🌰 harvest

Rosa
Rose

The genus *Rosa* includes four rather different groups of garden plants. The highly bred, repeat flowering 'hybrid tea' and 'floribunda' roses require very artificial growing conditions to bloom to best effect (but they provide excellent food for deer, if you happen to have these!) and are inclined to various foliage ailments. These species of rose are not considered here; neither are the climbing sorts, although some are really excellent if allowed to run riot through trees. The two groups which are featured here are some of the old fashioned shrub roses and a selection of the species roses.

Shrub roses

Rosa 'Golden Wings'

The shrub roses only have a single period of bloom, although occasionally all may produce a few late flowers. They thrive on a wide range of soil types, except very wet and acidic soils.

These roses are best in full sun, but they will tolerate light to moderate shade. They can be propagated by grafting or budding – the techniques that are used for their commoner cousins. However, they are usually more easily rooted from semi-hardwood cuttings in summer, or, for the species roses, by seed.

Old fashioned roses

Old fashioned roses are useful in shrub beds, but they can be grown in dedicated beds if preferred. Most have strongly fragrant flowers but do not provide any fruiting features and have only modest foliage. Despite their name, some are modern selections but in the tradition of the old forms. The group includes a number of different types, such as the alba, bourbon, damask, gallica, noisette and china roses, but modern hybridizers have crossed between these groups to reduce the practical value of these names.

soil	Will tolerate all garden soils except wet and very acidic ones
site	Prefers a position in the garden with sun and moderate shade
general care	Roses are fairly easy to maintain and cultivate as long as they are kept well manured
pruning	Little pruning is needed except to remove old stems; aim for 2–3 year old stems
pests & diseases	Various foliage diseases can affect them, but rarely seriously; similarly with various insect pests

Rosa 'Buff Beauty'

	SPRING	SUMMER	AUTUMN	WINTER	height 5yrs (m)	height 10yrs (m)	spread 5yrs (m)	spread 10yrs (m)	petal colour	
Rosa 'Buff Beauty'		● ●			1.2	1.2	1.2	1.2		Double flowers, lightly scented
R. 'Cardinal Richelieu'		● ●			1	1	1.2	1.2		Gallica form; double flowers, fragrant
R. 'Celeste'		●			1.2	1.5	1	1.2		Alba rose; double flowers, fragrant
R. 'Frühlingsgold'		●			1.5	2	1.5	2		Modern shrub; scented, vigorous arching habit
R. 'Frühlingsmorgen'		●			1.2	2	1	1.5		Modern shrub; scented, leaves greyish green
R. 'Golden Wings'		● ● ● ●			0.9	1.1	1	1.3		Modern shrub; single flowers, large (12cm)
R. 'Heritage'		● ● ● ●			0.9	1.2	0.9	1.2		Modern shrub; double flowers, lemon-scented
R. 'Louise Odier'		● ● ● ●			1	2	0.8	1.2		Bourbon group; double flowers, fragrant
R. 'Madame Alfred Carrière'		● ●			2	3	2m	3		Noisette group; almost a climber
R. 'Maiden's Blush'		●			0.9	1.2	0.7	0.9		Alba group; double flowers, fragrant

● *flowering*

Species roses

Apart from the flowers, which are generally single and fragrant, these roses have attractive fruits. Most of the plants featured here are forms or hybrids of *Rosa rugosa*. These have very large single flowers which are followed by large red heps or hips. The fleshy part of the hip is rich in vitamin C. The stems are vigorously prickly, and coupled with their suckering habit (when on their own roots) they make excellent hedging and barrier plants. They should be cut back hard in spring and will flower in mid-summer. The 'Rugosa' roses are well adapted to light sandy soils, and maritime habitats. *Rosa moyesii* and its hybrid 'Geranium' have attractive single flowers, but are better for the flask-shaped fruits which persist long into winter. *Rosa primula* and *Rosa xanthina* 'Canary Bird' both have attractive yellow flowers in late spring; they also both have very appealing feathery leaves, but dismal black hips. *Rosa rubiginosa* has beautifully formed pink flowers but is worth growing for the fragrant foliage alone; this is apple-scented, especially after it has been dampened by a shower.

Rosa 'Rosarie de l'Hay'

Rosa rugosa

Rosa xanthina 'Canary Bird'

	SPRING	SUMMER	AUTUMN	WINTER	height 5yrs (m)	height 10yrs (m)	spread 5yrs (m)	spread 10yrs (m)	petal colour	
Rosa 'Blanche Double de Coubert'		flowering	harvest		1.2	1.5	1	1.2		Rugosa form; not reliable for fruiting
R. 'Geranium'		flowering	harvest	harvest	1.5	2.5	1	1.5		Single flowers; hips orange-red
R. moyesii		flowering	harvest	harvest	2	3.5	1.5	2.5		Single flowers; hips red
R. primula	flowering				1.2	2.5	1	2		Single flowers, scented; leaves fern-like
R. 'Rosarie de l'Hay'		flowering	harvest		1.2	2	1	1.5		Rugosa form; flowers strongly scented, single
R. rubiginosa		flowering	harvest		1.2	2	1.2	2		Also called *R. eleganteria*; apple-scented
R. rugosa		flowering	harvest	harvest	1	1.5	1	1.5		Suckering shrub with prickly stems
R. rugosa 'Alba'		flowering	harvest		1	1.5	1	1.5		Flowers pale pink in bud
R. rugosa 'Rubra'		flowering	harvest	harvest	1	1.5	1	1.5		Flowers purplish-red
R. xanthina 'Canary Bird'	flowering				1.2	2.5	1.2	2.5		Flowers musk-scented; leaves greyish green

 flowering harvest

Rosmarinus
Rosemary

This kitchen herb makes an excellent spring flowering shrub and it is worth growing for this alone, although even in the shrub border it will provide the garnish to accompany spring lamb. The leaves are narrow and evergreen, normally carried on a rather stiff upright bush. They are delightfully aromatic and a fragrant oil is distilled from the foliage.

The flowers are normally some shade of blue, but white- and pink-flowered forms are recorded. They have the typical Labiate-type two lipped corollas. Rosemary is a native of the northern shore of the Mediterranean and is related to Lavandula. Accordingly, it requires a hot sunny site with good drainage to perform at its best, and is happy (once established) on dry sites and those of low fertility. It dislikes wet and heavy soils.

In the garden, Rosmarinus can be used in shrub or mixed borders, as a hedge and in the

Rosmarinus officinalis 'Sissinghurst Blue'

soil	Will tolerate well drained soils; good for chalky or stony sites
site	The best position for this plant is in a hot, sunny site where it will thrive
general care	Very easy to cultivate. It must have good drainage but, once established, it is happy on poor sites
pruning	Trim to keep in shape – best performed shortly before cooking roast lamb!
pests & diseases	Although it is fairly trouble-free from pests and diseases, it can be damaged by hard winters

Rosmarinus officinalis

kitchen garden. The prostrate forms, such as 'McConnell's Blue', can be used in a rockery, or tumbling over a container on a patio.

Rosemary will grow on a wide range of soil types, including chalky ones. The forms are most easily propagated by semi-hardwood cuttings in summer.

	SPRING	SUMMER	AUTUMN	WINTER	height 5yrs (m)	height 10yrs (m)	spread 5yrs (m)	spread 10yrs (m)	petal colour	
Rosmarinus officinalis	● ●				0.6	1	0.6	1		Narrow, evergreen leaves, aromatic
R. officinalis var. albiflorus	● ●				0.6	1	0.6	1		White-flowered variant
R. o. var. angustissime 'Benenden Blue'	● ●				0.6	1	0.6	1		Semi-erect, collected by Collingwood Ingram
R. officinalis 'Majorca Pink'	● ●				0.6	1	0.6	1		Pink-flowered form
R. officinalis 'McConnell's Blue'		● ●			0.2	0.3	0.6	1		Prostrate form, winter protection in cold areas
R. officinalis 'Miss Jessop's Upright'	● ●				0.6	1.2	0.6	1.2		Vigorous, grows to 2m
R. officinalis 'Severn Sea'	● ●				0.6	1	0.6	1		Spreading habit with arching branches
R. officinalis 'Sissinghurst Blue'	● ●				0.6	1	0.6	1		Upright habit

● *flowering*

Rubus

It is difficult to give **Rubus** a common name; should it be 'raspberries', 'blackberries' or 'dewberries', which suggest the tasty fruit, or 'brambles', which is many people's immediate thought at the mention of Rubus. The small selection of species listed here encompasses all of these, but much more besides.

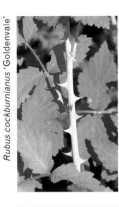

Rubus cockburnianus 'Goldenvale'

The flowers of *Rubus* 'Benenden' are large white dog-rose flowers but with none of the prickles. With double pinky-red flowers and fresh-green pinnate leaves there is *Rubus spectabilis* 'Olympic Double', which is a suckering shrub. Again it has few prickles, perhaps its only drawback is that it can sucker rather too freely on light sandy soils. However, *Rubus biflorus*, *Rubus cockburnianaus* and *Rubus thibetanus* do justify the 'bramble' epithet. Their joy in the garden is in the white-washed stems, which are only developed in the first autumn and last to create an effective winter display. Finally, there is *Rubus tricolor* which shares the reddish bristles but is evergreen and makes a vigorous, hugging

soil	A very unfussy plant, as it is at home in any type of garden soil
site	Position in the garden where there is sun or light shade
general care	A very easy plant to cultivate and look after. Some can sucker and most will tip-layer
pruning	Remove two year old stems after flowering or fruiting
pests & diseases	Relatively trouble-free. Pests and diseases do not usually cause any problems

Rubus tricolor

ground cover plant. It is excellent for filling odd corners or banks.

An important part of Rubus is that generally the stems are biennial; they grow vigorously in the first summer and then flower and fruit in the second. They should be managed by removing the two year old stems at the end of their second summer. Rubus thrive on all garden soils. They can be propagated by semi-hardwood cuttings in summer, but most will 'tip-layer'. They can also be propagated by root cuttings.

	SPRING	SUMMER	AUTUMN	WINTER	height 5yrs (m)	height 10yrs (m)	spread 5yrs (m)	spread 10yrs (m)	petal colour	
Rubus 'Benenden'	● ●				1.8	2	1.8	2		Palmate leaves, non-spiny stems
R. biflorus	●				1.8	2	1.8	2		Stems covered in waxy white wash first winter
R. cockburnianus	●				1.8	2	2	3		Stems covered in waxy white wash; fruit black
R. cockburnianus 'Goldenvale'	●				1.8	2	1.8	2		Yellow-green leaves
R. henryi var. bambusarum	●				1.8	2	1.8	2		Black fruit; evergreen with three leaflets
R. phoenicolasius	●				1.5	2	1.5	2		Stems with reddish bristles; fruits bright red
R. spectabilis 'Olympic Double'	●				1.2	1.8	1.5	2.5		Double flowers; fruit orange-yellow
R. thibetanus	●				1.8	2	2	3		Stems blue-purple with waxy bloom; fruit black
R. tricolor	●				0.2	0.4	2	4		Good ground cover for sun and shade

● *flowering*   *harvest*

R

Flowering Shrubs

Ruscus & Danae

Butcher's broom

These two genera are closely related, and this is why they are treated together here. Ruscus is the more common in cultivation, while Danae originates from the Middle East and is not found so readily. These plants are members of the Lily family and are scarcely shrubs. They are related to the Asparagus and, like these, the new growths are eaten in parts of Europe.

What appears to be foliage is actually modified stems (cladodes). The true leaves are small brown scale-like structures. The flowers are carried in the middle of the cladodes, in the axils of the leaves. In *Ruscus aculeatus* the flowers are carried on separate male and female plants, and are dull white. The fruits on female plants are globose or oblong bright red berries. These are long lasting, often persisting throughout winter and into the next spring. In *Danae racemosa*, the plants are hermaphrodite, with both male and female flowers on the same bush, and orange-red in colour. This plant has fresh green and softer foliage, than the dark green and hard, prickly foliage of *Ruscus aculeatus*.

Both these genera are very shade tolerant. They thrive on a wide range of soils, especially calcareous soils. They are very useful for filling a dank corner but can also be grown in full sunlight where they will make a stronger display. The name 'Butcher's broom' comes from the use of the cut stems to make brooms. The most effective method of propagation is simple division in spring, but the seeds can be germinated.

Ruscus aculeatus

soil	Will tolerate any well drained soil, including chalky ones
site	Position in the garden wherever there is sun or some shade
general care	Generally fairly easy to cultivate and look after. Beware of prickly stems of *R. aculeatus*
pruning	None required, but old stems can be cut to ground level in late winter
pests & diseases	Relatively trouble-free. Pests and diseases do not usually cause any problems

Danae racemosa

	SPRING	SUMMER	AUTUMN	WINTER	height 5yrs (m)	height 10yrs (m)	spread 5yrs (m)	spread 10yrs (m)	petal colour	
Danae racemosa		●	🌰	🌰	0.6	1	0.6	1	▨	Glossy green foliage; orange-red/red berries
Ruscus aculeatus	●		🌰	🌰	0.6	1	0.6	1	☐	Dull green spiky foliage; bright red berries

● flowering   🌰 harvest

Salix

Willow
or sallow

The genus Salix contains several hundred species, ranging from minute shrubs to large trees. The larger forms are featured in *Trees & Shrubs*, also in this series of books, and only a selection of the smaller to medium shrubs are included here. With this number of species, identification of willows can be difficult. It is made even harder because many of them hybridize promiscuously and there are separate male and female plants.

The gender of a willow can be an important horticultural point; there are both male and female weeping forms of *Salix caprea*, the common goat willow, and both were grown in the past as the 'Kilmarnock willow'. The male plant is attractive, with his showy yellow catkins before the leaves, whereas the female form, 'Weeping Sally', has rather drab flowers and no redeeming features.

When grafted onto a stem, the Kilmarnock willow is good as a small weeping shrub for a lawn or for a prominent position in a bed. *Salix hastata* 'Wehrhahnii' is another male form, combining the silky silver, later yellow catkins with sea-green foliage into a small bush to 1m (3ft). *Salix helvetica*, with grey-green and white leaves, makes an even smaller shrub for the

soil	Best on moist, well drained soils, but will tolerate moderately wet conditions
site	Plant where there is plenty of sun, but in no more than light shade
general care	Very easy to cultivate and look after but this certainly isn't a plant for dry soils
pruning	No strict requirements. Simply prune to restrict and to reshape
pests & diseases	Various fungi and insects will eat the leaves but usually without causing lasting damage

Salix caprea 'Kilmarnock'

rock garden. *Salix lanata* is another plant for the rock garden, with silvery-grey hairy leaves.

Most willows are easily propagated by cuttings, whether soft, semi-hardwood or hardwood, or by layering the stems of prostrate ones. However, some should be grafted onto a rootstock.

Flowering Shrubs

	SPRING	SUMMER	AUTUMN	WINTER	height 5yrs (m)	height 10yrs (m)	spread 5yrs (m)	spread 10yrs (m)	petal colour	
Salix caprea 'Kilmarnock'	● ●				1.5	1.5	1	2		Weeping shoots; male plant
S. hastata 'Wehrhahnii'	●				0.6	1	0.6	1		Sea-green foliage; male plant
S. helvetica	●				0.3	0.6	0.2	0.4		Leaves grey-green above, silvery hairy beneath
S. lanata		●			0.5	1	0.8	1.5		Silvery leaves

● *flowering*

Salvia
Sage

The sages are a large group but most are annuals or perennials; even the woody ones are often sub-shrubs, with a woody base from which herbaceous shoots are thrown each year.

The common sage, *Salvia officinalis*, is widely used as a culinary herb and makes an attractive low shrub, both for the semi-evergreen foliage and the white, pink, violet or purple colour of the flowers. The name, *Salvia* – to save – refers to its various medicinal uses. The flowers are in whorls along a flowering stem; they are the typical two lipped Labiate flower, and come in a range of colours.

Sages are useful as part of shrub, mixed and herbaceous borders provided they have full sun. They are an essential element of a herb garden. Sages grow on all soils provided they have good drainage. Water at the roots over winter is liable to kill even the hardier sorts. They are neither long term plants nor particularly hardy.

Salvia microphylla 'Maraschino'

Salvia officinalis 'Tricolor'

soil	Any well drained soil is good for this plant; water logging is fatal
site	Position in a warm, sunny spot in the garden for best results
general care	Generally fine, but ensure that water does not collect around the roots at any time
pruning	Prune only to remove winter or other damage, or to pick for the kitchen
pests & diseases	Slugs and snails can affect the new growth, but apart from that, fairly trouble-free from pests and diseases

	SPRING	SUMMER	AUTUMN	WINTER	height 5yrs (m)	height 10yrs (m)	spread 5yrs (m)	spread 10yrs (m)	petal colour	
Salvia aurea		● ● ●	● ●		1	1	1	1		Evergreen, tender; also called *S. africana-lutea*
S. elegans 'Scarlet Pineapple'	● ●			● ●	2	2	1	1		Sub-shrub; needs a frost-free environment
S. fulgens		● ● ●			1	1	0.9	0.9		Sub-shrub; leaves rich green, white beneath
S. greggii		● ●	● ●		0.5	0.5	0.5	0.5		Evergreen shrub or sub-shrub
S. guaranitica		● ●	● ● ●		1	1.5	0.5	0.6		Sub-shrub, tender
S. guaranitica 'Blue Enigma'		● ●	● ● ●		0.9	0.9	0.9	0.9		Fragrant flowers
S. involucrata 'Bethelii'		● ●	● ● ●		1.5	1.5	1	1		Sub-shrub with velvety leaves
S. microphylla 'Cerro Potosi'		● ● ● ●	●		0.9	0.9	0.9	0.9		Evergreen shrub
S. microphylla 'Maraschino'		● ● ● ●	●		0.9	0.9	0.9	0.9		Cherry-red flowers
S. officinalis		● ●			0.8	0.8	1	1		Semi-evergreen shrub
S. officinalis 'Icterina'		● ●			0.8	0.8	1	1		Leaves yellow and green variegated
S. officinalis 'Purpurascens'		● ●			0.8	0.8	1	1		New leaves red-purple
S. officinalis 'Tricolor'		● ●			0.8	0.8	1	1		Grey-green leaves, zones of cream and pink/purple

● *flowering*

Santolina

Holy flax

This genus is a member of the Compositae family, which includes sunflowers and dandelions. The flowers are in small button-like heads carried above the foliage on long stalks in mid- to late summer.

Santolinas are mainly grown for the pinnatisect leaves (i.e. leaves which are divided almost to the midrib at several places), which are grey-green to silver and often aromatic. Santolinas make small evergreen shrubs and can be trimmed to make effective mini-hedges, for use in the rock garden or to divide small areas. They can also be trimmed to form a carpet of foliage, or a dash of colourful foliage in a border.

They are shrubs of hot, dry and sunny sites in the Mediterranean region, and have an overriding need for good drainage. They are also better on poor soils than highly fertile ones. The forms listed below should be hardy provided you can give them these conditions. They are easily propagated from semi-hardwood cuttings in summer and it is prudent to take cuttings each summer in case of winter losses. Grown for their best foliage, they will need trimming periodically through the summer and all forms benefit from trimming in autumn.

Santolina chamaecyparissus

Santolina chamaecyparissus 'Lemon Queen'

soil	This plant will tolerate very well drained soils of low fertility
site	Position in a warm, sunny spot in the garden for best results
general care	Enjoys hot conditions, so expect some winter losses and take precautionary cuttings as insurance
pruning	Trim as needed and reshape in autumn; rejuvenate old bushes in spring
pests & diseases	Relatively trouble-free. Pests and diseases do not usually cause any problems

	SPRING	SUMMER	AUTUMN	WINTER	height 5yrs (m)	height 10yrs (m)	spread 5yrs (m)	spread 10yrs (m)	petal colour	
Santolina chamaecyparissus		● ●			0.5	0.5	1	1		Flowerheads 1cm; grey-green leaves
S. chamaecyparissus 'Lemon Queen'		● ●			0.6	0.6	0.6	0.6		Compact, lemon-yellow flowers
S. pinnata subsp. *neopolitana*		●			0.75	0.75	1	1		Grey-green aromatic foliage; flowerheads 2cm
S. p. subsp. *neopolitana* 'Edward Bowles'		●			0.75	0.75	1	1		Grey-green aromatic foliage; flowerheads 2cm
S. rosmarinifolia		●			0.6	0.6	1	1		Leaves bright green; flowerheads 2cm

 *flowering*

Sarcococca
Sweet box

These shrubs are valuable for their sweetly scented winter flowers. They form evergreen, often suckering shrubs and are related to the true box (Buxus).

The flowers have showy, off-white to cream male flowers at the tip with inconspicuous female flowers at the base. The fruit is a fleshy drupe, which ripens to red, purple or black. Sarcococca are useful both for their season of flowering and their ability to waft their fragrance over a wide area at an otherwise dull season.

Sarcococca confusa makes an upright shrub to 2m (6ft) and has black fruits following the very fragrant flowers. *Sarcococca hookeriana* var. *digyna* also has black fruits, but this is a spreading and suckering shrub to a metre (3ft). *Sarcococca hookeriana* var. *humilis* is lower growing, to 0.3–0.5m (1–1½ft) and in the right conditions can form a clump several metres (yards) across. *Sarcococca ruscifolia* makes a suckering shrub to a metre (3ft) but has red fruits, although these are somewhat lost amongst the foliage.

All Sarcococca grow on a wide range of soils, needing good drainage, but will thrive on acidic sands to chalky soils. They are also good in dry shade and in polluted atmospheres. They

soil	Well drained soils, not too fertile, including acidic and chalky ones
site	Prefers shade – only in full sun if on a moisture-retentive soil
general care	Position in the garden where the winter fragrance of the flowers can be appreciated
pruning	No special pruning required, except to restrict or reshape the plant
pests & diseases	Relatively trouble-free. Pests and diseases do not usually cause any problems

Sarcococca hookeriana var. digyna

will grow in full sun but here they need adequate soil moisture. *Sarcococca hookeriana* var. *humilis* is also very useful as a ground cover. They can be propagated by semi-hardwood cuttings in summer, by removal of suckers in late winter and by seed. Young plants are tasty to slugs and snails.

Sarcococca ruscifolia

	SPRING	SUMMER	AUTUMN	WINTER	height 5yrs (m)	height 10yrs (m)	spread 5yrs (m)	spread 10yrs (m)	petal colour	
Sarcococca confusa			● ● ●	🌰 🌰 🌰	1	1.5	0.6	1		Dense rounded bush; leaves glossy dark green
S. hookeriana var. *digyna*			● ● ●	🌰 🌰 🌰	0.6	1	1	1.5		Fruits black/blue-black; leaves mid-/dark green
S. hookeriana var. *humilis*			● ● ●	🌰 🌰 🌰	0.4	0.6	0.6	1		Glossy, evergreen leaves
S. ruscifolia			● ● ●	🌰 🌰 🌰	0.6	1	0.6	1		Dark red fruits; leaves dark glossy-green

● flowering   🌰 harvest

Skimmia

This is a small genus of evergreen shrubs which have very fragrant flowers. The common forms in cultivation are either male or female, and you need both sexes to produce the fruit. This can be white, such as in *Skimmia japonica* 'Kew White', but is most often red, such as *Skimmia japonica* 'Veitchii'.

Some of the less common species have black fruits. The fruits are green in late spring and colour by autumn; they can often be found providing colour well into the next year.

Male clones are worth growing both for their fragrant flowers and also to pollinate the female plants. Good male forms are *Skimmia confusa* 'Kew Green' and *Skimmia japonica* 'Fragrans'. However, if you have space for only one plant and are not on a chalky soil, choose *Skimmia reevesiana* 'Robert Fortune' (it is also listed as a form of *Skimmia japonica*), as this is a hermaphrodite and will produce the

crimson-red fruits when grown on its own. Apart from this form, Skimmia will grow on all well drained soils, including chalk soils.

Skimmia are useful for the very fragrant flowers in spring and the long lasting fruits. *S. confusa* 'Kew Green' thrives in full sun but the others are best in dappled to moderate shade. In the garden, they are useful to fill space beneath established trees or in other shady spots, as well as in shaded borders. They are propagated by semi-hardwood cuttings, preferably with some heat from beneath, in late summer. They can also be raised from seeds sown in the spring.

Skimmia japonica

soil	Likes well drained soils, including chalk (except for *S. reevesiana*)
site	Prefers a position in the light with a moderate amount of shade
general care	Fairly easy to look after. Plant both sexes to ensure the females carry the showy fruits
pruning	Pruning is rarely required for this plant, as it is fairly slow growing
pests & diseases	Relatively trouble-free. Pests and diseases do not usually cause any problems

	SPRING	SUMMER	AUTUMN	WINTER	height 5yrs (m)	height 10yrs (m)	spread 5yrs (m)	spread 10yrs (m)	petal colour	
Skimmia confusa 'Kew Green'	● ●		🍂 🍂 🍂		0.6	1	0.6	1		Male form; will grow in full sun
S. japonica	● ●		🍂 🍂 🍂		0.6	1	0.6	1		Can grow to 6m over a long time
S. japonica 'Fragrans'	● ●		🍂 🍂 🍂		0.6	1	0.6	1		Male form, lily-of-the-valley scent
S. japonica 'Kew White'	● ●		🍂 🍂 🍂		0.6	1	0.6	1		White-fruited form
S. japonica 'Nymans'	● ●		🍂 🍂 🍂		0.6	0.9	1	1.5		Female selection, freely fruiting
S. japonica 'Veitchii'	● ●		🍂 🍂 🍂		0.6	1	0.6	1		Brilliant red fruits; often listed as 'Formanii'
S. reevesiana 'Robert Fortune'	●		🍂 🍂 🍂		0.6	1	0.6	1		Hermaphrodite, fruits dull crimson-red

● flowering   🍂 harvest

Spiraea

For a genus with such small flowers – scarcely any have individual flowers larger than a centimetre (½in) – Spiraea makes quite a show. The reason is the sheer number of flowers. In *Spiraea japonica*, the flowers are carried at the end of the current year's shoots in many branched clusters; they are normally pink.

The forms of this species can be hard trimmed in spring and will give a magnificent display from mid- to late summer. *Spiraea japonica* also has larger leaves than found in most species and there are a number of forms selected for the colour of the foliage; in 'Candle Light' the leaves are pale yellow, in 'Fire Light' the new leaves are orange coloured before maturing to green and then turning red in autumn, whereas 'Golden Princess' does both –

Spiraea japonica 'Fire Light'

soil	Well drained soils, yet prefers moisture-retentive and of moderate fertility
site	The best position for this plant is in the sun or very light shade
general care	Spiraea is very easy to cultivate and generally maintain as they can grow in most garden soil types
pruning	*S. japonica* can be cut back hard in spring (Group 2); trim others after flowering
pests & diseases	Relatively trouble-free. Pests and diseases do not usually cause any problems

bronze-red new leaves which are bright golden yellow all summer.

In the garden, Spiraea are deciduous shrubs useful for shrub beds but can also be used for other functions, such as informal hedges of low screens. They thrive on all well drained soils. They can be propagated by seed (which is very fine and should be sown directly onto damp compost), or softwood or semi-hardwood cuttings in early summer.

	SPRING	SUMMER	AUTUMN	WINTER	height 5yrs (m)	height 10yrs (m)	spread 5yrs (m)	spread 10yrs (m)	petal colour	
Spiraea 'Arguta'	● ●				1	2	1	2		Masses of white flowers on arching branches
S. japonica 'Anthony Waterer'		● ● ●			1	1.5	1	1.5		Bronze-red leaves; when new, creamy-white
S. japonica 'Candle Light'		● ● ●			1	1.5	1	1.5		Pale yellow leaves
S. japonica 'Fire Light'		● ● ●			0.8	1	0.8	1		New foliage orange coloured
S. japonica 'Gold Mound'		● ● ●			0.5	0.8	0.5	0.8		Yellow foliage and small heads of flowers
S. japonica 'Golden Princess'		● ● ●			0.8	1.2	0.8	1.2		New leaves bronze-red, then golden yellow
S. japonica 'Little Princess'		● ● ●			0.3	0.5	0.5	1		Small green leaves
S. japonica 'Nana'		● ● ●			0.3	0.45	0.4	0.6		Small green leaves
S. nipponica 'Snowmound'	● ●				1	2	1	2		Neat upright bush to 3m
S. thunbergii	● ● ●				1	1.5	1.2	2		Dense habit, can be semi-evergreen
S. vanhouttei	●				1	2	0.8	1.5		Upright habit

● *flowering*

Stephanandra

This small genus of deciduous shrubs is related to Spiraea. The Latin name refers to the ring of anthers which are arranged like a crown around the capsule. Like its relative, Spiraea, Stephanandra's individual flowers are small, but in bloom there is more of a subtle beauty – not the 'Bridal wreath' display that is so captivating in Spiraea.

In the garden, the species of Stephanandra are useful for the neatly cut foliage, which often turns orange and other tints in autumn, and in the neat habit. *Stephanandra incisa* 'Crispa' makes a low mound of a bush to 0.6m (2ft), with crinkled leaves. It will root wherever the shoots touch the ground and can be used as ground cover; it is particularly good as ground cover in full sun but for this use it does require a moisture retentive soil.

Stephanandra tanakae is taller, making a bush to 2m (6ft) or so, with shining brown twigs and larger leaves which also turn orange in autumn. Both species are excellent on all well drained garden soils and in full sun to moderate shade. They can be propagated by softwood or semi-hardwood cuttings in summer, or by hardwood cuttings from late autumn. They often sucker and these can be removed and grown on; the same applies where they have naturally layered. *Stephanandra incisa* can also be propagated by root cuttings in early spring.

Stephanandra tanakae

soil	Well drained to moist soils, including both acidic sands and chalky soils
site	Sun to moderate shade; in full sun it needs more moisture in the soil
general care	Because this plant needs its moisture, mulch to maintain a moist and fertile soil
pruning	Prune after flowering, aiming to keep branches for up to three years (Group 1)
pests & diseases	Relatively trouble-free. Pests and diseases do not usually cause any problems

	SPRING	SUMMER	AUTUMN	WINTER	height 5yrs (m)	height 10yrs (m)	spread 5yrs (m)	spread 10yrs (m)	petal colour	
Stephanandra incisa 'Crispa'		●			0.5	0.6	1	2		Low habit; leaves lobed with wavy margin
S. tanakae		● ●			1.2	2	1.2	2		Can make 3m in height

● *flowering*

Symphoricarpos

Snowberry

These have tiny bell-shaped or funnel-shaped flowers of white and pink. Although we scarcely notice the flowers, they are rich in nectar and very attractive to bees. Where these have done their business, the fruits, in the form of white or pink berries, develop. They are ripe from autumn onwards and often last well into the new year, as they are not relished by birds.

soil	Tolerates well drained soils, including sands, gravels and chalky ones
site	Prefers to be planted in a position with sun as well as moderate shade
general care	Best in fertile soils, so mulch to maintain fertility and keep the soil moist during the summer
pruning	Little required, except to remove wayward and crossing branches
pests & diseases	Relatively trouble-free. Pests and diseases do not usually cause any problems

Bear in mind that the berries give rise to mild stomach upsets, which probably explains why birds ignore them, and their juice can irritate the skin. The berries appear to be in clusters, which is the meaning of the Latin name.

Snowberries have a number of uses in the garden. They sucker freely and are useful for filling odd corners, especially as they will grow beneath trees and in shade. They are also good ground cover in the open, generally making low spreading bushes. *Symphoricarpos chenaultii* 'Hancock' is especially good for this purpose, as are similar forms.

Symphoricarpos can also be used for informal hedging, providing colour from the fruits after the leaves have fallen in autumn. The suckering habit also makes them suitable for stabilizing banks, and they are tolerant of maritime conditions. *Symphoricarpos orbiculatus* 'Foliis Variegatus' is attractive for the small leaves which have an irregular yellow margin.

Snowberries are very tolerant of soil conditions, although most naturally occur on sands and gravels. The forms can be propagated in a variety of ways. Removal of suckers is often the easiest, but they will strike from softwood, semi-hardwood and hardwood cuttings in season.

These plants can also be grown from seed, but in order to do this the seeds must first be separated from the juicy flesh surrounding them.

Symphoricarpos chenaultii 'Hancock'

S

Flowering Shrubs

	SPRING	SUMMER	AUTUMN	WINTER	height 5yrs (m)	height 10yrs (m)	spread 5yrs (m)	spread 10yrs (m)	petal colour	
Symphoricarpos chenaultii 'Hancock'		●	🌰🌰	🌰	0.8	1.2	1	2		Fruits dark peach; useful for ground cover
S. doorenbosii 'Mother of Pearl'		● ●	🌰🌰	🌰🌰🌰	1	1.8	1.2	2.5		Arching shoots loaded with shiny white fruits
S. orbiculatus 'Foliis Variegata'		● ●	🌰		0.8	1.5	1	2		Fruits dark purple-red; best in full sun

● *flowering*   🌰 *harvest*

Teucrium
Shrubby germander

This genus contains a large number of perennials, sub-shrubs and shrubs and comes from hot dry climates. However, the only woody species commonly cultivated is *Teucrium fruticans*. This makes an evergreen bush with arching white-woolly shoots bearing fragrant grey-green leaves.

The flowers are carried in summer and are in terminal racemes. The individual flowers are pale blue in colour and have a five-lipped corolla with four protruding stamens. It is excellent in mild gardens where it can be used to make informal hedges, withstanding light clipping. In cooler settings, it is best in a sheltered spot in a shrub bed or against a wall. It needs good drainage and full sun.

Teucrium can be propagated by seeds or by softwood or semi-hardwood cuttings in summer.

Teucrium fruticans

Ulex
Gorse

Gorse is a common shrub of lowland heath and waste ground. It has distinctly spiny – some would say viciously spiny – shoots and almost no leaves. Photosynthesis is carried out through the green shoots. It is either a valued shrub for wild barren places or a weed.

Few consciously cultivate it for their gardens, although the quality and quantity of flower is outstanding, with open flowers present at all times of the year in mild maritime areas. The plant featured here, whilst it is a form of the common *Ulex europaeus*, is a sterile double flowered form, 'Flore Pleno'. It also has the benefit of making a smaller and more compact bush, holding the flowers for longer. It will grow on any neutral to acidic soil but is best on the most barren sands and gravels; on fertile sites it will become lank and dismal. It demands full sunlight, or no more than light shade.

Ulex europaeus 'Flore Pleno'

soil	Teucrium: any well drained soil. Ulex: barren sand and gravels – not too fertile
site	Teucrium: prefers a sunny position. Ulex: likewise, but will tolerate light shade
general care	Teucrium: needs to have shelter in cooler gardens. Ulex: watch out for the spiny shoots
pruning	Teucrium: Can be hard pruned in late winter (Group 2). Ulex: clip after main flowering
pests & diseases	Both are relatively trouble-free. Pests and diseases do not usually cause them any problems

	SPRING	SUMMER	AUTUMN	WINTER	height 5yrs (m)	height 10yrs (m)	spread 5yrs (m)	spread 10yrs (m)	petal colour	
Teucrium fruticans		● ● ●			0.6	1	1	2		Evergreen; aromatic grey-green leaves
T. fruticans 'Azureum'		● ● ●			0.6	1	1	2		Selection with darker blue flowers
Ulex europaeus 'Flore Pleno'	● ●				0.6	0.8	0.7	1		Sterile form with semi-double flowers

● flowering

Vaccinium

Blueberry *or*
Blaeberry
or Bilberry

These members of the Ericaceae or Heather family have small white bell-shaped flowers, sometimes with a pink tinge. The fruit is a violet blue berry (but ranging from black to stunning turquoise in different species) which is edible and widely used, such as for flavouring yoghurts.

In the garden, the taller growing bilberries, such as *Vaccinium corymbosum*, are frequently consigned to the fruit garden. However, their colourful flower and attractive autumn colour make them highly suited to the shrub border. The cowberry, *Vaccinium vitis-idaea*, is a small ground cover form with small, deciduous box-like foliage and red berries. The other two are also evergreen; *Vaccinium floribundum* has attractive new foliage. *Vaccinium glauco-album* has leaves which are a vivid blue-white on the underside and grey-green on the top.

The requirement which all Vaccinium share is for a fertile, acidic and generally moist soil. They will take full sun if they have sufficient soil moisture but are better in light shade. Some species thrive in bog conditions. In the garden they can be used in borders, with the smaller species such as *Vaccinium glauco-album* and *Vaccinium vitis-idaea*, used as ground cover.

soil	Enjoys acidic fertile or sandy soils, but avoid lime or chalky conditions
site	Prefers to be planted in a position with sun as well as moderate shade
general care	Generally fine as long as you feed with Ericaceous fertilizer to maintain an acidic soil
pruning	Minor tidying or reshaping only should be required, no drastic cutting back
pests & diseases	Relatively trouble-free. Pests and diseases do not usually cause any problems

Vaccinium arctostaphylos

Vaccinium cylindraceum

	SPRING	SUMMER	AUTUMN	WINTER	height 5yrs (m)	height 10yrs (m)	spread 5yrs (m)	spread 10yrs (m)	petal colour	
Vaccinium arctostaphylos		● ● 🥜	🥜		1	1.5	1	1.5		Deciduous shrub
V. cylindraceum		●	● 🥜		1	1.5	0.8	1.2		Semi-evergreen; flowers green red-tinged
V. corymbosum	●	●	🥜 🥜		1	1.5	1	1.5		Deciduous shrub; fruit tasty, edible, blue-black
V. floribundum		●	🥜 🥜		0.7	1	1	1.5		Red fruit; evergreen shrub
V. glauco-album	●	●	🥜 🥜		0.3	0.5	0.7	1		Suckering spreading shrub; fruit blue-black
V. vitis-idaea	●	●	🥜 🥜		0.2	0.2	0.7	1		Creeping deciduous shrub; fruit bright red

● *flowering*   🥜 *harvest*

Viburnum
Guelder rose

This genus contains perhaps 150 different species, plus many garden forms. They are grown in the garden for a number of reasons. All of them have attractive flowers in large corymbs; in many the flowers give off a pleasing perfume which scents the garden air.

Viburnum rhytidophyllum

Viburnum farreri and its hybrid *Viburnum bodnantense* are useful for flowering over the winter period, and are well sited if positioned so that the scent can drift indoors. Even more attractive in flower are the several forms of *Viburnum burkwoodii* and *Viburnum carlesii*. These make medium sized evergreen shrubs which are very fragrant when in bloom in the first half of the year. However, not all the species have fragrant flowers to attract pollinators. There are species which mimic the gaudy ray-florets seen in Hydrangea to draw attention to otherwise less striking blooms. *Viburnum plicatum* has several very floriferous forms of this type, making tiered branches with the showy flowers standing above. This flower type is also seen in the guelder rose, *Viburnum opulus*.

Viburnum are also very attractive in fruit. This ranges in colour from red, such as in guelder rose, *Viburnum opulus*, turquoise in *Viburnum davidii* and red, ripening to black, in *Viburnum rhytidophyllum*. When growing Viburnum for their fruiting effect, always plant two or three different plants to ensure adequate cross-pollination. This is especially important with *Viburnum davidii*, where some forms appear to be predominantly male or female.

Viburnum come as both deciduous species and as evergreen species. The deciduous ones are useful for their often striking autumn colour, with species such as

soil	Well drained, moderately fertile soils, including chalky ones
site	Prefers to be positioned in a sunny site with moderate shade
general care	Easy to cultivate and look after. Mulch to maintain soil fertility and to conserve moisture
pruning	Hard, in spring/after flowering, to remove weak, damaged or crossing branches
pests & diseases	Aphids and honey fungus can cause problems, but apart from these, relatively trouble-free

Viburnum burkwoodii

Viburnum plicatum 'Pink Beauty'

wayfaring tree (*Viburnum lantana*), giving rich maroon colours. The evergreens provide foliage throughout the year, with *Viburnum rhytidophyllum* having some particularly bold foliage.

In the garden, Viburnum can be used in shrub beds and in woodland gardens, where the taller growing forms, such as *Viburnum*

V

Flowering Shrubs

Viburnum carlesii

rhytidophyllum, can make small trees. They can also be used as ground cover – *Viburnum davidii* once established will smother weeds and produce its exquisite fruits on the large and curiously veined leaves. *Viburnum bodnantense*, *Viburnum farreri* and *Viburnum tinus*, are valuable for the flowers which are carried during the winter period. *Viburnum plicatum* and its forms are especially attractive either as specimen shrubs or in a prominent bed.

Viburnum thrive on all well drained soils, tolerating chalky sites as well as acidic ones. They are much better on fertile sites, but they will grow in full sun to moderate shade. Viburnums can be raised from seed, or from cuttings, either softwood or semi-hardwood in summer. They can also be layered.

	SPRING	SUMMER	AUTUMN	WINTER	height 5yrs (m)	height 10yrs (m)	spread 5yrs (m)	spread 10yrs (m)	petal colour	
Viburnum bodnantense 'Charles Lamont'	flowering		flowering	flowering	1	1.5	0.6	1		Upright deciduous bush
V. bodnantense 'Dawn'	flowering		flowering	flowering	1	1.5	0.6	1		Upright deciduous bush
V. bodnantense 'Deben'				flowering	1	1.5	0.6	1		Upright deciduous bush
V. burkwoodii	flowering		harvest		1	1.5	1	1.5		Evergreen shrub, fragrant flowers
V. burkwoodii 'Anne Russell'	flowering		harvest		1	1.5	0.8	1.2		Deciduous shrub; fragrant flowers
V. burkwoodii 'Park Farm Hybrid'	flowering		harvest		1	1.5	1	1.5		Evergreen shrub; some turn red/orange in autumn
V. carlesii	flowering		harvest		1	1.5	1	1.5		Deciduous shrub often turning red in autumn
V. carlesii 'Aurora'	flowering		harvest		1	1.5	1	1.5		Flowers pink, red in bud
V. cinnamonifolium		flowering	harvest		1.2	2	1.2	2		Evergreen shrub or small tree, can make 5m
V. davidii		flowering	harvest		0.6	1	0.8	1.2		Shrub with three-veined leaves, fruit turquoise
V. farreri	flowering		harvest		1.2	2	1	1.5		Deciduous shrub; fruit red berry
V. farreri 'Candidissima'		flowering	harvest		1.2	2	1	1.5		White flowered form with green new leaves
V. globosum 'Jermyns Globe'		flowering	harvest		1.2	2	1.2	2		Metallic blue fruits
V. hillieri 'Winton'		flowering	harvest		1.2	2	1	1.5		New foliage copper coloured, fruit red
V. lantana		flowering	harvest		1.2	2	1	1.5		Deciduous shrub giving good autumn colour
V. opulus		flowering	harvest		1.2	2	1	1.5		Deciduous shrub, leaves lobed like many acers
V. opulus 'Aureum'		flowering	harvest		1	1.5	0.9	1.2		Deciduous; leaves tend to burn if in full sun
V. opulus 'Compactum'		flowering	harvest		0.8	1.2	0.8	1.2		Deciduous; dwarf form
V. plicatum 'Lanarth'		flowering			1.2	1.8	1	1.8		Deciduous; large sterile flower heads
V. plicatum 'Mariesii'		flowering			1.2	1.8	1	1.8		Deciduous; tiered branches; few fruits
V. plicatum 'Pink Beauty'		flowering			1.2	1.8	1	1.8		Deciduous; flowers turn pinkish tinge with age
V. 'Pragense'		flowering			1.2	1.8	1	1.8		Evergreen shrub to 3m in height
V. rhytidophyllum		flowering			1.2	1.8	1	1.8		Evergreen; leaves with impressed veins, glossy
V. tinus	flowering	harvest		flowering	1.2	1.8	1	1.8		Evergreen shrub, to 3m or so in height
V. tinus 'Purpureum'	flowering	harvest		flowering	1.2	1.8	1	1.8		Young foliage dark, bronzy purple

flowering   harvest

Vinca
Periwinkle

These make trailing shrubs or sub-shrubs and are evergreen, thus providing useful ground cover, although they can become invasive. They will grow happily in full sun to quite dense shade, spreading widely and rooting as they go.

soil	All garden soils except those which become seriously dry in summer
site	Sun for flowering – sun or moderate shade for ground cover
general care	To prevent these plants becoming invasive in the garden, cut back hard in spring
pruning	The only pruning required is cutting them back to control their spread
pests & diseases	Apart from being prone to rust fungi, these are relatively trouble-free from pests and diseases

The flowers can be quite showy, with the petals joined into a tube with five widely spreading or star-like lobes. In colour they are usually bright blue, but dark plum-purple in *Vinca minor* 'Atropurpurea', lavender-blue in *Vinca minor* 'La Grave', and white, in *Vinca minor* form *alba* and 'Gertrude Jekyll'. Flowering can be rather sparse and spasmodic in shade and in this respect they are much happier when in full sun. The flowers are carried over an extended period, from late spring into autumn. The Greater periwinkle, *Vinca major*, grows up to 0.5m (20in) in height, and can go even higher when it can 'prop' itself against a wall. The Lesser periwinkle, *Vinca minor*, is lower growing, rarely taller than 0.2m (8in) and makes a better ground cover for shade.

Vincas thrive on almost all soils, except those which are too dry. They are very easily propagated, either by division or separation of pieces that have rooted as they wander, which should be carried out either in autumn or spring, or by taking cuttings in summer.

Vinca minor 'La Grave'

	SPRING	SUMMER	AUTUMN	WINTER	height 5yrs (m)	height 10yrs (m)	spread 5yrs (m)	spread 10yrs (m)	petal colour	
Vinca major		● ● ● ●	●		0.4	0.4	1	2		Evergreen; can spread indefinitely
V. major 'Variegata'		● ● ● ●	●		0.4	0.4	1	2		Leaves richly margined creamy white
V. minor	● ●	● ● ● ●	●		0.2	0.2	1	2		Low growing evergreen
V. minor forma alba	● ●	● ● ● ●	●		0.2	0.2	1	2		White-flowered form
V. minor 'Argenteovariegata'	● ●	● ● ● ●	●		0.2	0.2	1	2		Leaves blotched with white
V. minor 'Atropurpurea'	● ●	● ● ● ●	●		0.2	0.2	1	2		The flowers have an almost black sheen
V. minor 'Gertrude Jekyll'	● ●	● ● ● ●	●		0.2	0.2	1	2		Compact form
V. minor 'La Grave'	● ●	● ● ● ●	●		0.2	0.2	1	2		Large flowers

Flowering Shrubs

 flowering

Vitex
Chaste-tree

This shrub needs a warm site to give its best, as the flowers are only produced at the end of hot summers.

The flowers are violet and fragrant. The leaves are palmate with five or seven separate leaflets, resembling the leaf of cannabis. Whilst they also have an aromatic pungent odour, the only reported medicinal benefit is the use of the seeds in the past to cure venereal diseases. They should be located in full sun in a well drained soil, and in the wild are characteristically found on river gravels. They can be propagated by semi-hardwood cuttings in summer.

Vitex agnus-castus

soil	Vitex: any well drained soil, both acidic and chalky. Weigela: well drained, fertile
site	Vitex: in the hottest spot for best flowering. Weigela: sun to light shade
general care	Vitex: remove any winter cold damaged shoots in spring. Weigela: fertilize for maximum flower production
pruning	Vitex: prune hard in spring (Group 2). Weigela: cut back to ground level after flowering
pests & diseases	Vitex: relatively trouble-free from pests and diseases. Weigela: general pests of woody plants

Weigela and Diervilla

Weigela has regular flowers born on short leafy twigs on last year's wood, whereas the related genus Diervilla has flowers which are distinctly two-lipped and are carried at the end of the current season's growths.

Weigela has been included in Diervilla in the past and may occasionally be found under this name. They are related to the

Weigela 'Eva Rathke'

honeysuckles. In the garden Weigela is useful for the spring or early summer flowers, adding colour to shrub beds. *Weigela florida* 'Variegata' is one of the best variegated types of these plants. Weigelas require good drainage and fertile soils for the best results.

	SPRING	SUMMER	AUTUMN	WINTER	height 5yrs (m)	height 10yrs (m)	spread 5yrs (m)	spread 10yrs (m)	petal colour	
Vitex agnus-castus			● ●		2	3	2	3		Deciduous shrub, useful for autumn flowering
Diervilla sessiflora		● ● ●			0.8	1.5	1	1.5		Deciduous suckering shrub
D. splendens		● ● ●			0.8	1.5	1	1.5		Deciduous suckering shrub
Weigela 'Briant Rubidor'	● ●				1	2	1	2		Best in light shade; deciduous shrub
W. 'Eva Rathke'	● ●				1	1.5	1	1.5		Dark crimson flowers
W. florida 'Variegata'	● ●				1	2	1	2		Deciduous, leaves grey-green, white margin
W. middendorfiana	● ●				0.9	1.5	0.9	1.5		Deciduous; leaves fresh green
Weigela 'Victoria'	● ●				1	1.8	1	1.8		Deciduous; leaves fresh green

● *flowering*

Flowering Shrubs

Xanthoceras

This deciduous plant makes a shrub or occasionally a small tree. It has pinnate leaves and thrives on hot, dry very sunny sites.

The chief beauty is provided by the flowers. These are bell-shaped, 2.5cm (1in) across, with star-shaped petals. In colour they are white with a carmine eye and are carried in erect panicles on last year's shoots, thereby somewhat resembling the horse chestnut.

The fruit is a three-valved capsule. This makes an excellent flowering shrub for suitable sites. It will grow on a wide range of soil types, including acidic ones and chalky sites. The simplest method of propagation is seed, but where this is not available the plants can be raised from root cuttings. Suckers can also be removed.

Xanthoceras sorbifolium

soil	Xanthoceras: well-drained, both acidic and chalky. Zenobia: acidic, fertile soils
site	Xanthoceras: prefers to be in the sun. Zenobia: enjoys both the sun and light shade
general care	Xanthoceras: needs sunny site to flower well next year. Zenobia: remove flowing shoot tips after flowering
pruning	No pruning needed for either plant, except to control or reshape Zenobia
pests & diseases	Both plants are relatively trouble-free. Pests and diseases do not usually cause any problems

Zenobia

This shrub is in the heather family and needs an acidic site with a fertile soil which does not dry out in summer.

Zenobia pulverulenta

The flowers are bell-shaped, like large lily-of-the-valley flowers, and are also fragrant. Zenobia makes a shrub to 2m (6ft) and is either deciduous or semi-evergreen. The new foliage has a glaucous-white bloom. In the garden it can be sited in either full sun or light shade, but if the soil dries out, or it is not possible to give adequate watering in summer, it is best in some shade. It can be propagated by sowing the small seeds onto the top of damp compost, but semi-hardwood cuttings in mid-summer allow the best forms to be grown.

X
Z

	SPRING	SUMMER	AUTUMN	WINTER	height 5yrs (m)	height 10yrs (m)	spread 5yrs (m)	spread 10yrs (m)	petal colour	
Xanthoceras sorbifolium	●	●	🌰 🌰		1.2	2.5	1	2	☐	Deciduous shrub for hot sunny sites
Zenobia pulverulenta		● ●			1	1.8	0.9	1.5	☐	Deciduous/semi-evergreen; fragrant flowers

Flowering Shrubs

● flowering   🌰 harvest

Heaths, Heathers & Ling

The heathers are a rather uniform group of plants which belong to several genera in the botanical family of Ericaceae. The genera covered here are Calluna, Cassiope, Daboecia and Erica. The reasons for giving the heathers a separate section is that they have very similar requirements in terms of soil, site and care, and that they are mostly grown as low ground cover plants.

Some other members of this family have been featured on earlier pages, most notably the four pages of Rhododendron. The entry on the opposite page, Zenobia, also belongs to the family. These make larger plants and can be associated with a wide range of other plants. They fit well into shrub and mixed beds and do not need planting in large drifts in order to be effective.

Most heathers require fertile, acidic conditions. This is universally true of all the above genera except that there are a number of species in Erica which will grow happily on neutral to alkaline soils. They like adequate soil moisture but do not really like it too wet. Even the native forms which seem to be growing on boggy conditions will usually be found to be growing on a small hummock which raises them above the swamp, and some of them actually have specialized adaptations for the day when their bog dries out.

Heathers need to be associated in drifts. Single plants of this and that variety rarely look better than neglected urchins. Depending upon the space available, think in terms of five to ten plants as a minimum for each variety in a block. Unless you buy large plants, five to ten plants will cover only a single square metre (yard).

Some plants associate very well with heathers. Some of the Clematis, especially the *Clematis texensis* forms and hybrids, such as 'Gravetye Beauty', can look very good wandering through a planting of heathers. Another choice shrub which can be planted with them to provide flower, white berries and autumn leaf colour is *Sorbus reducta*.

Calluna
Ling, Heather

Calluna is closely related to Erica, although its calyx is coloured and longer than the petals, and it has four small bracts at its base. The genus comprises only the single species, *Calluna vulgaris*. The species is widespread, being found in Europe, as far east as Siberia, and down to Morocco and the Azores.

This species likes dry acidic conditions, and has been found growing on soil with a pH of 1.9 (most plants fail below a pH of 4.5). It can, perversely, also be found growing on the top of chalk downland, but it only survives there because it can grow in pockets of acidic clay above the chalk. In the garden it is valuable as ground cover and for planting in drifts. The flowers are carried on the current season's growths from mid-summer into mid-autumn. They are purplish-pink and rich in nectar, making excellent honey. There are also white

Calluna vulgaris 'Spring Cream'

soil	This plant tolerates any acidic, well drained soil type
site	Prefers sun; in shade it becomes lank and dismal. Also tolerates salt spray
general care	Weed carefully when establishing the plant to ensure that no perennial woods gain a foothold
pruning	Trim in spring before growth begins, removing last summer's dead flowerheads
pests & diseases	Phytophthora root rot can cause problems on waterlogged soils; also prone to grey mould

Calluna vulgaris 'Spring Torch'

flowered forms in cultivation. Its flowers are not the only reason for growing Calluna. Many of the garden selections have gold, red or other coloured foliage, giving colour to the bold drifts at all seasons of the year.

Calluna will grow vigorously on fertile soils, but soon becomes lanky and fit only for

	SPRING	SUMMER	AUTUMN	WINTER	height 5yrs (m)	height 10yrs (m)	spread 5yrs (m)	spread 10yrs (m)	petal colour	
Calluna vulgaris 'Anniemarie'		●●	●●	●	0.3	0.5	0.4	0.6		Double flowers, good for cutting
C. vulgaris 'County Wicklow'		●●	●●	●	0.15	0.25	0.25	0.35		Double flowers, prostrate habit
C. vulgaris 'Dark Beauty'		●●	●●	●	0.15	0.25	0.3	0.45		Dark green foliage
C. vulgaris 'Firefly'		●●	●●	●	0.3	0.45	0.3	0.45		Terracotta foliage in summer, red in winter
C. vulgaris 'Flamingo'		●●	●●	●	0.2	0.3	0.2	0.3		New foliage in spring is pink or red tipped
C. vulgaris 'H.E. Beale'		●●	●●	●	0.3	0.5	0.4	0.6		Double flowers, good for cutting; clay soils
C. vulgaris 'J.H. Hamilton'		●●	●●	●	0.1	0.1	0.15	0.25		Dwarf form with double flowers
C. vulgaris 'Robert Chapman'		●●	●●	●	0.15	0.25	0.4	0.65		Double flowers; foliage gold in summer
C. vulgaris 'Silver Knight'		●●	●●	●	0.3	0.4	0.2	0.25		Downy silver-grey foliage; purple-grey in winter
C. vulgaris 'Spring Cream'		●●	●●	●	0.3	0.3	0.4	0.45		Mid-green foliage, cream-tipped in spring
C. vulgaris 'Spring Torch'		●●	●●	●	0.25	0.4	0.4	0.6		Green leaves – cream, orange/red tips in spring
C. vulgaris 'Wickwar Flame'		●●	●●	●	0.3	0.5	0.4	0.65		Gold foliage, turning red in winter

● *flowering*

making into besom brooms. It can be regularly clipped in spring before the new growth starts and this will enable plants on lush sites to be kept going for a number of years. However, it is at its best when growing on a poor substrate, such as sandy gravels and acidic rubble, with some organic matter added. A few forms, such as 'H.E. Beale', will grow satisfactorily on clay but it is happier with good drainage.

On soils of low fertility, it is predominantly a shrub 20–50cm (8–18in) in height, but on rich soils or when drawn up in shade it may make 0.9m (3ft). The forms are easily propagated by taking semi-hardwood cuttings in summer, using shoots about 5cm (2in) in length. Established plants can also be layered.

Cassiope

This genus has small wiry shoots which carry disproportionately large white bell-shaped flowers in late spring or summer. They are low shrubs, rarely more than 15cm (6in) in height.

Cassiope demand a moist humus-rich site, such as a choice spot in a rock garden. When well grown, they are most attractive and worth the effort, but they do require plenty of moisture during the growing season and will not tolerate any chalk or lime in the soil. They will grow in either full sun, especially if kept moist, or in partial shade, and are best in a sheltered spot. They can be

Cassiope 'Muirhead'

soil	These shrubs prefer moist, humus-rich, acidic soils
site	Sun with moist soil; partial shade if soil only damp with side shelter
general care	Keep adequately moist during the summer but without waterlogging the plants
pruning	No pruning or cutting back is required for this particular shrub, unless reshaping
pests & diseases	Relatively trouble-free. Pests and diseases do not usually cause any problems

propagated by softwood or semi-hardwood cuttings in summer, preferably rooting them under mist. They can also be layered.

	SPRING	SUMMER	AUTUMN	WINTER	height 5yrs (m)	height 10yrs (m)	spread 5yrs (m)	spread 10yrs (m)	petal colour	
Cassiope 'Badenoch'	●	●			0.1	0.1	0.1	0.1		Low, mound-forming habit
C. 'Edinburgh'	●				0.1	0.2	0.1	0.2		Perhaps the easiest of the Cassiope to grow
C. 'Muirhead'	●				0.1	0.1	0.1	0.1		Low, mound-forming habit
C. 'Randle Cooke'	●				0.1	0.15	0.1	0.2		Mat-forming

 flowering

Daboecia
St Daboc's heath

These dwarf evergreen shrubs have urn-shaped flowers which are carried in small racemes above the foliage from early summer into late autumn.

Daboecia require acidic humus-rich soils with good drainage for their best growth; although they will not tolerate lime, they will survive in neutral soils. In the garden, they are useful for ground cover and in

soil		Well drained humus-rich acidic to neutral soils, but not soil with lime
site		The most preferable site would be in the sun or partial shade
general care		Easy to care for provided you ensure that they are kept moist and do not dry out during the summer
pruning		Clip in the early spring to shape and remove spent flowerheads
pests & diseases		Phytophthora root rot can be a problem, but apart from that, these plants are fairly trouble-free

drifts in heather beds. They are best in full sun, but will cope with partial shade. They are propagated by semi-hardwood cuttings in summer.

Daboecia cantabrica f. *alba*

	SPRING	SUMMER	AUTUMN	WINTER	height 5yrs (m)	height 10yrs (m)	spread 5yrs (m)	spread 10yrs (m)	petal colour	
Daboecia cantabrica f. *alba*		● ● ●	● ● ●		0.2	0.4	0.3	0.5	☐	Dark glossy green leaves
D. cantabrica 'William Buchanan'		● ● ●	● ● ●		0.2	0.4	0.3	0.5	■	Purple-crimson flowers

Erica
Heather

This is the most variable of the heathers, and also the largest genus, with some 700 species. Most of these are found in southern Africa and are not hardy. The plant's main features are its prominent bell-shaped corolla, which does not fall but withers as a brown corpse around the developing seed vessel, and the leaves, which are carried in whorls.

Erica erigena 'Irish Dusk'

The majority of the species in cultivation fit with the other heathers. They are suitable for planting in drifts – either with others of their sort or other varieties – or with dwarf conifers. These forms are low growing. Most of these forms demand acidic conditions, being best on moist but well to reasonably drained soils. However, there are a number of species which defy the common family abhorrence of lime and will grow, even thrive, on chalky soil. These include *Erica carnea*, *Erica darleyensis* and *Erica erigena*. This group of

Erica vagans 'Mrs D.F. Maxwell'

● flowering

Erica darleyensis 'Kramer's Rote'

Erica darleyensis 'Silberschmelze'

species (which will also grow on acidic soils) are also useful in their flowering period, from late autumn into mid-spring.

However, not all Ericas are only small growing shrubs. Some can make quite sizeable small trees. The commonly cultivated species in this group is *Erica arborea*, which will make 6m (20ft) or so in height with an open sprawling habit. The forms 'Albert's Gold' and 'Estrella Gold' have bright yellow new foliage. These

forms, however, require soils on the acidic side of neutral.

Ericas are plants of sun, doing far less well in more than the lightest shade. They do like adequate soil moisture, but not boggy conditions. These plants are propagated by semi-hardwood cuttings in summer.

soil	Well drained soils; most require acidic conditions but some tolerate chalky soils
site	For best results, plant in a warm, sunny position in the garden
general care	Adequate water during the summer; feed with a half-strength liquid fertilizer every month in summer
pruning	Trim before growth begins for summer flowering species and at the end of flowering for others
pests & diseases	Phytophthora root rot can affect these shrubs on wet sites, so avoid over-watering

	SPRING	SUMMER	AUTUMN	WINTER	height 5yrs (m)	height 10yrs (m)	spread 5yrs (m)	spread 10yrs (m)	petal colour	
Erica arborea var. *alpina*	● ●				1	6	0.4	0.8		Needs acidic conditions; flower honey-scented
E. arborea 'Albert's Gold'					1	2	0.4	0.8		Needs acidic conditions; rarely flowers
E. arborea 'Estrella Gold'	● ●				0.6	1.2	0.4	0.75		Needs acidic conditions; foliage lime-green
E. carnea 'Ann Sparkes'	● ●			●	0.15	0.15	0.3	0.45		Grows on both acidic and mildly alkaline soils
E. carnea 'Foxhollow'	● ●			●	0.15	0.15	0.3	0.4		Grows on both acidic and mildly alkaline soils
E. carnea 'Myretoun Ruby'	● ●			●	0.15	0.15	0.3	0.45		Grows on both acidic and mildly alkaline soils
E. carnea 'Springwood Pink'	● ●			●	0.15	0.15	0.3	0.4		Grows on both acidic and mildly alkaline soils
E. carnea 'Springwood White'	● ●			●	0.15	0.15	0.3	0.45		Grows on both acidic and mildly alkaline soils
E. carnea 'Vivelli'	● ●			●	0.15	0.15	0.3	0.45		Grows on both acidic and mildly alkaline soils
E. cinerea 'C.D. Eason'		● ●	● ●		0.3	0.6	0.4	0.7		Needs acidic conditions
E. cinerea 'Pink Ice'		● ●	● ●		0.1	0.2	0.2	0.35		Needs acidic conditions; deep green foliage
E. darleyensis 'Arthur Johnson'	● ●			●	0.15	0.3	0.3	0.6		Grows on both acidic and mildly alkaline soils
E. darleyensis 'Darley Dale'	● ●			●	0.15	0.3	0.3	0.5		Grows on both acidic and mildly alkaline soils
E. darleyensis 'Kramer's Rote'	● ●			●	0.15	0.3	0.3	0.6		Will grow on both acidic and alkaline soils
E. darleyensis 'Silberschmelze'	● ●			●	0.15	0.3	0.3	0.6		Will grow on both acidic and alkaline soils
E. erigena 'Irish Dusk'	● ● ●		● ●	● ●	0.3	0.6	0.3	0.45		Will grow on both acidic and alkaline soils
E. erigena 'W.T. Ratcliff'	● ● ●				0.45	0.75	0.3	0.55		Will grow on both acidic and alkaline soils
E. vagans 'Mrs D.F. Maxwell'		● ●	● ●		0.15	0.3	0.3	0.45		Needs acidic conditions
E. vagans 'Valerie Proudley'		● ●	● ●		0.1	0.15	0.2	0.3		Needs acidic conditions; foliage bright yellow

● *flowering*

Dwarf Conifers

Few dwarf conifers have flowers or fruits, but they are nonetheless valuable in the flowering garden and provide a number of useful functions. The range of size of 'dwarf conifers' varies from real pygmy varieties, which grow perhaps a centimetre (⅓in) per annum, to slow growing forms which may make 5m (16ft) to even 10m (33ft), only doing so much less quickly than the normal forms of the same species. The real pygmy forms are only suitable for alpine houses. The forms featured in this section cover plants making 25cm (10in) in ten years, up to those making a couple of metres (6ft) in ten years. The larger growing conifers are featured in a companion volume in this series, *Trees & Shrubs*.

Dwarf conifers have pronounced form, whether flat and ground hugging as in *Juniperus horizontalis*, or conical with twisted silver leaves (needles), as in *Abies koreana* 'Silberlocke'. Most are evergreen, as are all the forms listed here. However, there are a few uncommon dwarf forms of deciduous conifers, especially of the larches (Larix). Apart from habit forms, the great value of dwarf conifers is in the variety of their foliage colours. These are mainly golds or glaucous blues.

Dwarf conifers can be used as specimen plants. They can be set in a sea of grass, but are much better if the medium is gravel – if nothing else, at least it does not need cutting! They can also be used with paving, or to cover manholes, and they associate very effectively with heathers and dwarf shrubs. Dwarf conifers can also be used with larger growing shrubs, especially the taller growing forms, but care is needed to ensure that the dwarf conifers are not smothered. They can also be used in pots on a patio. Perhaps the best conifer for this use is *Platycladus orientalis* (still often sold as *Thuja orientalis*), which will relish hot dry conditions.

Some dwarf conifers are inclined to revert, producing shoots of normal vigour. Generally these shoots should be removed, although when the normally prostrate *Abies nordmanniana* 'Golden Spreader' forms a normal leader, my response is to keep the leader and enjoy the delight of a miniature upright form of this vigorous species.

Abies
Silver fir

The silver firs have given only a few dwarf forms but these include three of the very best. The forms listed here prefer an acidic soil.

The two dwarf forms of *Abies balsamea*, 'Hudsonia' and 'Nana' both make irregularly rounded small bushes, to a metre (3ft) in thirty years. The slow growing *Abies koreana* 'Silberlocke' has the needles twisted so that the glaucous white underside is revealed. *Abies lasiocarpa* 'Arizonica Compacta' is also slow growing rather than truly dwarf and makes a typical conical silver fir. Its great beauty is in its blue-grey leaves.

  Dwarf forms of silver fir are best in full sun but will tolerate light shade. They can be propagated by cuttings of two year old shoots taken in mid-winter and put in a frame, preferably with heat from beneath.

Abies koreana 'Silberlocke'

soil	Abies: acidic to neutral soils, including clays. Cedrus: acidic to chalky, including clays
site	Abies: sun or light shade. Cedrus: sun; will grow in light shade but performs badly
general care	Abies: keep weeds under control, feed and mulch to maintain healthy foliage. Cedrus: mulch to keep moist
pruning	Abies: remove any aberrant shoots. Cedrus: no pruning required
pests & diseases	Abies: aphids and red spider mite can be a problem. Cedrus: can be troubled by honey fungus

Cedrus
Cedar

The cedars will grow on chalk and limestone, as well as on acidic soils. Once established, they withstand drought. They need full sunlight and will not make satisfactory plants in shade. The dwarf forms share these characteristics.

Cedrus deodara 'Feelin' Blue'

Those which are part of *Cedrus deodara* have pendulous tips to the shoots and long needles. In 'Feelin' Blue' the plant makes a rather flat bush with blue-grey foliage. 'Golden Horizon' is also spreading and flat topped but with golden foliage. *Cedrus libani* 'Sargentii' is also a pendulous selection of a tree which normally has an upright or spreading habit.

	SPRING	SUMMER	AUTUMN	WINTER	height 5yrs (m)	height 10yrs (m)	spread 5yrs (m)	spread 10yrs (m)	petal colour	
Abies balsamea 'Hudsonia'					0.3	0.6	0.3	0.6		Forms dense, irregular mound with flat top
A. koreana 'Silberlocke'	●	◎ ◎ ◎ ◎			0.7	1.2	0.5	1	▨	Slow growing; produces violet-blue cones
A. lasiocarpa 'Arizonica Compacta'					0.7	1.2	0.5	1		Conical habit with blue-grey foliage
A. nordmanniana 'Golden Spreader'					0.3	0.6	0.3	0.6		Slow growing form, light golden yellow foliage
Cedrus deodara 'Feelin' Blue'					0.4	0.6	0.6	0.8		Blue-grey foliage
C. deodara 'Golden Horizon'					0.4	0.6	0.6	0.8		Yellow-green foliage, blue-green in shade
C. libani 'Sargentii'					0.4	0.6	0.6	0.8		Needs training, otherwise sprawls over ground

● *flowering*   ◎ *harvest*

Chamaecyparis

Cypress

The cypresses form tall trees and have given rise to a large number of cultivars. Many of these are tree forms, but that still leaves some hundreds of dwarf and slow growing forms. Foliage colour ranges from gold, such as in *Chamaecyparis obtusa* 'Crippsii', through silvery glaucous, as in *Chamaecyparis lawsoniana* 'Bleu Nantais', to steel-blue in *Chamaecyparis pisifera* 'Boulevard'. These all make conical bushes, with the last two in particular being slow growing rather than dwarf.

Forms which make a dwarf rounded bush to 1m (3ft) in height include *Chamaecyparis lawsoniana* 'Gimbornii' and *Chamaecyparis lawsoniana* 'Minima Glauca' – although they will take 25 years to make this height! Both of these have glaucous blue-green foliage.

Chamaecyparis lawsoniana 'Gimbornii'

Chamaecyparis thyoides 'Rubicon', has a similar growth rate and grey-green juvenile foliage which turns deep plum-purple in winter. Much more distinctive, and very attractive when well grown, is *Chamaecyparis*

Chamaecyparis lawsoniana 'Ellwood's Pillar'

pisifera 'Filifera Aurea'; the foliage here is not in flattened sprays but is reduced to golden-yellow whip-like strands which are pendulous under their own weight.

	SPRING	SUMMER	AUTUMN	WINTER	height 5yrs (m)	height 10yrs (m)	spread 5yrs (m)	spread 10yrs (m)	petal colour	
Chamaecyparis lawsoniana 'Bleu Nantais'					1	1.5	0.4	0.7		Conical habit with vivid silvery-blue foliage
C. lawsoniana 'Broomhill Gold'					1.2	2.5	0.4	0.8		Narrow columnar habit, bright gold foliage
C. lawsoniana 'Chilworth Silver'					1	1.5	0.4	0.7		Broadly columnar, dense, silvery blue foliage
C. lawsoniana 'Ellwood's Gold'					1	1.5	0.4	0.6		Columnar form, yellow foliage at tips of shoots
C. lawsoniana 'Ellwood's Pillar'					1	1.5	0.3	0.5		Narrow columnar form, blue-grey foliage
C. lawsoniana 'Ellwoodii'	●				1.2	2.5	0.5	0.8	■	Feathery grey-green foliage; can make 10m
C. lawsoniana 'Gimbornii'					0.3	0.5	0.4	0.7		Globose form to 1m by 1.2m
C. lawsoniana 'Minima Glauca'					0.3	0.5	0.3	0.5		Sea-green foliage, dense
C. obtusa 'Crippsii'	●				1	1.5	0.8	1.2	■	Rich, golden yellow foliage in fern-like sprays
C. obtusa 'Fernspray Gold'	●				1	2	0.7	1.2	■	Foliage in golden-yellow fern-like sprays
C. obtusa 'Nana Aurea'					0.25	0.4	0.25	0.4		Golden yellow foliage, dome shaped habit
C. obtusa 'Nana Gracilis'					1	1.5	0.4	0.7		Conical habit, foliage in flat dark green sprays
C. pisifera 'Boulevard'					1	2	0.5	0.8		Needs moist soil or develops brown patches
C. pisifera 'Filifera Aurea'					0.7	1.2	0.7	1.2		Dome shaped with golden whip-like strands
C. pisifera 'Squarrosa Sulphurea'					1.5	2.5	1.2	1.5		Conical habit with sulphur-yellow foliage
C. thyoides 'Ericoides'					0.6	1	0.4	0.7		Soft sea-green foliage turning bronze in winter
C. thyoides 'Rubicon'					0.2	0.4	0.2	0.4		Bun-shaped bush, deep plum-purple in winter

● *flowering*

In the garden, the small globe forms are best treated as plants for mulched beds, for tubs or for the rock garden; in mixed or shrub beds they are liable to be swamped by faster growing plants. The upright growing forms need siting where their shape highlights their appearance.

The larger growing forms, such as *Chamaecyparis obtusa* 'Crippsii' are excellent for shrub beds or to provide the framework for a mixed border.

Cypresses are easily clipped provided you remember one fact: they cannot make new growth except from existing 'green' foliage.

The cypresses need good sunlight to make effective bushes. They are tolerant of soil type, from acidic sands to fairly thin soils over chalk. However, they will not tolerate any hint of waterlogging.

soil	This plant can tolerate most types of well drained soil
site	Performs well in a sunny position but can also perform in light shade
general care	Keep slowest forms weed-free and sufficiently watered in summer, as any foliage killed will not be replaced
pruning	Only prune this shrub by clipping into existing live foliage
pests & diseases	Phytophthora root rot can kill them after a short period of waterlogging. Honey fungus is also a problem

Chamaecyparis pisifera 'Squarrosa Sulphurea'

Microbiota

This genus contains just the one species. It makes an excellent ground cover conifer, thriving in a wide range of sites, provided it has good drainage.

The foliage is in wonderful arching sprays. In summer these are grey-green, but in winter the foliage turns to bronze; at this stage it can almost look as if it is dead, but it is in fact extremely tough. In the garden it makes good ground cover for awkward corners. It can be propagated by cuttings from mid-summer to early spring.

Microbiota decussata

soil	This plant prefers any type of soil as long as it is well drained
site	Will tolerate being planted in sun to light shade in the garden
general care	Very easy to maintain and cultivate as this is an extremely tough species, as long as it has good drainage
pruning	No serious pruning required except to restrict its growth or reshape it
pests & diseases	Relatively trouble-free. Pests and diseases do not usually cause any problems

Juniperus
Juniper

Junipers include some large trees and many small shrubs. In the garden they provide tough evergreens. The foliage is naturally blue-green or grey-green, but garden selections have added gold to the range. In shape, junipers include very prostrate forms, especially the selections of *Juniperus horizontalis*, such as 'Blue Chip'; these spread over the ground surface, rising no more than 30cm (12in) above it.

Junipers make excellent ground cover plants and will control weeds as they go; they are especially good if used with a gravel mulch. Prostrate forms of *Juniperus communis*, such as 'Green Carpet' and 'Repanda', and the selections of *Juniperus squamata*, 'Blue Carpet' and 'Blue Star' are similar, if not so vigorous, but with brighter coloured foliage.

Most junipers make upright spreading bushes. Included here are the several forms of *Juniperus pfitzeriana*, *Juniperus*

Juniperus squamata 'Holger'

Juniperus squamata 'Blue Carpet'

soil	Well drained soils, whether chalky or acidic; good on dry sites once established
site	Junipers thrive best in full sunlight or, at most, light shade
general care	Very easy to maintain and cultivate. Propagate with cuttings of current year's growth in early autumn
pruning	None required. Cut back only to restrict spread or reshape for your garden
pests & diseases	Phomopsis fungi can kill the twigs on junipers, but apart from this they are fairly trouble-free

	SPRING	SUMMER	AUTUMN	WINTER	height 5yrs (m)	height 10yrs (m)	spread 5yrs (m)	spread 10yrs (m)	petal colour	
Juniperus chinensis 'Blue Alps'					1	1.5	1	1.5		Steel-blue foliage
J. communis	●	🌰🌰🌰🌰🌰			1	2	1	2	☐	Bluish fruit; yellow flowers
J. communis 'Compressa'					0.3	0.6	0.1	0.1		Miniature pencil-shaped form
J. communis 'Green Carpet'					0.1	0.2	0.6	1		Dense ground cover form, bright green foliage
J. communis 'Repanda'	●				0.1	0.2	0.6	1	☐	Bronze-tinged foliage in winter; yellow flowers
J. horizontalis 'Blue Chip'	●				0.1	0.2	1	2	☐	Bright blue foliage; yellow flowers
J. pfitzeriana 'Gold Coast'					0.4	0.8	1	2		Flat topped, with golden foliage
J. pfitzeriana 'Kuriwao Gold'	●				0.7	1.2	0.3	0.5		Golden green foliage, upright habit
J. sabina 'Tamariscifolia'	●				0.5	0.7	1	1.5	☐	Bright green, spreading foliage; yellow flowers
J. squamata 'Blue Carpet'					0.1	0.2	0.6	1		Blue-grey foliage, spreading
J. squamata 'Holger'					1	2	1	2		Sulphur-yellow new growth
J. virginiana 'Grey Owl'	●				0.6	1	0.7	1.2	☐	Silvery-grey foliage; yellow flowers

● flowering   🌰 harvest

Juniperus pfitzeriana 'Gold Coast'

chinensis 'Blue Alps', *Juniperus sabina* 'Tamasicifolia' and *Juniperus virginiana* 'Grey Owl'. These slowly grow to about 4m (13ft) in height or spread.

Generally, junipers are best if trimmed into live foliage, but they have a limited ability to make new growth from bare shoots if hard pruned on one side only.

The other habit form present in the dwarf junipers is the narrow upright exclamation mark. There are several forms of *Juniperus communis* which fit this category, of which 'Compressa' is featured here.

All the junipers thrive best in full sunlight, although they will take light shade. They are very catholic in their soil preferences, except for water logged and poorly drained soils.

Junipers can be propagated by taking ripe cuttings of the current year's growths in early autumn and rooting them over the next six to nine months in a cold frame.

Picea
Spruce

The dwarf forms of spruce make slow growing bushes which are useful for their somewhat spiky shoots. *Picea abies* 'Nidiformis' makes a nearly prostrate spreading bush. The branches are initially ascending then arch out, leaving a nest-shaped central depression with several tiers of foliage.

soil	This plant prefers acidic to lightly alkaline, well drained soils
site	Sun or light shade are the preferred conditions for spruces
general care	Remove any reversions to vigorous growth in order to keep spruces healthy and for the best results
pruning	Spruces do not require any pruning, beyond the regular removal of reversions
pests & diseases	Aphids can be a problem on spruces, causing needle-loss and death of foliage; spray with suitable insecticide

'Nidiformis' will make a feature in a gravel or heather bed. *Picea abies* 'Little Gem' is a sport from 'Nidiformis' and also has dark green foliage. It makes a bun-shaped plant, requiring planting in a trough or on a rock garden. 'Alberta Globe' is a sport which makes a globose dense bun.

These plants will all grow on acidic to slightly alkaline soils of good drainage. They are not suitable for thin soils over chalk. They can be propagated by cuttings in late summer.

Picea abies 'Reflexa'

	SPRING	SUMMER	AUTUMN	WINTER	height 5yrs (m)	height 10yrs (m)	spread 5yrs (m)	spread 10yrs (m)	petal colour
Picea abies 'Little Gem'					0.2	0.4	0.2	0.4	Bun-shaped
P. abies 'Nidiformis'					0.25	0.5	0.4	0.7	Nest shaped, ascending spreading branches
P. abies 'Reflexa'					0.1	0.2	0.6	1.2	Spreading prostrate habit
P. glauca var. *albertiana* 'Alberta Globe'					0.2	0.4	0.2	0.4	Bun-shaped
P. glauca var. *albertiana* 'Conica'					0.4	0.8	0.2	0.4	Cone shaped; can make 4–5m in 40–50 years
P. pungens 'Globosa'					0.3	0.6	0.3	0.6	Flat-topped; glaucous-blue foliage

● *flowering*

Pinus
Pine

The dwarf pines are useful for their foliage; the needles (in those featured here) are in pairs and add variety to the garden. *Pinus densiflora* 'Alice Verkade' and *Pinus heldreichii* var. *leucodermis* 'Compact Gem' both make slow growing forms. 'Alice Verkade' has dense bright green foliage. 'Compact Gem' has long needles, to 10cm (3in), on a plant which grows only a few centimetres (inches) per annum.

Pinus mugo is a species which in thirty or so years can make 4–6m (13–20ft) and has rigid dark green needles. It is thus slow growing, rather than dwarf. However, 'Gnom', 'Humpy', 'Mops' and 'Ophir' are bun-shaped selections of true dwarf character, with the foliage of 'Ophir' turning golden-yellow in winter. *Pinus sylvestris* 'Beuvronensis' makes a flat-topped or rounded bush to 1m (3ft) and has glaucous grey-blue foliage. *Pinus sylvestris* 'Watereri' is good as a young tree, with its bluish foliage. It is a slow but steady grower, making 8m (25ft) in about fifty to sixty years.

These pines all need full sunlight to flourish. They will grow on any well drained soil, with *Pinus mugo* being excellent on chalk and limestone sites. Apart from *Pinus mugo*, which can be raised from seeds sown in the spring, the forms need to be grafted onto seedling rootstocks in late winter.

Pinus mugo 'Humpy'

soil	Well drained soils, from acidic sands to chalk and limestone sites
site	These particular shrubs need as much full sun as possible to flourish
general care	Incredibly easy plants to cultivate and look after, especially once they are established
pruning	No pruning needed except perhaps to trim back to desired size and shape
pests & diseases	Can suffer from honey fungus; also, the leaves can be affected by various insects and leaf fungi

Pinus sylvestris 'Watereri'

	SPRING	SUMMER	AUTUMN	WINTER	height 5yrs (m)	height 10yrs (m)	spread 5yrs (m)	spread 10yrs (m)	petal colour	
Pinus densiflora 'Alice Verkade'					0.3	0.5	0.3	0.5		Dense bright green needles
P. heldreichii var. leucodermis 'Compact Gem'					0.2	0.3	0.2	0.3		Dark green 10cm needles
P. mugo	●		🌰 🌰		1.2	2	1	1.5	▢	Will make 4–6m or so; produces cones
P. mugo 'Gnom'					0.3	0.6	0.3	0.6		Rounded mound-forming bush
P. mugo 'Humpy'					0.1	0.2	0.1	0.2		Very dwarf form with short needles
P. mugo 'Mops'					0.3	0.6	0.3	0.6		Rounded bun-shaped bush
P. mugo 'Ophir'	●				0.25	0.3	0.25	0.5	▢	Foliage turns golden-yellow in winter
P. sylvestris 'Beuvronensis'	●				0.3	0.6	0.4	0.7	▢	Glaucous grey-blue foliage, miniature tree
P. sylvestris 'Watereri'	●		🌰 🌰		0.5	1	0.5	1	▢	Slow growing but steady; produces cones

● *flowering*   🌰 *harvest*

Platycladus
Biota

This genus has long been treated as part of Thuja, but differs in that the cones have prominent hooked bosses. It also has large round and wingless seeds and a notable absence of any delectable scent to the foliage, which is in erect flat sprays. Nevertheless, many nurseries may still list these forms as *Thuja orientalis*.

This genus is excellent for hot dry situations. *Platycladus orientalis* 'Aurea Nana' makes a dense globose bush with erect sprays of light golden-green foliage. It occasionally flowers, with the immature cones glaucous green. *Platycladus orientalis* 'Rosedalis' makes a dense ovoid bush which has very soft juvenile foliage; this is bright canary yellow in spring, maturing to sea-green and in winter turns plum-purple.

Platycladus are very tolerant of all but waterlogged soils. They can be propagated by ripe cuttings taken in autumn, or at most other times of the year.

Platycladus orientalis 'Aurea Nana'

soil	Platycladus: well drained – even chalks and gravels. Podocarpus: acidic/alkaline
site	Platycladus: sun; tolerates hot dry conditions. Podocarpus: sun or shade
general care	Platycladus: very easy to look after and cultivate. Podocarpus: quite hardy, but some can be tender
pruning	None required for either. Platycladus: will not make new growth from live foliage
pests & diseases	Both plants are relatively trouble-free. Pests and diseases do not usually cause any problems

Podocarpus
Foot yew

This group of mainly tropical to subtropical trees contains a small number of low growing hardy evergreens. They are valuable for rock gardens but can also be used as ground cover or associated with heathers.

Podocarpus lawrencei 'Blue Gem'

The plants are either male or female. *Podocarpus lawrencei* 'Blue Gem' makes a low spreading and vigorous ground cover; it has blue-green foliage. *Podocarpus nivalis* has a similar growth habit but olive-green leaves. They thrive on both acidic and alkaline soils, including fairly shallow soils over chalk. They can be propagated by seed but unless both sexes of the same species are present, these will produce hybrids. Cuttings in late summer will root.

	SPRING	SUMMER	AUTUMN	WINTER	height 5yrs (m)	height 10yrs (m)	spread 5yrs (m)	spread 10yrs (m)	petal colour	
Platycladus (Thuja) orientalis 'Aurea Nana'	●				0.8	1.5	0.7	1		Light yellow-green foliage in erect sprays
P. (Thuja) orientalis 'Elegantissima'					0.3	0.5	0.2	0.4		Juvenile soft foliage, canary yellow in spring
Podocarpus lawrencei 'Blue Gem'	●		🌰		0.2	0.3	0.6	1.2		Fruit has a red fleshy receptacle at the base
P. nivalis	●		🌰		0.2	0.3	0.6	1.2		Olive-green foliage

● flowering   🌰 harvest

Thuja
Red cedar

Thuja is a small genus of cypress-like trees. *Thuja occidentalis* from eastern North America makes a slow growing tree which has given rise to a large number of cultivars, and the taller growing *Thuja plicata* from the west of North America has added a few more.

A delightful aspect of all Thuja species is the deliciously aromatic foliage; it is strongest when the foliage is crushed but can be detected by brushing the hand against the foliage. Thuja are very adaptable. They will tolerate poor drainage, often growing naturally in bogs, but in these sites they do grow very slowly. That said, they much prefer fertile soils with good drainage, whether acidic or alkaline in nature.

Tsuga
Hemlock

The hemlocks are a small genus of evergreen conifers. They have given some excellent forms which can be used to make specimen shrubs or dot plants.

The three forms listed here all belong to *Tsuga canadensis*. 'Cole's Prostrate' is a vigorous form which makes an effective

Thuja occidentalis 'Tiny Tim'

soil	Thuja: acidic to alkaline, good on sands/chalk. Tsuga: acidic to chalky. Both well-drained
site	Thuja: likes sun to moderate shade. Tsuga: happy in sun or quite dense shade
general care	Thuja: very easy, generally looks after itself. Tsuga: keep soil moist but not wet during the summer
pruning	No particular pruning requirements needed for either plant
pests & diseases	Thuja: scale insects and aphids; *Keithia* can be a problem in nurseries. Tsuga: generally disease free

ground cover. 'Fantana' has wide spreading branches which carry ostrich-feather-like plumes irregularly set. 'Jeddeloh' has arching and rather stiff branches radiating out from a depressed centre. They can be propagated by cuttings from late summer or autumn.

Tsuga canadensis 'Jeddeloh'

	SPRING	SUMMER	AUTUMN	WINTER	height 5yrs (m)	height 10yrs (m)	spread 5yrs (m)	spread 10yrs (m)	petal colour	
Thuja occidentalis 'Danica'	●				0.2	0.3	0.2	0.3	■	Dense globose plant; foliage in erect sprays
T. occidentalis 'Hetz Midget'					0.1	0.2	0.1	0.2		Very slow growing, bun-shaped dwarf
T. occidentalis 'Tiny Tim'					0.1	0.2	0.1	0.2		Slow-growing form making rounded dwarf bush
T. plicata 'Stoneham Gold'					0.5	1	0.3	0.5		Slow-growing narrow conical bush
Tsuga canadensis 'Cole's Prostrate'					0.1	0.1	1	2		Ground hugging
T. canadensis 'Fantana'	●				0.3	0.6	0.6	1	□	Erect branches arch out, pendulous at tips
T. canadensis 'Jeddeloh'	●				0.7	1.2	0.8	1.5	□	Erect-arching branches, nest-shaped centre

● flowering

Architectural Plants

'Architectural plants' is a term used to describe those planted for the boldness of their impact, usually foliage. The companion volume in this series of books, *Architectural Plants*, discusses the full range of such plants. This page is simply a taster, and suggests plants that go well with flowering planting schemes.

Yucca flaccida 'Golden Sword'

Agave americanum

Agave americanum and its form 'Variegata' have glaucous foliage which is carried from a basal rosette until one day it sends a single flowering shoot several metres (yards) into the air, and then dies. *Cordyline australis* is slow growing but can ultimately make a tree to 8m (25ft) or so. It is liable to be cut by cold winters. The flowers are carried in large terminal panicles in early summer and are fragrant. The trunk has a single stem until the plant flowers, and then branches every time it flowers. *Yucca filamentosa* is a stem-less plant which produces large erect panicles 1–2m (3–6ft) with creamy-white individual flowers 5–7cm (2–3in) in length. In 'Bright Edge' the normally glaucous leaves have a narrow golden-yellow margin. *Yucca flaccida* is similar, with 'Golden Sword' having a broad band of creamy-yellow along the leaf midrib, and 'Ivory' has particularly showy and large panicles of creamy-white flowers which have a green stain. *Yucca gloriosa* will develop a single stem to 2.5m, with few side branches, and has stiff and very sharp-pointed leaves and creamy-white flowers. These plants like well drained sites in full sun. They are propagated by offsets.

soil	These plants prefer well drained soils, either acidic or alkaline	
site	Most architectural plants favour a sunny position or a little light shade	
general care	In cold gardens, these types of plant will benefit from added winter protection	
pruning	Easy to maintain, as pruning is generally not required for these architectural shrubs	
pests & diseases	Relatively trouble-free. Pests and diseases do not usually cause any problems	

	SPRING	SUMMER	AUTUMN	WINTER	height 5yrs (m)	height 10yrs (m)	spread 5yrs (m)	spread 10yrs (m)	petal colour	
Agave americanum		☀			0.8	2	1.5	3	▓	Grey-green spiny margined leaves
A. americanum 'Variegata'		☀			0.8	2	1.5	3	▓	Leaves edged white
Cordyline australis	☀				1	2	1.5	1.5	☐	Flowers fragrant, will make 8m in mild areas
C. australis 'Purple Tower'	☀				1	2	1.5	1.5	☐	Deep plum-purple leaves
C. australis 'Red Star'	☀				1	2	1.5	1.5	☐	Bronzy-red leaves
C. australis 'Sundance'	☀				1	2	1.5	1.5	☐	Yellow leaves with a pink base and midrib
C. australis 'Torbay Dazzler'	☀				1	1.5	1.5	1.5	☐	Leaves with a creamy white margin
C. australis 'Torbay Red'	☀				1	2	1.5	1.5	☐	Deep burgundy-red leaves
Yucca filamentosa		☀ ☀			0.8	1	1	1.2	☐	Slightly glaucous leaves
Y. filamentosa 'Bright Edge'		☀ ☀			0.8	1	1	1.2	☐	Leaves with narrow, golden-yellow margin
Y. flaccida 'Golden Sword'		☀ ☀			0.8	1	1	1.2	☐	Leaves with central broad creamy-yellow band
Y. flaccida 'Ivory'		☀ ☀			0.8	1	1	1.2	☐	Flowers in large panicles, stained green
Y. gloriosa		☀ ☀ ☀			0.8	1.5	1	1.2	☐	Leaves very sharp-pointed

☀ *flowering*

Troubleshooting

Growing a varied range of shrubs and trees attracts an equally varied selection of pests, diseases and other problems. The following diagram is designed to help you diagnose conditions suffered by your shrubs or trees from the symptoms you can observe. Starting with the part of the shrub or tree that appears to be most affected – leaves or stems – and by answering successive questions 'yes' [✓] or 'no' [✗], you will quickly arrive at a probable cause. Once you have identified the cause, turn to the relevant entry in the directory of pests and diseases for details of how to treat the problem.

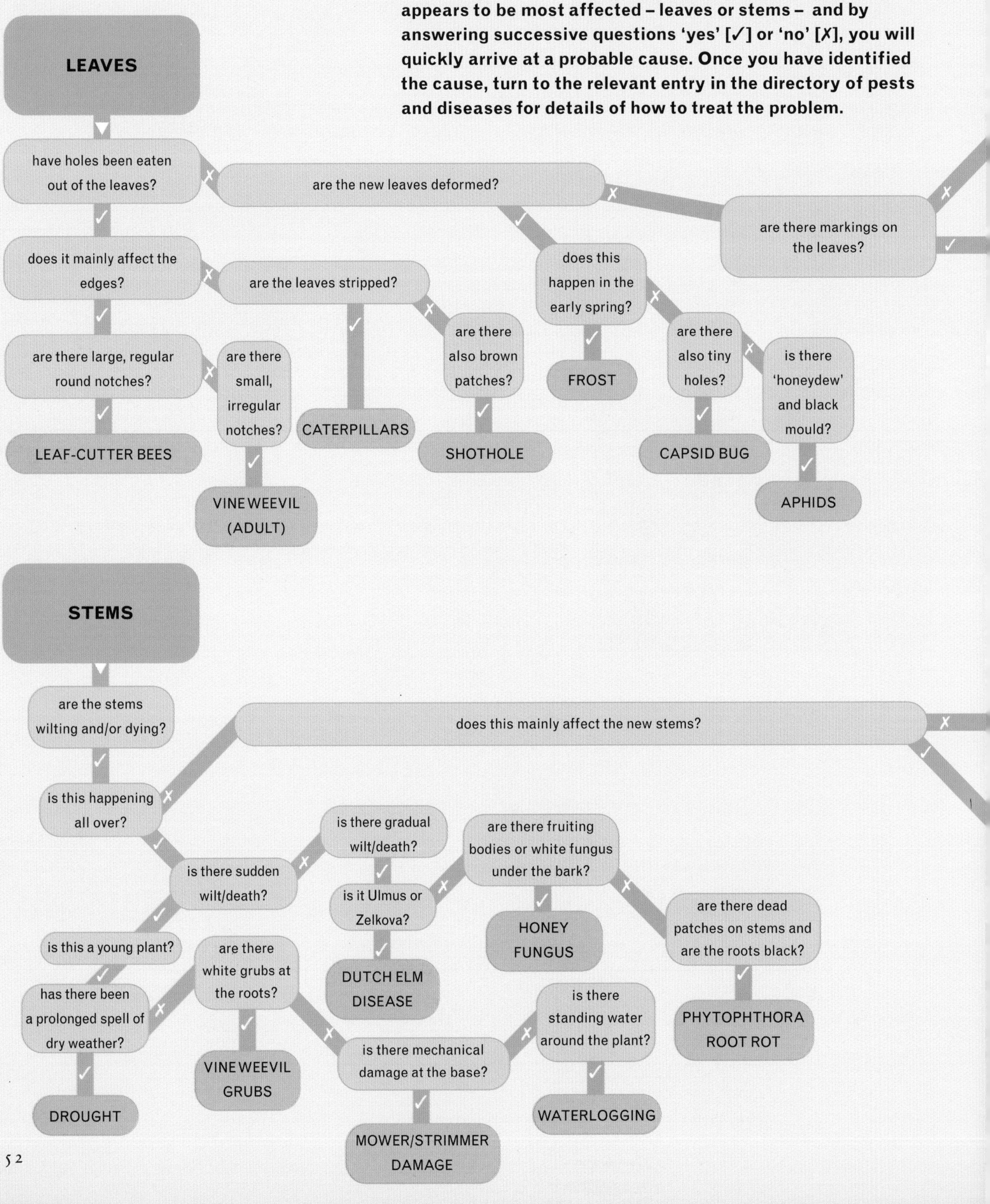

LEAVES

have holes been eaten out of the leaves?

are the new leaves deformed?

are there markings on the leaves?

does it mainly affect the edges?

are the leaves stripped?

does this happen in the early spring?

are there large, regular round notches?

are there small, irregular notches?

are there also brown patches?

FROST

are there also tiny holes?

is there 'honeydew' and black mould?

LEAF-CUTTER BEES

CATERPILLARS

SHOTHOLE

CAPSID BUG

APHIDS

VINE WEEVIL (ADULT)

STEMS

are the stems wilting and/or dying?

does this mainly affect the new stems?

is this happening all over?

is there gradual wilt/death?

are there fruiting bodies or white fungus under the bark?

is there sudden wilt/death?

is it Ulmus or Zelkova?

HONEY FUNGUS

are there dead patches on stems and are the roots black?

is this a young plant?

are there white grubs at the roots?

DUTCH ELM DISEASE

is there standing water around the plant?

PHYTOPHTHORA ROOT ROT

has there been a prolonged spell of dry weather?

is there mechanical damage at the base?

VINE WEEVIL GRUBS

WATERLOGGING

DROUGHT

MOWER/STRIMMER DAMAGE

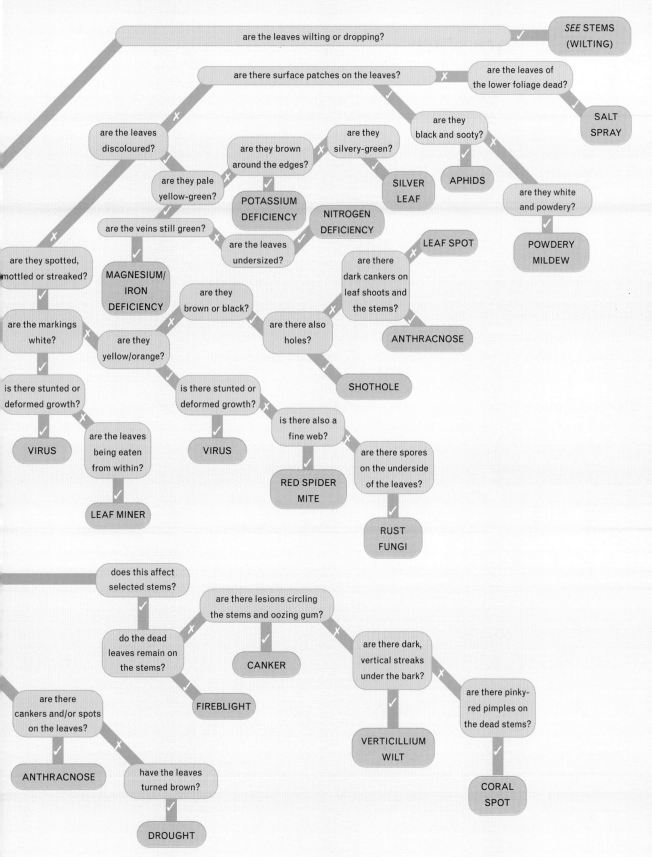

are the leaves wilting or dropping? — ✓ → *SEE* STEMS (WILTING)

are there surface patches on the leaves? — ✗ → are the leaves of the lower foliage dead? — ✗ → SALT SPRAY

are the leaves discoloured? — ✗

are they black and sooty? → APHIDS

are they white and powdery? — ✓ → POWDERY MILDEW

are they brown around the edges? — ✓ → POTASSIUM DEFICIENCY

are they silvery-green? → SILVER LEAF

are they pale yellow-green? → NITROGEN DEFICIENCY

are the leaves undersized? — ✓

are the veins still green? — ✓ → MAGNESIUM/ IRON DEFICIENCY

LEAF SPOT — ✗

are there dark cankers on leaf shoots and the stems? — ✓ → ANTHRACNOSE

are they spotted, mottled or streaked? — ✓

are they brown or black? — ✗

are there also holes? — ✗ → SHOTHOLE

are the markings white? — ✓

are they yellow/orange? ✗

is there stunted or deformed growth? — ✓ → VIRUS

are the leaves being eaten from within? → LEAF MINER

is there stunted or deformed growth? — ✓ → VIRUS

is there also a fine web? — ✓ → RED SPIDER MITE

are there spores on the underside of the leaves? → RUST FUNGI

does this affect selected stems? — ✓

are there lesions circling the stems and oozing gum? — ✗

do the dead leaves remain on the stems? — ✓ → FIREBLIGHT

CANKER — ✓

are there dark, vertical streaks under the bark? — ✗

are there cankers and/or spots on the leaves? — ✗ → ANTHRACNOSE

have the leaves turned brown? — ✓ → DROUGHT

VERTICILLIUM WILT — ✓

are there pinky-red pimples on the dead stems? — ✓ → CORAL SPOT

153

Pests & Diseases

Insect problems

Flowering shrubs are susceptible to a number of different pests and diseases, some of which can prove fatal. However, the majority of conditions can be treated successfully, as the following pages explain.

Vine weevil

Vine weevil can be a major problem on many flowering shrubs. The adult weevil is a black beetle nearly 1cm (⅜in) in length. It feeds on foliage after dark, making U-shaped notches in the leaves. However, the foliage damage is minor. The real damage is caused by vine weevil grubs – white maggot-like caterpillars, growing to 1cm (⅜in). The grubs eat the roots and bark below ground, up to just above ground level. This often kills the plant. Squash adults after dark and control the grubs by spraying the soil with either a solution of microscopic nematode worms (a biological control), or a chemical preparation.

Aphids

Aphids are sap-sucking insects. They come in a large number of different species, ranging from green to black or white to a waxy wool. They quickly build up large colonies during the summer months. They can cause death of shoot tips when present in large numbers, but are more of a problem for the honeydew they secrete. If control is necessary on a small scale spray with a contact insecticide. Use one that only kills aphids, leaving their predators to mop up those missed by the spray. Killing both aphids and their predators is likely to lead to a new problem, as the aphids breed much faster than their predators.

Red spider mites

Red spider mites are also sap-sucking insects which can cause weakening and death of leaves. They are scarcely visible to the naked eye because they are less than half a millimetre in length, but they spin a silky protective coat which is more visible. There are several different species of red spider mite which affect different groups of plants. They can be treated using a chemical spray such as derris or malathion, and this may need to be applied as often as twice a week. Alternatively, you could introduce natural insect predators – the best is *Phytoseilus persimilis* – which can be obtained by mail order through garden centres. Mites flourish in hot, dry conditions, so alter these wherever possible to protect your plants.

Scale insects

Scale insects are sap-sucking insects which protect themselves with a protective scale and also by a waxy wool. Different species afflict different shrubs, mainly sucking the sap from the trunks and branches of the plants, rather than from their leaves. These pests do not normally present a serious problem – although there is some evidence that they can reduce the growth rate of plants – but a heavy infestation can appear unsightly. Scale insects can be eradicated by washing the stems of the affected shrub with a soapy solution that removes the protective wax covering the insects.

Caspid bugs

Capsid bugs are green or brown insects, approximately 0.6cm (¼in) in length, which suck the sap from the buds and the young foliage of some flowering shrubs. These pests insert a toxic saliva into the plants they attack that causes areas of the expanding leaves to be killed. In Fuchsia sometimes the problem can be so serious that it can lead to the failure of flowering. Capsid bugs can be controlled by spraying with a systemic insecticide (that is, one which is moved around within the plant), during the summer months.

Caterpillars

Caterpillars come in a vast range of shapes and sizes, readily eating the foliage of most shrubs, although most are only found on a restricted range of hosts. If unchecked, they would eat all the foliage of many plants, but fortunately most caterpillars are themselves eaten by something else (whether a parasitic wasp or a blue tit) and the actual harm done is rarely of more than passing significance. Also, those that survive turn into butterflies or moths. Therefore, it should not generally be necessary or desirable to control them on shrubs, although this can be achieved by the use of sprays, including the biological *Bacillus thuringiacus*.

Leaf cutter bees

Leaf cutter bees make neat semi-circular holes in the margins of leaves. They are solitary, non-stinging insects which are useful for pollinating flowers and rarely cause any actual harm. The pieces of leaf are carried back to holes in the ground, usually on banks, where they are used to feed their grubs. The damage that these creatures cause is usually slight and they generally do not require any form of control. However, if they are a persistent nuisance and you do need to get rid of them, try swatting them as they land on your plants.

Leaf miners

Leaf miners eat the centre of leaves, leaving dead or discoloured patches, but they cause little actual damage. However, the tracks that they leave behind on leaves as they burrow through them can be unsightly, so you might want to bring them under control. These pests are difficult to get at, so the best method of dealing with them is to use a systemic insecticide.

Fungal problems

Wilt

Wilt diseases cause the death of foliage and shoots by blocking the water conduction system. The commonest examples are Dutch elm disease and verticillium wilt. The disease often does not transfer from the current year's affected water conduction tissues into the new tissues laid down next year, so if the branch or shrub is not killed, they can recover unless re-infected. Some control is possible by removing affected branches, cutting back well beyond signs of infection or damage. The disease will show as a staining of the outer ring of wood. Sterilize the blade between cuts so as not to pass on the infection.

Leaf spot

Leaf spot diseases cause the death of patches of leaves, which either remain as black or 'tar' spots, or fall away as 'shot holes'. Remove affected leaves at the first sign and burn them. Leaf spot can also be controlled by the use of systemic fungicides containing copper.

Anthracnose

Anthracnose diseases are caused by fungi which kill new leaves and shoots. Different species occur on a range of shrubs. They are more prevalent in cold wet summers, but generally new growth is made which is unaffected and the shrub quickly recovers. Anthracnose can also cause cankers on the stems of some flowering shrubs. If you need to control this condition, remove all affected parts of the plant and burn them. Then, spray the shrub with benomyl or a copper-based fungicide.

Mildew

Mildew can cause serious harm to soft young foliage and in bad cases will kill plants, as is the case with powdery mildew on certain Rhododendron. The fungi form a white powdery covering and do not need damp conditions. Control is possible at an early stage by spraying with a fungicide.

Rust fungi

Rust fungi have a complex and interesting life style. In a 'perfect' case, each rust fungus passes different stages of its lifecycle on unrelated genera. However, the Buxus rust does not have an alternate host. Damage is only produced on the primary hosts, taking the form of many rust, purplish brown, orange or yellow coloured masses of spores and causing the loss of leaves. Fungal sprays can control the condition.

Cankers

Cankers are lesions that appear on the stem or bark of flowering shrubs which are caused by a fungus or bacterium. If the stem of the plant becomes girdled by cankers, its distal portion may be starved and killed, which results in symptoms similar to those of wilt diseases. The best solution to this problem is to remove the affected branch of the shrub.

Fireblight

Fireblight is a bacterial disease which kills shoots, and occasionally whole plants. It is restricted to Cotoneaster and other genera in the apple subfamily (Maloideae) of the rose family (Rosaceae). Infection is usually via the flowers or new leaves. It can be controlled by removing affected shoots at least 60cm (2ft) below any signs of the disease, sterilizing the blade of the secateurs between each cut on a rag soaked in methylated spirits.

Silver leaf

Silver leaf is a fungal disease which occurs in many woody plants, except in the conifers. It infects the wood, causing a brown discoloration of the current season's wood; often, but not always, the foliage on the affected branch takes on a leadened or silver sheen. The fungus usually enters the wood through pruning wounds. In mild cases, prune out the affected branches or see whether they recover naturally. In severe cases, remove the plant.

Coral spot

Coral spot disease is identified by the coral or pink rounded pustules on the bark. The fungus can kill healthy tissue but is normally associated with stressed, dying or dead branches. It can be a problem on stressed trees and shrubs, such as those recently moved or growing in waterlogged soils, but is rarely serious on healthy specimens. Remove affected shoots and attend to any stress by ensuring that newly planted shrubs are adequately watered, and attend to drainage if waterlogging is considered a problem.

Phytophtora

Phytophthora are a group of single-celled or yeast-like fungi which are spread through water, and are most famous for the potato blight. Phytophthora root disease kills the roots of many shrubs, including Calluna, Chamaecyparis, Erica and Rhododendron, causing the sudden death of the shrub. If the soil is poorly drained, address the problem, but the disease can occur after temporary flooding due to heavy rain. Because the disease does not produce fruit bodies, it is extremely difficult to confirm and can be mistaken for other conditions.

Honey fungus

Honey fungus is a group of fungi which vary in their severity. They can all colonize dead and nearly dead tissue, but some can kill healthy trees. Some shrubs, such as Chamaecyparis, Ligustrum and Pinus, are susceptible and can be killed at any age. The fungus can be identified by the white mat of mycelium produced between the bark and the wood of an infected shrub. Resin may exude from the bark just above ground level. The best control for this problem is the removal of dead roots, but unfortunately this is seldom practical in most situations. A phenol-based product is sold as a control measure.

Non biological agents

Nutrient deficiencies

Nutrient deficiencies in flowering shrubs can cause discoloration of leaves, smaller leaves and less growth. A shortage of nitrogen will show by the smaller shoots and pale or yellow-green leaves which become red, purple orange or yellow as they mature and fall early. Fertilizer can be given for immediate but short term relief. The best solution is to increase the organic matter in the soil, which allows regulated release of nitrogen by soil bacteria. Phosphorus deficiency can give similar symptoms.

Potash (potassium) deficiency shows as scorch of the leaf margin, with the margin becoming brown or grey-brown. This can be corrected by giving potassium as a feed. Both magnesium and iron can be deficient on alkaline soils, due to their being unavailable for plant roots. The use of chelated forms of iron can assist.

Salt spray

Salt spray can kill the foliage of some flowering shrubs. It is especially common along roadsides as a result of de-icing salt applied in winter; any parts of the plant splashed by passing cars will be killed, but foliage on the opposite side and higher up the plant will normally survive. Salt spray also occurs in coastal gardens, and occasionally storms can bring salt spray many miles inland.

Drought

Drought can cause immediate symptoms on the soft leaves of deciduous shrubs. At an early stage, the leaves will recover overnight, but as the drought becomes more severe leaves are lost and those remaining develop dead patches between the veins, and the twigs die back. The leaves of evergreens are much tougher and may not show immediate damage. However, they may be just as badly affected, so keep a close eye on them.

Frost damage

Frost damage occurs when the foliage or stems of a plant are frozen; this causes water to be withdrawn from the cell contents. Rapid thawing can exacerbate the damage, which is why walls that face the sun in the morning are not suitable for some shrubs. Frost damage most often takes the form of killed foliage, especially emerging leaves, and shoots. However, it can distort new leaves if they are not killed. In the case of long-lasting leaves, for example where all the leaves are produced in one whorl at the shoot tip, the effect can be apparent for two or three years. Frost can also cause the bark to split in many shrubs.

Waterlogging

Waterlogging can cause the death of roots, especially the fine roots which actually absorb water! If it occurs during the summer, the shrub can quickly die from lack of water despite standing in water. Waterlogging over winter can be even more invidious. The shrub starts to leaf out (flush) in the spring and may develop a full or nearly full crop of leaves. However, because it is drying the soil faster than it can extend new roots into the soil, the foliage suddenly dies. By that time, there is little that can be done. Try severely reducing the shrub, so that the few living roots are in balance with the quantity of foliage and water; if this fails, improve the drainage before planting the replacement. Less severe waterlogging is one cause of twigs dying back.

Index of Plants

This index lists the plants mentioned in this book by their common names where applicable and their Latin names in all other instances

General Index

Acknowledgements

Author's acknowledgements:
I wish to record my thanks to all the people, in many countries, who have helped me to learn more about trees, shrubs and other plants. There are too many of you to list individually, but you will know who you are, and thank you. Also, to thank Heather for her support, understanding and patience. – Keith Rushforth

The majority of photographs in this book were taken by Tim Sandall. A number of others were kindly contributed by the following individuals and companies and are credited in full below:

John Feltwell/Garden Matters: pp 79(B); 95(T) (Steffie Shields); 130(B)

Keith Rushforth: pp 48(R); 53(x2); 56; 59(T); 96(BR); 99(T); 111(B); 125(R); 128–129; 136(T)

Key: T = Top; B = Bottom; R = Right

The publishers would like to thank Coolings Nurseries for their cooperation and assistance with the photography in this book, including the loan of tools and specialist equipment. Special thanks go to: Sandra Gratwick, Garry Norris, Ian Hazon and Brian Archibald. Coolings Nurseries Ltd., Rushmore Hill, Knockholt, Kent, TN14 7NN.
Tel: 00 44 1959 532269; Email: coolings@coolings.co.uk; Website: www.coolings.co.uk

Thanks are also due to the Sir Harold Hillier Gardens and Arboretum and Hampshire County Council, for allowing photographs for this book to be taken on their premises